DEMARCATING
The DISCIPLINES

GLYPH TEXTUAL STUDIES
(new series)

SERIES EDITORS: Wlad Godzich, Henry Sussman, Samuel Weber

VOLUME 1: Demarcating the Disciplines

VOLUME EDITOR: Samuel Weber

CONSULTING EDITORS: Christie Vance McDonald,
Rainer Nägele, Lindsay Waters

GLYPH TEXTUAL STUDIES 1

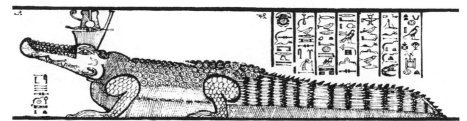

DEMARCATING
The DISCIPLINES

Philosophy
Literature
Art

University of Minnesota Press ~ Minneapolis

Published by the University of Minnesota Press,
2037 University Avenue Southeast, Minneapolis MN 55414

The illustration on the cover and title page, an Egyptian crocodile
from the Ptolemaic period, is reproduced through the courtesy
of the Walters Art Gallery, Baltimore.

Printed in the United States of America

Library of Congress Cataloging in Publication Data
Main entry under title:

Demarcating the disciplines.

(Glyph textual studies ; 1)
1. Literature—Study and teaching—Addresses,
essays, lectures. I. Weber, Samuel, 1940-
II. Series.
PN59.D45   1985   807   84-28057
ISBN 0-8166-1397-4
ISBN 0-8166-1398-2 (pbk.)

Chapter 3, "Asterion's Door," Copyright © 1985 by Malcolm Evans,
originally written in 1980.

The University of Minnesota is an equal-opportunity educator and employer.

CONTENTS

PREFACE

With this volume *Glyph* begins, belatedly, a new stage in its existence. A change in publisher—from Johns Hopkins University Press to the University of Minnesota Press—is accompanied by a change in focus. In the future *Glyph* will be an annual publication organized around specific issues, of which *Demarcating the Disciplines* is an initial instance. This shift reflects transformations that have affected the intellectual context in which we are situated. When we first began publication some eight years ago, our primary concern was with providing a forum in which established notions of *representation* could be problematized and explored, with particular reference to the specific situation of North American "critical theory." Since this time, the greater currency of such concerns has brought with it new problems and priorities which, we are convinced, can best be articulated by a publication that focuses upon particular questions emerging out of the contemporary critical landscape.

In an indirect way the project as we have formulated it resembles a historical one, for in part it will consist in reassessing movements and accomplishments of the recent past that were not visible when they were taking place. Nevertheless, it is important to note how this ongoing reassessment differs from a historical endeavor, with all its attendant periodizations: to situate the recent critical past is not to affirm the distance separating us from that past; the project conceived for *Glyph* consists in remapping the critical landscape rather than simply offering an objectified inventory of the given movements and conceptions that reside there. The very words and concepts at our disposal—"theory" and "criticism," for example—cannot be exempt from this re-examination. Perhaps "glyph" itself most accurately describes the activity we envision: *glyph* is both inscription and the act of inscribing, and the propulsion of *Glyph* as a critical project will derive from the movement such an intersection implies. The issues of future volumes include "The Question of War," "On Kant's Third Critique," "The Interface of Word and Image," and "In Disregard of Philosophy: Heterological Practices."

Glyph has never tried to be all things to all people. One of its distinguishing features has been a practice informed by a twofold conviction: first, that intellectual work in general, and in particular that being pursued in the areas in which we are primarily engaged, is inevitably *partial*, in all the senses of the term; and second, that a publication that *assumes* its partiality, not merely as a burden but as a challenge, can produce a different sort of inquiry and of writing from that commonly accepted and encouraged in the American academic establishment. To pursue and elaborate this *parti pris* while resisting, as much as possible, the facile solutions of eclecticism and sectarianism — this has defined the activity that we resume with this publication.

If, after such a long period of interruption, there still persists an expectation that *Glyph* has a function to perform today, it is, we are convinced, tied to this activity. Leaving to others the ambition of covering the whole, we will be more than satisfied if we can continue to lay a small but significant *part*.

INTRODUCTION

Samuel Weber

In the spring of 1983, Jacques Derrida gave a lecture in Frankfurt on "The Principle of Reason and the Pupils of the University," an English translation of which has been published in *Diacritics*. Following his talk, Jürgen Habermas asked Derrida if he could provide "a philosophical justification" for what, to Habermas as to many others in the audience that evening, can only have seemed to be a quite bizarre and arbitrary concern for institutional questions. That the author of *De la grammatologie*, for whom there was "nothing outside of the text," should now be addressing something as evidently extratextual as the University, will undoubtedly seem to many, and not just in Frankfurt, as a surprising turn of events.

And yet, even if one is unacquainted with Derrida's writings of the last decade, in which this "turn" has gradually emerged with increasing insistence, an attentive reading of *Of Grammatology* would reveal traces of what was to come. Indeed, it was precisely the importance assigned to the notion of *trace* that also entailed the question of its *institution*, as the minimal condition of any sort of legibility, including that of deconstruction itself. Derrida's "object" in *Of Grammatology* was of course not entities in themselves — "writing," "speech" — but an *institutionalized system of interpretation* in which precisely the question of the institution itself had come to be obliterated. Indeed, this is one, if not perhaps the major, effect of what Derrida was describing as the Metaphysics of Presence: the obfuscation of institution as an indispensable, but also inevitably problematic part of the articulation of meaning. If difference is construed to be a function of identity, and ultimately of presence, institutions can be viewed as the form in which the latter specifies or actualizes, expresses or represents itself. Institutionalization is thus conceived to be the repetition or reproduction of what, in and of itself, is already constituted and articulated in its identity.

Once however the values of presence and identity are indeed problematized, as functions or effects of "traces," of a "graphics of supplementarity," the following question must sooner or later be addressed: how, in ever-changing situations, does such a "function" or "effect" *take place*?

Whereas the earlier, more classically deconstructive writings of Derrida—up to *Dissemination*, which can be seen as a kind of pivot—sought to demonstrate the problematic status of certain major attempts, in the Western intellectual tradition, at systematic closure, i.e., at institutionalization, his subsequent writings have carried this demonstration further and, in a certain sense, in a different direction. Having established a certain structural instability in the most powerful attempts to provide models of structuration, it was probably inevitable that Derrida should then begin to explore the other side of the coin, the fact that, *undecidability notwithstanding*, decisions are *in fact* taken, power *in fact* exercised, traces *in fact* instituted. It is the highly ambivalent *making* of such *facts* that has increasingly imposed itself upon and throughout the more recent writings of Derrida as well as upon the field of problems and of practices associated with his work.

To this imposition, the current volume of *Glyph* bears witness; it consists in a series of studies that seek, in different ways, to explore the relation between *the reading and writing of texts* and *the operations of the institution*. The focus, as has generally been the case for *Glyph*, is upon the discipline of literary studies, but this limitation is more a part of the *problem* addressed than of its solution. The fact that, in the English-speaking world at least, the question of representation—*Glyph*'s point of departure—has been articulated most extensively within the disciplines of literary studies is an example of that institutional constraint without which nothing is possible, but which also tends to assimilate the practices it permits and to absorb their transformative potential.

However different the essays in this volume may be, they concur in a double, if ambivalent recognition: that the question of the institution points us toward constraints that define, albeit in negative fashion, the possibilities of change.

For many years, the prevailing strategy of our established institutions of learning and of inquiry was to deny their own coercive, constitutive power. Or rather, to justify it in terms of objects, values, and a paradigm of knowledge that were held to be above and beyond question. One might argue about particular works or concepts, about the specific meaning of literary texts, but not about the presumption that literature *exists*, and that ultimately a poem should not *mean*, but *be*. But at the same time that it was seeking to establish, or confirm, this attitude, the New Criticism so often decried today, was also working to subvert the *being* of literature precisely by demonstrating its resources to *mean* in ways that defied or exceeded the unity and identity of a being, a literary work. Hence the reproach so often directed at a critic such as Empson, for excessive, even anarchic ingenuity: could he not see, after all, that his "ambiguities" were merely abstract possibilities, not realized in the texts he was pretending to read?

Today, such anarchy, loos'd upon the world, has made it more difficult, less self-evident for literary scholars (and others) to take the identity of their objects for granted, without at least posing the question of that *granting*.

But the most recent strategy of legitimation, identifying not the work but the "interpretive community" as the source of literary value, merely inverts the previous scheme, by placing the principle of identity not in the literary object but in the critical subject; the latter is construed as no less unitary than was the New Critical Work and, indeed, probably as far more static than were texts rewritten in terms of ambiguity, paradox, and irony. If Stanley Fish refuses to accept the notion of ambiguity, for instance, it is in the name of a conception of diversity far more monolithic in its refusal to think the significance of conflict than were ever the New Critics.

The advocates of such a notion of "interpretive communities" would do well to reread the text in which the term was first developed, in English at least: Josiah Royce's *Problem of Christianity*. Royce, in attempting to account for the formation of the Christian Community of Interpretation, was forced to acknowledge a certain transcendent element without which the community could never get itself together: it was only by virtue of a force, a figure, (and a voice—that of Jesus— that came from without, that the Community could find its way together, into a unity. The voice, in whose name the Community of Interpretation always seeks to speak, marks its relation to an exteriority that it can never simply appropriate, since it defines the limits of its property and of its identity. This is also why, in reproducing itself, any "community" inevitably reproduces its relation to a certain outside. The only decisive question concerns the *kinds* of relations to alterity that *particular* communities are capable of institutionalizing, their capacity to articulate constitutive ambivalences, and their ability to entertain alteration.

The texts in this volume all address this question: from Derrida's account of Hegel, attempting to normativize philosophy as a quasi-natural, hierarchical institution, as irreversible as the "ages" of man — to Ruth Salvaggio, recounting in an almost anecdotal manner the confrontation of a college teacher of literature with a strange and remarkable undergraduate paper — what we have assembled here are protocols of an alteration at work in what is perhaps the beginning of an institution turning itself inside out.

DEMARCATING
The DISCIPLINES

1

THE AGE OF HEGEL

Jacques Derrida

Translated by Susan Winnett

" . . . and if I may be permitted to evoke my own experience . . . I remember having learned, in my twelfth year – destined as I was to enter the theological seminary of my country – Wolf's definitions of the so-called *idea clara* and that, in my fourteenth year, I had assimilated all the figures and rules of syllogism. And I still know them."

And he still knows them.

Hegel in his twelfth year. You can see the scene from here.

And he still knows them. And he remembers – with a suppressed smile, no doubt with a twinkle in his eye. It would be wrong for you to overlook Hegel's sense of humor, the fact that he recalls old Wolf's *idea clara* and all the syllogistic formalities; in short, the whole machine. With the implication: I'm playing games; I'm being ironic: I would never say anything like this in my *Greater Logic*. But perhaps I would, after all, since if there is as much modesty as coyness in my irony, this irony does indeed serve my argument; the seriousness of the concept is not absent for a moment.

All the same. Hegel in his twelfth year. That doesn't happen every day.

In 1822 he is fifty-two years old. He has all his "great works" behind him, particularly the *Encyclopedia*, and the still very recent *Philosophy of Right* of Berlin,[1] without which the scene you think you are witnessing would be (in its essentials, as he would say) indecipherable.

At the age of fifty-two, he speaks of his twelfth year. He was already a philosopher. But just like everyone is, right? That is, not yet a philosopher since, in view of the corpus of the complete works of his maturity, this *already* will have been a *not yet*.

If we don't think through the conceptual, dialectical, speculative structure of this *already-not-yet*, we will not have understood anything (in its essentials, as he would say) about the *age* (for example, that of Hegel). Or about any age whatsoever, but especially and *par excellence* that *of* philosophy or *for* philosophy.

All the same, what a scene, this *Ecce homo* in the ministerial mail. It must have packed enough power, however trivial it might seem. For, at the end of the same century, another *Ecce homo*, sufficiently Hegel's contemporary to feel himself endlessly accountable, adopts him as a principal adversary.

Under the cover of the *already-not-yet*, autobiographical confiding enlists the anecdote in a demonstration, treating the issue of (the) age as a figure in the phenomenology of the mind, as a moment in the logic. He has opened up the family album to just the right place for the minister, to whom he will — we should add — certainly have spoken of his private life. The album will have been opened to just the page and in just such a manner so that no single illustration is detachable from the interminable, continuous philosophical discourse that opens the album and that permeates every image. The scene becomes difficult to envision as soon as we interpolate: "You see, Your Excellency, That's-me-in-my-twelfth-year-between-eleven-and-thirteen-years-That's-me-in-the-photograph-there-in-my-first-connection-with-philosophy-I-read-much-I-was-very-gifted-I-knew-all-that-already-I-was-very-gifted-but-basically-just-like-everyone-else-don't-you-think-besides-it-wasn't-yet-really-philosophy-just-old-Wolf-the-syllogistic-formulas-and-then-an-exercise-of-memory-already-me (that is, Hegel) but-not-yet-Hegel (that is, me), etc."

It seems at first a comic sidelight, a pleasurable bonus for this false confidence to have been addressed to a Minister. It is part of a report, a "special report," commissioned by the Ministry, by a State bureaucracy in the process of organizing the nationalization of the structures of philosophical education by extracting it, based upon a historical compromise, from clerical jurisdiction. We shall have to return to this techno-bureaucratic region of Hegelian confiding. It is indispensable if we are to understand the philosopher-civil-servants of today, who no longer address their letters to the prince, the king, the queen, or the empress, but rather whose reports now and then make their way more or less directly to those upper echelon civil servants marked by the ENA[2] (who, like Hegel's interlocutors, are often more cunning, *ostensibly* more open to "contemporary philosophy" than are the powers-that-be within the University). It is indispensable if we are to understand that the philosopher-civil-servants of today belong to what I call the age of Hegel.

In the *Philosophy of Right* Hegel did not simply propose a theoretical deduction of the modern State and of its bureaucracy. He did not simply comprehend, in his fashion, the role of the *formation* of civil servants and of the pedagogical structures when placed in the service of the State. He did not take merely a theoretical interest in the transmission, through instruction, of a philosophy, the rationality of which was supposed to culminate most universally and most powerfully in the concept of the State, with all the wrinkles, stakes, and convolutions of such a "paradox." Very quickly and very "practically" he found himself implicated, advancing or foundering, with more or less confidence, in the techno-bureaucratic space of a highly determined State. And he gave an account of this determination.

But we're getting ahead of ourselves. Let's keep our ears tuned to the resonances of this confidence. It is private, since it has to do with a childhood memory confided in a letter by a singular philsopher who remembers, and who remembers his memory—what he learned by heart and still remembers. And yet, this confidence is so little private that it is addressed to the offices of a Ministry, to the technocracy of a State, and to its service, in order to help it put into practice a concept of the State that informs the entire letter.

THE CORRESPONDENCE BETWEEN HEGEL AND COUSIN

Twenty-two years later, in France, in a context that, although different in many respects, remains analogous and contiguous, Cousin, too, will add his confidence to the file. His age will be touched upon. (He was not so precocious: "Without being a particularly slow learner, I took my degree in philosophy at the age of 19.") This took place in the House of Peers (*Chambre des Pairs*), in the famous discourse on "The Defense of the University and of Philosophy" (*La défense de l'université et de la philosophie*).[3] The Peers wanted to abolish the teaching of philosophy in the *collèges*[4] and professed concern about the effects on young minds of contact with philosophy. The jist of Cousin's reply: Definitely not; since philosophy teaches natural certitudes (for example, the existence of God, the freedom or immortality of the soul), in principle, it can never be too early to begin. In other words, as long as the contents of instruction reinforce, as it were, the predominant forces, it is best to begin as early as possible. And the contradictory unity that reconciles the predominant force with itself and constitutes the basis of historical compromise is a mutually desired contract between the secular State and Religion. Cousin exclaims: "They will object: Are 15- and 16-year-olds to audit metaphysics? I reply, yes, of course . . . ." Let's

5

put aside for the time being the definition of the young philosopher as an *auditor* and the issue of aural education. Let's focus on the fact that it is the teaching of *metaphysics* which causes the objection of age to be raised, at least apparently so, and insofar as a distinction is drawn between metaphysics and dogmatic theology. It remains to be seen how the content of metaphysics is determined. Cousin, who declares himself in favor of its instruction, would seem more audacious than Hegel, who, at the moment he proposes to extend and improve the *preparation* for the study of philosophy offered in the *lycées*, excludes metaphysics from such a propadeutic. He calls attention to the "higher reasons" that work "to exclude *metaphysics proper from the Gymnasium*." But once we have anlayzed this difference between Hegel and Cousin, we find it to be a mere detail within a fundamental analogy. Cousin's adversaries have nothing against allowing such disciplines as psychology and logic to be taught in the lycée on the same footing as the traditional humanities. But metaphysics — that name given to philosophy "proper" — is more worrisome. Rightly or wrongly, metaphysics seems more slippery (*retorse*), less malleable, "ideologically" less flexible. Which, generally speaking, is neither right nor wrong, but would demand a different analysis of the philosophical slip (*retors*) in this regard. Perhaps this scheme still operates in an analogous way: no one denies that young "auditors" should receive instruction in the "human sciences," which, while often related, even annexed to philosophy, are not philosophy "proper."

So we have Cousin — who once confided to Hegel that he did not seek a political career but was a truly persecuted liberal (let's not simplify, let's never forget, at least no more than was the case for Hegel), who became a *Pair de France*, State Counsellor, Director of the ENS (*Ecole normale supérieure*), Rector of the University, Minister of Public Education — the very same Cousin addresses his peers: "You exclaim, we have 15- and 16-year-olds auditing metaphysics! And I reply, "Of course, the soul and God at the age of 15 or 16. You seem, furthermore, to take some particular pleasure in the notion that the philosophers in our *collèges* are 15 or 16 years old. Without being a slow learner, I myself took my degree in philosophy at the age of 19, and none of my students was younger than 18. Don't you think that an 18- or 19-year-old who has mastered the humanities and rhetoric, as well as the physical sciences and mathematics, should be capable of understanding the simple and unambiguous deductions of *natural* truths?" I emphasize *natural*: it is always by insisting upon the 'natural', by naturalizing the content or the forms of instruction, that one "inculcates" precisely what one wishes to exempt from criticism. GREPH[5] must be particularly careful in this respect, since its tactics could expose it to this risk of naturalist mystification: by demanding that the age at which a young person begins the study of philosophy be lowered, and that the scope of instruction be extended, there is a risk of being understood (without intending it; but the adversary will do his best to further this impression) as suggesting that once prejudices and "ideologies" have been erased, what will be revealed is the bare truth of an "infant" always already ready to philosophize and *naturally* capable of doing so. Those modes of discourse that are currently held to be the most "subversive" are never entirely free of this naturalism. They always appeal to some sort of return to primitive desire, to the simple lifting of repression, to the unbinding of energy, or to the primary process. Cousin's version of naturalism is — here as elsewhere — immediately theological. The natural truths taught by metaphysics proceed from divine writings and will have engraved in the soul of the disciple that which the teacher of philosophy can only reveal through self-effacement: an invisible writing that he causes to appear upon the body of the pupil. Are the discourses of the GREPH always free of this schematization? Does it not return, necessarily, in a more or less disguised form? Cousin: "Do you believe that, at the age of 18 or 19, when one has entirely completed one's humanities and rhetoric [premises which GREPH has now denounced], when one is studying physics and mathematics, one is incapable of understanding the simple and solid proofs proceeding from the great natural truths! The more necessary these truths are for the moral life of man, the more God wanted them to be available to human reason. He has engraved them in the mind and in the soul with luminous characters, which a skilled master must endeavor to reveal rather than obscuring them beneath the hieroglyphs of ambitious science."

Along stages that are always idiomatic, we are guided back to the most durable tradition of the philosophical concept of teaching: revelation, unveiling, the discovered truth of the "already-there" (*déjà là*) according to the mode of "not-yet" (*pas encore*), a Socrato-Platonic anamnesis sometimes taken up by the philosophy of psychoanalysis. Throughout these specific determinations may be found, time and again, the same scheme, the same concept of truth, of a truth linked to the same pedagogical structure. But the interpretation of these specificities must not succumb to this determination, as though one had to settle for the discovery of the same beneath all variations. One should never settle for this but also never forget to take its power into account. At the age of Cousin (which is still ours as well), the question at issue is always, as it was for Plato, one of a double metaphoric of inscription: a bad writing (*une mauvaise écriture*), secondary, artificial, cryptic or hieroglyphic, voiceless, intervenes to obscure good writing (*la bonne écriture*); it overdetermines, occults, complicates, perverts, makes a travesty of the natural inscription of the truth of the soul. By effacing himself, the teacher (*maître*) is also promoting the unlearning of bad writing. But if this motif retains a certain "Platonic" allure, the specificity of its "age" marks itself by a profound "Cartesian" reference. My use of its (traditional) philosophical name is a matter of provisional simplification; ultimately, this specificity does not have a philosophical configuration. It is Cousin himself who sends us back to Descartes; what is at stake here is an accommodating interpretation of Cartesianism, an attempt both to confirm that the teaching of philosophy in France must refer to the Cartesian tradition (since *true* and *French* coincide, natural truth is also national), and also to demonstrate that, contrary to the allegations of certain adversaries of secular schools and State education, Descartes is not dangerous: Cartesian doubt, as we all know, remains provisional and methodic; it is not a skeptical doubt. The Commission of Peers concerned with the business of the law under debate had indeed subscribed to this statement, penned by the Duc de Broglie: "What is the philosophy which is and should be taught in France, not only because its origin is French, but also because it is really the true and sound philosophy? Most certainly that of Descartes."

Let us put aside for now the issue of philosophical nationality, its implications, and its effect upon the history of the nationalization of French education since the time of Cousin. We shall have to return to it elsewhere, so far as it concerns the case of France; here (and elsewhere) we will be concerned with its bearing on the case of the Prussian State. Let's also put aside the question of the asserted equation of a philosophy that is "really true" and one that is "sound." For the moment, I wish simply to emphasize the determination of truth as certitude, because this constitutes a common ground for Hegel and Cousin in its philosophical phenomenon. And Cousin needs it, as a decisive argument in imposing his discourse upon the majority of Peers in this tight struggle between two contradictory interests of the then-prevailing force. By thus insisting upon the value of certitude, we can begin to put the situation into some kind of systematic perspective that would take into account — in order to relate it to, put it to the test of, or construe it as derived from — the basic interpretation of the philosophical "age" as *epochality* (that is, a Heideggerian interpretation that designates the Cartesian event as one of certitude, as a reassuring foundation of subjectivity that becomes the basis of all post-Cartesian metaphysics until and including Hegel). This *epochal* interpretation, with all its machinery, could be connected (either as proof or as derivation) to the Hegelian, onto-teleological interpretation of the philosophical "age" as moment, form, or figure, totality or *pars totalis*, in the history of reason. We could then pose the question whether, in this form or in ancillary ones, such a debate could dominate, indeed could shed light on, the problematic of the structures of teaching we have expounded — whether that which we first recognize in terms of its regional determinants — psychophysiological, technical, political, ideological, (etc.) — could be rendered comprehensible by such a debate, or whether it would, instead, force us to revise our premises.

This detour through France will bring us back to Berlin. We shall travel the opposite route another time. Cousin was in the process of citing de Broglie: "This is how M. the Duc de Broglie puts it. If the philosophy taught in the schools of the University is the one that really should be taught there, if it is the sound, the true philosophy, then, it seems to me, all is for the best. How could such a philosophy constitute a dangerous teaching? Because, they say, Cartesian philosophy proceeds from doubt. . . . " Cousin goes on to demonstrate, without refinement but with due precision, that provisional doubt is destined to establish the existence of the soul and the existence of God. With confident oratorical skill and political rhetoric — we will never encounter its parliamentary equal — he amalgamates Descartes with Fénelon and Bossuet. And appropriately so, because if this amalgamation appears unrefined to a historian of philosophy, it is the refinement of *this* historian that is "crude," insofar as it blinds him to the nature of precisely those mechanisms that must be analyzed here. In regard to certain massive effects, in teaching and elsewhere, the difference between Descartes, Fénelon, and Bossuet may be negligible, and may be taken to be so when the situation demands; the texts will always authorize such amalgamations, and the efficacy of the alliance (or the alloy) that enables Descartes, Fénelon, and Bossuet to be amalgamated can be evaluated by means of the massive effects it produces. As well as by those elicited by Cousin's impeccable rhetoric. Here is the "age" as inferred from Descartes: "How could such a philosophy constitute a dangerous teaching? They attribute it to the fact that Cartesian philosophy begins with doubt — provisional doubt, to be sure — and proceeds in search, above all, of certainty; it is thus that it proclaims the distinction between and reciprocal independence of philosophy and theology. *These are excellent principles*, says Mr. Chairman (*M. le Rapporteur*). If they are excellent, it follows that they are simultaneously true and useful; it is, therefore, good to teach them. Please note that I am not the one who introduced the issue of the value of the principles of Cartesian philosophy into a parliamentary debate. I had no intention of turning this assembly into a philosophical academy. . . . Doubt, even provisional doubt, is not the true principle of Cartesian philosophy. Descartes' professed intention is to destroy the foundations of skepticism and to prove unshakeably the existence of the soul and the existence of God. . . . The principles of Cartesian philosophy are those of Fénelon's *Treatise on the Existence of God (Traité de l'existence de Dieu)* and Bossuet's *Treatise on the Knowledge of God and the Self (Traité de la connaissance de Dieu et de soi-même)*. The second of these two works was compiled for a pupil (*auditeur*) who wasn't yet fifteen years old, and whom Bossuet was educating to be a man and then a king—and not a philosopher. He also taught the Dauphin logic; his notebooks contain matter enough to shock our diffidence even today. Did he stop there? No. His aim was to impart to his august, but very youthful pupil not the elementary psychology that understanding allots to us, but rather that sound and strong metaphysics which, supported by reason and the soul, raises itself to God. But, it will be said, 'metaphysics for fifteen and sixteen-year olds? . . . ' "

With such a logic of certainty, based on *natural* and *native* grounds—here revealed in the language and history of a philosophy that is both *national* and yet sufficiently natural to be universal—Cousin could well have gone back much further than the age of sixteen. Why didn't he? In order to account for this "contradiction," and hence for its "logic," what must be addressed is the problem of ideology, of the Ideologues, and of the relation between Ideology and the "unchangeable givens with which we must begin," namely the existence, "in every civilized society," of "two classes of men" (Destutt de Tracy, *Observations upon the Current System of Public Instruction [Observations sur le système actuel d'Instruction publique]*). We shall return to this elsewhere. At the moment we are interested in situating the connection between, *on the one hand*, a particular problematic of the-age-for-the-teaching-of-philosophy as an allegedly natural state of development of the soul and body, and, *on the other hand*, a particular problematic of the-teaching-of-philosophy in the age of the State, at the moment when new social forces tend to divest the Church of the monopoly on education in order to confer this monopoly upon the State they are in the process of taking over [arraisonner]. The concept of the onto-encyclopedic *Universitas* is inseparable from a certain concept of this State. In the course of the struggle for the monopoly of public education, Cousin never ceased to reiterate: "If the University is not the State, then [our adversary] is correct. . . . Unless I am mistaken, however, it has been proved that the University is the State; that is to say, public power brought to bear on the instruction of the young." (The objections of numerous ministers and of M. le Vicomte Dubouchage: "That, exactly, is what we would contest.")

Cousin had begun, logically enough, by recalling that education is an institution and, consequently, that "to teach is not a natural right": "the State has not only the right to oversee teachers . . . it has the right to confer upon them the power of teaching . . . and public education as a whole constitutes an enormous social power which the State has the right and the duty not only to oversee, but also, to a certain extent, to direct from above. . . . The right to teach is neither a natural right nor a private activity; it is a public power." And in one of those agrégation-reports that the GREPH will have to reassemble into a (partial) corpus and then to analyse, Cousin in 1850 admonishes: "A professor of philosophy is a functionary of the moral order, appointed by the State for the purpose of cultivating minds and souls by means of the most *reliable* [*certains*] aspects [my emphasis, J. D.] of the science of philosophy."

Correspondence between Hegel and Cousin. Between 1822 and 1844, the birth of philosophy in the age of European civil service

Hegel's discourse on the State will have presided at this birth, to the extent, at least, that a discourse can be said to preside. This discourse on the State is also, inextricably, an onto-encyclopedic system of the *Universitas*; the power of this discursive machine and of the forces it serves no longer needs to be demonstrated. All the blows it has sustained — those inflicted by Marx, Nietzsche, Heidegger, and everything for which these names stand — all these blows, as violent and as *heterogeneous* as they seem, compared to each other as well as in their relations to the Hegelian program, continue to reverberate with it, to justify themselves in its terms, to negotiate within its space, and to risk being overcodified (surcodé) — even today — by the interchange into which it forces them. Even to the point, each time, of running the risk of merely reproducing it, with or without the "liberal" modifications we have observed in Hegel and Cousin.

THE HERITAGE OF HEGEL AND THE FUTURE OF HIS ESTABLISHMENT

Am I reading all this in(to) the image of the child Hegel, in(to) the exposure (*cliché*) of a disclosure (*confidence*) (" . . . if I am permitted to evoke my own experience . . . in my twelfth year . . . ")? Do we see the scene? No, not yet. This image, which we would be wrong to pounce upon, has been, up to a certain point, staged by Hegel. His hold on it is manifest, and the Hegelian manipulation of the performance (*représentation*) always acts itself out inside a bag full of negatives (*clichés*), which promises more than one surprise.

All the same, what a scene. Hegel didn't always eschew autobiographical confidences. In those philosophical works of his which we call "major" (but where are we to situate this letter? how are we to classify it in the hierarchy? must we indeed accept the principles of this hierarchy?), it happens from time to time that he talks /about/ himself[6], that he whispers private things into the reader's ear. About Antigone, for example, and the calm he acquires from the awful carnage. These confidences are always evoked or adduced by the philosophical necessity of demonstration. Here too, doubtless. But this time, it's the little Georg-Friedrich Wilhelm between the ages of eleven and thirteen.

A few years ago, in Strasbourg, I saw, or think I saw, a photo of Martin wearing short pants. Martin Heidegger. Must he not have trembled before Thinking or Philosophy? Mustn't his Masters or Pastors have delighted in provoking fear and promoting the delight engendered by fear in order that it discharge itself in laughter before the short pants of a great man defrocked (he, too, having emerged, as it were, like Hegel, from an unforgettable "Theological Seminary")? There, it wasn't Martin himself who displayed the photograph. Rather, his brother, "the sole brother," as one of Heidegger's dedications reads. The brother turned him this trick with the naive, affectionate mischievousness of someone swelling with pride at having written a booklet about the memories of a family, "Heidegger," but who also has (perhaps) something of a (deadly) grudge concerning his brother in short pants. In short pants, at an age when one has not yet learned philosophy, much less thought, there is no difference yet between two sole brothers.

Here, it's Hegel himself who, index finger on the seam of his breeches, proffers the exposure (*cliché*) to the Minister: here I am between the ages of eleven and thirteen. And he does it in the ripeness of age, at a moment when the philosopher (fifty-two years old) and his philosophy begin to speak of their death; at twilight. The next month (June 1822), addressing the same ministerial sponsor, in a spirit of exchange consistent with the ubiquitous exigencies of systematic philosophical rigor, Hegel speaks of "supplementary revenues," of his children, his death, his widow, and of the insurance he has taken out for the future. To Altenstein: "Your Excellency was generous enough, on the occasion of my appointment to the University of this city, to nourish my hopes that the development of the projects that Your Excellency envisages for the institutions of learning would afford him the opportunity to open up a new field of activity for me and to augment my future resources. I dare anticipate the realization of these benevolent promises only in connection with Your Excellency's noble plans for the development of knowledge and the education of the young, and I regard the improvement of my own economic situation only as a subordinate element in this totality. Since, however, four and one-half years have passed since my appointment in Berlin, and since various domestic troubles have made my situation increasingly difficult, I have recalled Your Excellency's previous statements on my behalf; and Your Excellency's benevolent wishes authorize me to express to him the hopes to which these circumstances have given rise. I did not fail to acknowledge my gratitude when, as a consequence of the duties assigned me at the Royal Examination Commission [to which our letter of 22 April alludes as a legitimizing experience], I received supplementary resources. But this supplement is already almost entirely exhausted, owing to the fact that, as I approach old age, I am obliged to think of the future of my wife and children — all the more so, since I have devoted all my personal resources to my intellectual development (*formation*) which I now place at the service of the royal government. My insurance premium for the General Fund for Widows, in order that my heirs may receive 300 thalers per year, in addition to my mandatory contributions to the University Widows' Fund, amounts to an annual expenditure of 170 thalers. I cannot make this sacrifice year after year without two considerations imposing themselves on me: first, that if I do not die a professor of the Royal University, my contributions to the University Widows' Fund will be entirely lost; and second, that because of my insurance at the General Fund for Widows, my future widow and my children will not be able to count on the generous help of his Royal Majesty." We shall read the rest of this letter; it merits attention, as does this correspondence as a whole, but we should note immediately the contradiction Hegel confronts with such anguish and which he begs the Minister to help him resolve. This insurance fund for widows at the University (there could, of course, be nothing but widowed women [*veuves*] at a university open only to men, and preferably married men) already represents a socialization that should give the families of civil servants all necessary security. But since the fate of professors is determined by royal power (Hegel is afraid of not dying a "professor of the Royal University," he will do everything to die a professor of the Royal University), if Hegel were to lose his job before his death, he would have taken out this insurance for *nothing*: the University Widows' Fund would not pay (since he would not be a member of the University), nor would the King (since he had taken out insurance at the General Fund for Widows). It is acutely necessary to resolve this contradiction between the insufficiently developed rationality of civil society and a State that is still too determined in its particularity. As always, Hegel raises the contradiction to *catastrophic* proportions in view of the best resolution. In order to turn the situation around.

How could one not take out policies at the University Fund for nothing? So that, after all, there need never be a widow or children left unprovided after the death of the Philosopher; which is to say that there need never be a widow or children of the University; for is a widow who can still count on the revenues (on the returns) of her husband really a widow? Or indeed has she ever been one? And are children insured against the death of the father (capital or revenue) still children? Or rather, haven't they always been?

Hegel was reassured by Altenstein, the Minister, as early as the following month. By the State. But by a State still conferring special favors and acting by decree, one might say.

Yes. Nevertheless, this State did help its philosopher, the apologist for its rationality; the philosopher who, at least, conferred the justification of universal form upon the particular forces represented by *this* State, or rather, upon certain of its factions. Would it have helped him otherwise? And conversely, would Hegel have said just anything, would he have renounced the "internal" demands of the system (*Encyclopedia*, *Logic*, and especially the *Philosophy of Right of Berlin*), of the system at the height of its development, simply for the love of Marie, Karl, or Immanuel Hegel? All that, moreover, for a widow and children about whom he already thinks, as it were, posthumously, and thus with the paradoxical disinterestedness of the dead? How could all these particular interests (family or civil society) be reconciled so neatly with the system of the interests of reason, with the history of the system and the system of history, without becoming awkwardly cumbersome? That is the question. This unity is not easy to conceive, but we can neither omit any of the pertinent terms, forces, desires, or interests, nor relegate any of them to secondary status. We shall return to this.

In satisfying Hegel's demands the month following the letter about the *lycées*, Altenstein knew whom he was supporting. On 25 June he sent Hegel a letter informing him of what he had procured (travel reimbursements, 300 thalers for the previous year, 300 thalers for the current year, etc.). In order to secure these "extraordinary allotments," he had had to speak in praise of Hegel's philosophy *and* politics, in praise not only of his political philosophy, but of his *political influence* — of his political influence in a difficult situation, in an atmosphere of considerable student unrest. Altenstein knows exactly what *he has to say*, even if what he actually thinks is more complex: "Certainly I need not expand upon Hegel's merits as a man, a university professor, or a scholar. His scholarly merits are widely recognized. He is undoubtedly the most profound and most solid philosopher in Germany. But his value as a man and as a university professor is even *more important* [my emphasis, J. D.]. His influence upon the young is infinitely salutary. With courage, seriousness, and competence, he has opposed the pernicious infiltration of a philosophy without depth, and he has dashed the presumptions of the young. His opinions render him worthy of the highest esteem and this fact — combined with his salutary influence — is recognized even by those who have nothing but disdain for anything that has to do with Philosophy" (6 June 1822).

Hegel knows all this. Practically every thread in this skein where "private interests" and the interests of historical reason, special interests and the interests of the State, the interests of a particular state and the universal historical rationality of the State are so conveniently intertwined. He had just recently expounded this in the *Philosophy of Right*; and he knows, at the moment with which we are concerned, how his *Philosophy of Right* "had thoroughly scandalized the demagogues" (Letter to Duboc, 30 July 1822). And when he thanks Altenstein, the terms of his gratitude serve to define the locus of the exchange and of the contract, the insurance of the one and the assurance of the other: "As regards subsequent developments in my situation, I must refer myself most respectfully to the sage judgment of Your Excellency with the same spirit of absolute confidence in which I responded to the summons to enter the service of the Royal State. In my work, for which freedom and serenity of mind are particularly necessary, I need not fear being troubled in the future by extrinsic cares, now that Your Excellency's benevolent promises have relieved me of my worries, and now that manifold and unequivocal evidence has secured for me the reassuring conviction that possible misgivings regarding philosophy on the part of the high authorities of the State — misgivings readily occasioned by false tendencies within philosophy itself — have not only remained foreign to my public activity as a professor, but also that I myself have labored, not without commendation and success, to aid those young people studying here to think properly, and thus to render myself worthy of the confidence of Your Excellency and of the Royal Government" (Berlin, 3 July 1822).

Having taken out all this insurance and reassurance — on the Heirs (of Hegel), on the State (of Prussia), on the University (of Berlin) — he does not forget Bavaria, where he participates in the lottery. In July, after having congratulated Niethammer on the budget for public instruction adopted by the Bavarian State Legislature ("the other branches don't concern me"), after informing his correspondent of the disciplinary measures against "demagogic" instructors under consideration in Berlin (a week before dispatching the Letter about the Gymnasium. Hegel continues: "The brilliant state of the Bavarian budget reminds me that I am still in possession of Bavarian lottery tickets, of whose fate I have heard nothing. . . . I take the liberty of attaching a scrap of paper on which I have jotted down their numbers, and would ask your son — since he works in the Department of Finance — to make inquiries in this matter. . . . " He then alludes to the difficulty of receiving approval in matters of philosophy, theology, and Christianity: "It is in applying concepts and reason to matters concerning the State that one encounters the most difficulty [in gaining this approbation], but I myself have already made it very clear that I have no desire to ally myself further with our gang of libertarian apostles. But there is no sense in worrying any more about those who are on the other side."

And indeed, if, because of his political behavior as well as of his political philosophy, Hegel would seem to uphold the State against a "gang" of "demagogues," this support is conditional, complex, and an entire strategic reserve can make Hegel pass for an enemy in the eyes of those "who are on the other side." We have plenty of signs of this strategic reserve, of the recourse it might find in the system of the philosophy of right, of the concrete effects it had back then in the political arena. For obvious reasons, we shall have to limit ourselves, in a moment, to those which are legible in the "Letter about the Gymnasium."[7]

Ecce homo, it is I between the ages of eleven and thirteen. The man who says this is not simply a mature man, already contemplating death, thinking about the University Widows' Fund, and of a time post-Hegel (will he ever have thought of anything else?). It is Hegel the philosopher, who is not an adult like any other, one mature man among others. It is a philosopher who presents himself as the first adult philosopher, the first to think the beginning and end of philosophy, truly to think them through conceptually. It is the philosopher of a philosophy which thinks itself (*qui se pense*) as having left childhood behind, which claims to think, within its own history, all the ages of philosophy, all of time and the entire teleology of its maturation. And which, therefore, has nothing but childhoods in its past, and in particular, childhoods under representation, if representation is, *already without yet being*, "the thought that conceives." The child, Hegel, is thus more serious, more amusing, more singular, singularity itself: not impossible, nor inconceivable, but practically unimaginable. He did everything to render it unimaginable, until the day when — until the close of the day when, anxious about the future of the teaching of philosophy in the State, anxious as well about the future of his widow and his sons, he evokes, for argument's sake, his childhood; he remembers, he says he remembers, that which he already remembered between the ages of eleven and thirteen. For *already* it was but a matter of memory or understanding, not of speculative thought.

The scene seems all the more comical for its absolute lack of braggadocio, which — were there even the faintest suspicion of it — would have to be neutralized, legitimized, and thereby effaced with whatever good reasons we would then invoke. And indeed, the comical element is a result precisely of the *good reasons* with which Hegel can authorize himself to say such things in all modesty. First of all, it is true, he must have been very, very gifted. We have only to read his works — so well known and extremely profound, as Altenstein reminds the Chancellor. And then, we have the additional testimony about that brilliant schoolboy who read so very much and recopied long passages of the things he read. And again, if he offers himself as an example (*pour exemple*) but not as exemplary (*en exemple*); if he plays with the example the way, elsewhere, he teaches the *Beispiel*,[8] it is in order to render apparent the essence of a possibility: every normally healthy child could be Hegel. At the moment when the old Hegel remembers the child Hegel, but also thinks him and conceives him in his truth, this child Hegel plays, no doubt, like all children, but plays here the role of a figure or of a moment in the pedagogy of the mind. Moreover, the anecdote serves to support a thesis; it is intended to carry a conviction and pave the way for political decisions. It justifies itself, thereby effacing its anecdotal singularity by invoking an older common experience (*die allgemeine ältere Erfahrung*). It is this common experience that certifies that this instruction does not exceed the intellectual powers (*Fassungskraft*) of high school students. Finally, this capacity, to which the little, eleven-year-old Hegel bears witness, is *not yet* a philosophical capacity as such (that is, a speculative capacity), but rather, a memory, the memory of certain lifeless contents, contents of understanding (*entendement*), contents that are forms (definitions, rules, and figures of syllogisms). And this not-yet propagates its effects throughout the letter, permeates the entire pedagogical machinery that Hegel proposes to the Minister. This *not-yet* of the *already*, as we shall see, interdicts precisely that which it would seem to promote, namely, the teaching of philosophy in the Gymnasium.

When Hegel says that he still remembers the *idea clara* and syllogistics, we note a mixture of coyness (refinement and play, the put-on puerility of the great mathematician who feigns astonishment that he still remembers his multiplication tables), a certain affected tenderness for the remnants of the child in himself; most of all, a portion of irony in his challenge to pedagogic modernity, "a challenge directed at current prejudices against autonomous thought, productive activity." And what is more current (even today, for the age of Hegel will have lasted that long) than the monotonous pedagogic modernity that takes issue with mechanical memorization, mnemotechnics, in the name of *productive* spontaneity, of initiative; of independent, *living* self-discovery, etc.? But Hegel's irony is double: He knows that he has, elsewhere, objected to mnemotechnic formalism and learning "by heart." We cannot, therefore, suspect him of being simply and *generally* a partisan of such techniques. It is a question, precisely, of age, of the order and teleology of acquisition, of *progress*. And this progress, from age to age, is not only that of the schoolboy in the Prussian Gymnasium. We discover its stages and its sequence in the history of philosophy. The age of formalism and quantitative technique — the age of Leibniz, for example — is that of "incapable childhood" (*unvermögende Kindheit*), as the *Greater Logic* puts it. But on the other hand, the modernist theme of productive spontaneity remains just as abstract, and hence childish (for the child is more abstract than the adult, like a concept still undetermined), just as empty or incapable as are formalism and mechanical memory insofar as they have not been worked through, sublated. The entire "system" of speculative dialectics organizes this childhood anamnesis to suit the minsterial project — its conformism, respectful and sometimes inane; its irony; its coyness; its imperturbable thoroughness.

I've been somewhat precipitous in foregrounding this scene, removing it from the context of a Report (*Rapport*) which frames it and exceeds it substantially. Why? In order to be a step ahead of impatient readers, in order to anticipate the adversaries of the GREPH, those for whom the GREPH is first and foremost a gathering of eccentrics (oh yes) who would teach philosophy at the cradle: some call us destructive and antiphilosophical, while others accuse us of excessive zeal and panphilosophism at a time when, as everyone knows — for example, since Hegel — that philosophy is finished; which is to say that there is a virtual alliance between these two reactions. Nor will they hesitate to seize on this: "Now the GREPH claims to base an argument upon the fact that the great Hegel, between the ages of 11 and 13 . . . " etc. And they'll continue, doubtless: "Not satisfied simply with invoking the example of Hegel, the GREPH hopes to Hegelianize children, starting them on the *Greater Logic* or *The Philosophy of Right* in the sixth form . . . " etc. We are already familiar with such stereotyped objections, with the code of this reaction which, as always, begins with the fear of comprehending. Of comprehending that we are trying to get at something utterly different, as should already have become manifest and perhaps will become more so. For example, as we read this Letter of Hegel's.

I do not want to say how this "minor" text of Hegel's *should be read* — "by and in itself," in its "proper context," within the scene into which the GREPH has opted to translate and reproduce it. I do not want to say what *should be made* of this text (a point I make for the sake of those who believe that to read is, immediately, to do; or for those who, on the other hand, are equally certain that to read is not to do, not even to write; both are caught up in those oppositions — in the form of guardrails [*gardefous*] — whose practices, tendentiousness, finality, and directions for use are familiar by now). I do not want to say *what is needed*, nor do I want to say what is needed *according* to the GREPH. For in writing I am also addressing the GREPH, as, I presume, we all are here.[9] From the outset, the GREPH has defined itself as a locus of work and debate, and not as a center for the broadcasting of slogans or doctrinaire messages. It is probable that when we do reach agreement — in order to take a stance, to take political initiative, and to undertake appropriate actions — the GREPH will not shrink from "slo-gans" (*mot d'ordre*), which it does not consider simply to be the opposite of the concept: there is something of the slogan in every concept, and vice versa. Certainly, there was an initial agreement about the condi-tions of such a debate; about the new objects (excluded until now) that must be brought to light; about the old objects that must be seen in a new light; about certain forces that must be combatted. And this con-sensus still exists. But so does the initial openness (*ouverture*) of the debate. And it is in order to take part in such a debate — keeping in mind certain common assumptions   that I would like to develop cer-tain hypotheses and advance certain propositions, using, as my point of departure, an applied reading which might, for the moment, interest no one but myself. What is to be done with this Letter of Hegel's? Where is it to be situated? Where does it take (its) place? Evaluation is inevitable: is it a "major" text or a "minor" one? Is it a "philosophical" text? What status, as they say, do we grant it? What title? One of the tasks of the GREPH could be a critique (not only formal, but effective and concrete) of all existing hierarchies, of all the criteriology, implicit or explicit, that privileges certain evaluations and classifications ("major" or "minor" texts). Further: a general reelaboration of the en-tire problematic of hierarchies. Without such a reelaboration, no pro-found transformation will be possible. The force that dominates the process of classification and the institution of hierarchies allows us to read whatever it is interested in having us read (which it then labels major texts, or texts of "great import"); and it renders inaccessible whatever it is interested in underestimating, and which in general it *cannot read* (describing such texts as minor, or marginal). And this holds true for the discourse of the educator and for all his evaluatory procedures (grading; juries for examinations, competitions, theses; so-called supervisory committees; etc.); it is the evaluative standard determining all discourse: from that of the critic and the upholder of tradition to that determining editorial policy, the commercialization of texts, etc. And once again, it is not simply a matter of texts in print or on blackboards, but rather of a general textuality without which there is no understanding and no action. Reread the Preliminary Project of the GREPH: every sentence demands that the censured or devaluaed be displayed, that the vast holdings of a more-or-less forbidden library be exhumed from the cellars. And that there be a lack of respect for prevailing evaluations: not simply in order to indulge certain perverse bibliophilic pleasures (on the other hand, why not?); nor even in order better to understand what links philosophy to its institution, to its institutional underside and recesses (*dessous et envers*); but rather to transform the very conditions of our effective intervention in them. *Underside* or *recesses*, because it is not a matter of discovering today, belatedly, what has been known all along: that there is such a thing as a philosophical institution. Indeed, "Philosophy" ("*la*" *philosophie*) has always had a dominant concept to take this into account, and *institution* is at bottom the name it has reserved for this task. Underside and recesses, because we are not satisfied with what the institution reveals about itself: neither with what we can perceive empirically, nor with what we can conceive according to the law of the philosophical concept. Underside or recesses would no longer have a signification dominated by the philosophical opposition that continues to order discourse in terms of a concealed substance or essence of the institution, hidden beneath its accidents, circumstances, phenomena, or superstructures. Underside and recesses would designate, rather, that which, while still being situated within this venerable (conceptual and metaphoric) topos, might begin to extricate itself from this opposition and to constitute it in a new manner.

The critical reelaboration of this hierarchy and of this problematics of hierarchy must not be restricted to new "theorems" in the same language (*langage*). It requires that we also write in a language (*langue*) and that we operate according to schemes that can no longer be determined by the old divisions.

This is why the *overturning* (*renversement*) of the authorized hierarchy is not enough. This is why it is not enough to canonize "minor" texts or to exclude, and thereby devalue, "major" texts. The *same* philosophical program can lead to evaluative or classificatory statements that seem contradictory: this text is a "minor" text (for example: circumstantial, "journalistic," empirico-anecdotic, feebly philosophical, etc.); or the *same* text is a "major" text (addressing a "great" philosophical theme, engaging the great problematic tradition, manifesting all the signs of a profound theoretical responsibility, etc.). But are these statements contradictory? If the *same* premises lead to evaluations that are apparently contradictory, what does this tell us about the system of reading and hierarchization at work? If this system of reading has an essential rapport with "Hegelian philosophy," with everything this philosophy seems to collect, complete, configurate into its "age," then the "Letter" in which we are interested can no longer be a mere example, a case in point evoked to illustrate this question.

Hegel's Letter on the Gymnasium has, quite obviously, been treated as a minor text. And not only in France. The letter does not belong to the "scholarly" corpus of Hegel. It was not vouchsafed a place in the Correspondence. Even if we don't allege deliberate censorship or willful exclusion, how are we to believe this "omission" fortuitous or insignificant? But its necessity is the complicated product of factors that cannot be analyzed until we acknowledge the traditional marginalization (*minorisation*) of texts of this kind and of the entire system in which this takes place, as well as the complicated strategy involved in the relations between Hegel and royal power. This extreme philosophic and political complexity makes any attempt to situate this gesture in a particular, determinate context both difficult and ambiguous. And this holds true in our case — that of the GREPH today.

If this "special report" has more or less disappeared from the great circulation of philosophical texts, can this be explained entirely by reasons relating to its "form"? It is, to be sure, a letter. Of course, there is a venerable tradition of philosophical letters. But of what does this tradition consist and what does it preserve? Either "fictive" letters on topics that tradition has sanctioned as "great philosophical themes," or correspondence between philosophers, at least one of whom must be considered "great," and which treats subjects worthy of the great philosophical vein. Or perhaps letters written by a "great philosopher" to some worldly dignitary: the custodian of public power receives a philosophical message from a subject who is a philosopher (even if he is a foreigner, he occupies the position of the respectful subject of the King, the Queen, the Princess, or, we might say, the Prince-in-General) on a topic already designated as philosophical. Or, on a topic of great political philosophy, which amounts to the same thing. Because, until the age of Hegel, questions pertaining to scholarship or to the university were not located in the domain of large-scale politics (*la grande politique*). The question of education is not yet the business of a State occupied with recovering its power from the forces of feudalism. (The Altenstein episode is, in this respect, a transition of extreme historical complexity and considerable symptomatic value: although we cannot do so here, we must analyze it as closely and minutely as possible in order even to begin to "open up" this letter of Hegel's.) In the "great" tradition of philosophical letters, the great addressee is assumed to be a philosopher or a person of philosophical stature; the great philosopher speaks to him as an adult tutor. With the respect owed to a Prince by a subject, but with the authority of a subject who is a philosopher — educated, mature — a sort of specialized technician. Double dysymmetry. But the report (and rapport) is a double one and, at any rate, one does not speak of education as one would of a political matter; nor does one treat the teaching of philosophy as a problem of the State.

Besides these great philosophical letters, there are the private correspondences of the great philosophers: they are published because of their biographical-anecdotal interest and only insofar as they illuminate the lives of philosophers who have been granted admission to the Pantheon of Western Metaphysics. They are usually read as if they were novels or memoirs.

The tradition, as we have described it, cannot find a place for Hegel's "Letter." It is not really a "letter," although it bears all the external characteristics of one. It is addressed less to a person than to a function. It is a report (*rapport*) commissioned by a Ministry: commissioned by a very particular Ministry and a very particular Minister in a situation that is very difficult to analyze, even today; in a situation whose political interpretation is immediately and necessarily relevant to the fundamental stakes of all the political struggles in Europe during the 19th and 20th centuries. And in a situation in which Hegel's place can really not be determined without the simultaneous and structural cognizance of an entire general textuality, consisting (at least) of: (1) his "great" philosophical works, the most obvious being the entire *Philosophy of Right*, which is to say, at least that which Jacques d'Hondt calls the "three" philosophies of right[10]; (2) his other writings, that is, *at least* all his letters, even the secret ones, those which he hid from the police as an act of solidarity with certain victims of persecution; (3) his actual practice in all the complexity that has always been more or less evident, but which, as we know, cannot be reduced (far from it) during the Berlin period to that of an official and respectful (indeed, obsequious) philosopher of the State.

Interpreting the age of Hegel involves keeping in mind this boundless textuality, in an effort to determine the specific configuration that interests us here: the moment at which systematic philosophy—in the process of becoming philosophy of the State, of Reason as the State—begins to entail, more or less obviously, but essentially, indispensably, a pedagogical systematics governed by the necessity of entrusting the teaching of philosophy to state structures and civil servants. The business most certainly began before Hegel. The philosophical-pedagogic interventions of the French Ideologues at the time of the Revolution are signs of it, and we know the significance the French Revolution held for Hegel. But can we not date from the age of Hegel the most powerful discursive machine of this problematic? Is this not indicated by the fact that the Marxist, Nietzschean, and Nietzscheo-Heideggerian problematics that now dominate all questions concerning the relations of education and the State must still come to grips with Hegelian discourse? They cannot do without it: *at least* in regard to this problem of education and the State, of the teaching of philosophy and the State, which, it seems to me, no philosophy prior to the "age of Hegel"—no political philosophy, no philosophy of education—treated with the kind of irreducible historical specificity that interests us. Such is, at least, the hypothesis I submit for discussion. If my hypothesis is admissable, then any treatment of this "Report" as minor, any evasion or subordination of this *type* of text is tantamount to a failure to move beyond a prestatist problematics of education and of philosophical education. It involves a refusal to recognize the original irreducible configuration in which our questions are asked. And consequently a refusal to identify its borders and its exterior; a refusal, furthermore, to transform or transgress.

THE PRINCIPLES OF THE RIGHT TO PHILOSOPHY

What happens in this "Report"? Hegel is not simply the "great philosopher" consulted by the powers-that-be (*Le pouvoir*). He is summoned to Berlin by Altenstein, who offers him Fichte's chair. Altenstein, Minister of Public Instruction since 1817, incorporates the struggle (waged with suppleness, negotiation, and compromise) for the enforcement of mandatory schooling, recently adopted, for academic freedom, and for the defense of the universities against feudal powers. Engels will praise his liberalism. Along with Schulze, Director of Higher Education in his Ministry, a disciple and friend of Hegel's, freemason and courageous liberal, Altenstein occupies a very sensitive, precarious, vulnerable place in the budding bureaucracy, struggling against the forces of feudalism: that of a compromise formation. To the extent that he is allied with Altenstein and Schulze, Hegel is caught between the "feudalists" and the "demagogues," giving signs of allegiance to the "right" when the situation or the relation of forces seems to require that he do so, secretly protecting his persecuted friends on the "left." By addressing his report to Altenstein, he is not simply acting as a "realistic" philosopher, compelled to reckon with the powers that be, with the contradictions inherent in these powers, and with his interlocutor's strategy within these contradictions. It is not the powers-that-be (*Le pouvoir*) — considered as a monolithic whole — which are compelled to reckon with the Hegelian system; and indeed, Hegel will say nothing in his pedagogical-philosophical propositions that is not in keeping with this system, a system which, admittedly, can fold and turn in on itself without breaking. Only a *fraction* of the forces in power is represented in the summons to Hegel. At any rate, the space for the intricate negotiations between the forces in power (however contradictory they may be and however determined may be a particular stasis of contradiction) and Hegel's philosophical strategy must be open, possible, already practicable. Without this, no compromise, no implicit contract would even have been sketched. This space, like the topic upon which it depends, can construe itself neither within Hegel's *oeuvre* — as if something of the sort existed in a pure state — nor in what we could regard as the nonphilosophical realm exterior to it. Neither the "internal necessities of the system" alone nor the generally accepted opposition between "system" and "method" can account for the complexity of these contracts or compromises. They are neither simply *within* nor simply *external to* philosophy. (Engels: "That is how the revolutionary side of Hegelian doctrine is stifled by the contumescence of its conservative side . . . therefore, the internal necessities of the system themselves *alone are sufficient* explanation of how a profoundly revolutionary mode of thought can lead to a very moderate political conclusion." *Ludwig Feuerbach and the End of German Classical Philosophy*, p. 16. My emphasis. Is the distinction between "system" and "method" inherent in the systematic? Is it intraphilosophical? etc.)

The essential foundation of the contract is the necessity of making teaching — particularly philosophical teaching — into a structure of the State. But of which State? The State itself, as conceived in *The Philosophy of Right*, should no longer be at the disposition of a prince or a particular force as a form of private property engaged in a contract (§75, Note on Contracts and Marriage). But if the State is above civil society, the idea of the State is not a Utopia, and the Preface to the *Philosophy of Right* insists upon this in the famous paragraph about the philosophy that does not leap over its own time ("*Hic* Rhodus, *hic* Saltus," and then, "*Hier ist die Rose, hier tanze*"). This is not the place to reopen the debate about Hegelian philosophy as an official philosophy or a philosophy of the State. The elements (*données*) of this debate have consistently been too oversimplified for us to presume, here, briefly to reconstruct the overall problematic. The fact that Marx and Engels *themselves* judged it necessary to take violent exception to the simplifications that reduce Hegel to a mere philosopher of the State — this should be enough to put us on our guard against hasty conclusions. For the present, let us be content with locating the space of the strategic negotiations: between the Idea of the State as defined in the third part of *The Philosophy of Right* (reality as an act of substantial will, as a goal in itself, absolute, immobile, knowing what it wants in its universality, etc.) and personal subjectivity or particularity, whose most extreme forms the modern State has the power to perfect.

Within this space, Hegel seems to anticipate the ministerial request. Then, as now (the analogy would take us far, even though it must be handled with care), the Ministry wants to keep "philosophical teaching in the Gymnasium from losing itself in a babble of hollow formulas (*sich in ein hohles Formelwesen verliere*) or from transgressing the limits of school teaching." Then, as now, these two fears are related, if not confounded. What is the hollowness of formulas? What is babble? Who is to define it? From what point of view? According to what philosophy and whose politics? Does not every new or subversive discourse always constitute itself through rhetorical effects that are necessarily identified as gaps in the prevailing discourse, with the inevitable phenomena of discursive degradation, mechanisms, mimetisms, etc.? The relation of the "*Formelwesen*" to the alleged plenitude of the completed discourse will be definable only in terms of a strictly defined philosophy. Here Hegel is no more able than anyone else discoursing on babble to avoid proposing a philosophy — in this case the dialectic of speculative idealism — as a general criteriology that distinguishes between empty and full language in education. And which also determines the limit between schoolteaching and that which lies outside its domain. Nowhere in the letter is the question of this criteriology and these limits posed. Nor, furthermore, are either politics or the domain outside the school so much as mentioned. But it is in the answer to this unposed question that, as always, an educational system constructs or reforms itself.

Hegel — Hegel's philosophy — responds to the request, which we can here distinguish from the question: in order to avoid babble, to substantiate mind with content, with a good content such as is necessarily determined by the Hegelian system, and to begin there, to begin, indeed, with a content that has been recorded: with memory, with memory such that its concept is dialectically determined within the system ("for, in order to possess knowledge of any kind—even the highest sort—one must have memorized it [*im Gedächtnisse haben*]; regardless of whether this is to be a beginning *or* an end in itself." But Hegel goes on to justify his pedagogical proposition: *it is preferable that this be a beginning*, for "if it is a beginning, one has that much more freedom and inducement to think for oneself"). For Hegel, memory was both a beginning and an end; he remembers (his twelfth year) and remembers that he began by remembering that which he first learned by heart. But at the same time, this homology of the system (the dialectical concept of *Gedächtnis*) and of the autobiographical situation that gave Hegel the inducement and the freedom to think, this homology is to be enriched again by its pedagogical version: by beginning with teaching the content of knowledge, before even thinking it, we are assured of a highly determined prephilosophical inculcation which paves the way for good philosophy (*la bonne philosophie*). We know the schema, and the GREPH was quick to criticize certain of its current consequences.

In order to abide within the "limits of schoolteaching," this prephilosophical content will consist of the humanities (the Ancients, the great artistic and historical ideas of individuals and peoples, their ethics and their religiosity), classical literature, the dogmatic content of religion—so many disciplines that will be studied in light of the content that is essential to the preparation for speculative philosophy. Time and again, content is privileged in this propaedeutic, and the material part stressed over the formal part. The treatment reserved for religion and its dogmatic content is remarkable enough. Indeed, it defines fairly accurately the lines of negotiation. There is, of course, as we know, a war between Hegel and religious authority. The two parties indulged in violent verbal exchanges. Hegel was accused and suspected of even worse. But at the same time, his interest is in wresting religious instruction from the religious powers; the *Philosophy of Religion* defines the conditions and the perspectives of this reappropriation. At stake is the raising of religion to the level of speculative thought, making apparent those aspects of religion that are elevated and consummated in philosophy, as in their truth. The pedagogical version of this movement is not a mere corollary of the philosophy of religion, without which the Letter would be incomprehensible. It is, rather, central to it. In 1810, he had written to Niethammer: "Protestantism has less to do with a particular confession than with a superior, more rational spirit of reflection and of culture; its spiritual foundations are not a sort of training adaptable to this or that utilitarian purpose." This objection to pedagogical teaching or utilitarianism, as expressed in the Letter of 1822, is therefore indissociable from this Protestant philosophy-pedagogy. And in 1816,

Hegel writes again: "Protestantism is not entrusted to the hierarchical organization of a church, but is, rather, found only in a general intelligence and a general culture. . . . Our universities and our schools are our churches" (cited by d'Hondt, pp. 53–54). This implies that the teaching of religion, in its dogmatic and ecclesiastical contents, be carried out neither as a solely historical matter (*nur als eine historische Sache*), as an account (*récit*) of events, as a narration without a concept, nor, formally, as the abstractions of natural religion, the guarantees of abstract morality, or subjective fantasms. In other words, there is but one way to rescue the teaching of religion from the ecclesiastical authorities while, at the same time, upholding its *thought* content against the conscious or unconscious destructors (atheists, deists, Kantians, etc.) of religious truth: to teach religion as it is *thought* in a speculative manner in the *Phenomenology of Mind*, the *Philosophy of Religion*, or the *Encyclopedia* ("the contents of philosophy and those of religion are the same," §573, etc.). But *teaching* it as such can only be carried out in a teaching of the State, of a State that conducts its rapport with the Church according to the *Principles of the Philosophy of Right*. There again, the Letter of 1822 is legible only if we read, concomitantly, chapter 270 of the *Philosophy of Right* about "philosophical knowledge which recognizes that the conflict between the State and the Church has nothing to do with the content of truth and reason, but rather, only with their form." The place of "dogmatic content" in education is defined in a footnote: "Like knowledge and science, religion has as its principle its own form which is different from that of the State; they [religion, science, and knowledge] enter into the State partly as a means of educating [Mittel der Bildung] and of forming attitudes, partly insofar as they are essentially *ends-in-themselves*, by virtue of their outward existence. In both respects, the principles of the State relate to them in terms of *application*. A comprehensive, concrete treatise on the State would also have to deal with such spheres—as well as with art, mere natural phenomena, etc.—and to consider their relations to and positions within the State." And the last section of the same chapter situates the question of teaching at the center of the rapports between Church and State. The example of Protestantism plays a very important role here, although it is alluded to only parenthetically: it is the case in which there is no "particular content" that can remain exterior to the State, since "in Protestantism" there is no "clergy which would be the sole depository of Church doctrine, for [in Protestantism] there is no laity."

The same demonstration is possible for the other branches of knowledge that Hegel wishes to integrate into preparatory teaching

(empirical psychology and the basics of logic). It would refer the pedagogical proposition to its own foundation in the Hegelian system of
speculative dialectics, the relations between understanding and reason;
to the critique or to the resurgence of Kantianism, etc. In short, no *philosophy* except Hegel's can assume or justify such pedagogy — its structure, its progression, and its rhythm — and remain rigorously consistent.
Can we not say that the basis of negotiation with the ministerial request
was extraordinarily narrow? Does this not explain why the Altenstein-
Hegel episode was without issue (*sans lendemain*)?

Certain of the sharper features of this episode indeed remain without issue. But rather than constituting a philosophical, political, or
pedagogical revolution, it developed (like Hegelian philosophy) and accumulated a past; and to a large extent it has survived. It was quite necessary, in this negotiation between political forces and a philosophical
discourse, that an ideal and common line be drawn. In the most spec-
tacular case, that of religion, it was necessary that the European State,
in its new forms and in the service of new forces, reclaiming a certain
power from feudalism and from the Church, manage to remove teaching from the jurisdiction of the clergy, at the same time "preserving" religion and putting it in the right. Putting it in the right while refusing
it a certain, particular, determinate power, thinking it philosophically
in its truth (philosophy): this was the formula, Hegel's formula. Which
is neither to allege that Hegel responded so admirably and in such detail
(art or chance?) to a demand formulated *elsewhere*, in the empirical
field of historical politics; nor vice versa. But a possibility had been
opened to this common language, to all its secondary variations (for Hegel was not the only philosopher to propose his pedagogy, and the entire
systematic range of these variations remains to be studied), to its *trans-
latability*. This common possibility is legible *and* tranformable neither
simply within the philosophical system, if such a thing existed in a pure
state, nor in a domain simply foreign to any sort of philosophy.

Taken in its greatest singularity, the Altenstein-Hegel endeavor was
undoubtedly a failure; but the general structure that opened it and that
Hegel tried to keep open is where we find ourselves today, and it does
not cease to modify its modalities. This what I call the age of Hegel.

For at the moment when he seems to respond to the highly specific
demands of a particular faction of the then-prevailing powers, Hegel
means to distinguish their *particularity*: the national from the bureau-
cratic. For example, in order to liberate the time necessary for the
teaching of logic, he does not hesitate to propose encroaching upon the
"so-called teaching of German and German literature" (thus taking a
stand in a competition whose issues and stakes we know all too well —

between philosophy, "French," and French "literature"); or similarly, upon the juridical encyclopedia, distinct from the theory of right. What is behind this choice? In the eyes of Hegel, it is the precondition for the development of logic. For logic is what conditions "the *general* formation of the mind (*allgemeine Geistesbildung*)," "general culture." And it is general culture that should thrive in the gymnasium instead of its being oriented toward "training" for civil service or "professional" studies.

We can no more attempt an *immediate* analogical transposition of this "liberal" motif than of any other, especially if we are in search of some kind of guarantee or slogan. First of all, because we must draw a scrupulous distinction between a reading in its own context, its historical and political context (Hegel's complex and mobile strategy vis-à-vis the different forces then struggling for the power of the State and its bureaucracy, etc.), and its seemingly intraphilosophical context, which is neither simply permeable nor hermetically sealed, and which, according to specific constraints whose principle of analysis has yet to be formulated, is ceaselessly in operation within the historico-political sphere. And then, because this "liberal" motif, like all those motifs we can identify in this letter, is structurally equivocal. By loosening the hold of the "civil services," of a particular State, of the forces of civil society that control it and command the "professional" market, Hegel extends the domain of a "general culture" which, as we know, always remains highly determined in the contents it inculcates. Other forces of civil society manifest themselves here, and any analysis must be extremely vigilant in this regard. When we "repeat" Hegel's "liberal" utterance in the present situation directed against the hasty specialization and demands of the capitalist market, against the call to order issued to the Inspectors General who are supposed to "apply themselves in the service" of the Haby Reform,[11] against the inquisition of the Rectors into everything pertaining to "academic freedom" or the freedom of the universities, etc.), we should know that neither in Hegel's situation nor in our own can this utterance raise itself above the demands and commands of given forces in civil society; and that the relation between liberal discourse and the mobile, subtle, sometimes paradoxical dynamic of these forces must constantly be reevaluated. The Haby Reform invokes a wide range of "liberal" and neutralist themes which are not sufficient — far from it — to neutralize its most singular political and economic finality. Indeed, such themes contribute to it in very precise ways.

This equivocation is recapitulated everywhere, in accordance with a structural necessity. Let us take the example of (the) age, since it is our primary interest here. The GREPH has devised a strategy in this regard: it involves extending the teaching of philosophy (revised in both "form" and "content") to those levels prior to the final year of high school. In order to legitimize this extension, we had to, indeed, must still appeal to a logic currently accepted by the forces with which we are at odds and whose contradictions we hope to expose: why not grant philosophy that which is taken for granted in other disciplines, that is, the possibility of knowing the "progressivity" of education over a relatively long period? This provisional strategic argument borrowed from the logic of the adversary can expedite our approach to the Hegelian reference and compel us to propose the "Letter on the Gymnasium": does it not state that a child of 11 (for example, Hegel) is capable of access to very difficult philosophical content and forms? Does it not confirm that there is no natural age for philosophy and that, in any case, this age would not be adolescence? Does it not define a calculated "progressivity" — a "progressivity" organized teleologically, regulated according to a great systematic rationality, etc.?

Any and all services such argumentation might render are double-edged. They justify the extension we seek in terms of a "progressivity" considered natural: that is, naturally regulated by the Hegelian teleology of the rapports between nature and spirit, by the philosophical concept of (the) age that dominates both Reason in history and Hegel's entire pedagogy and theory of *Bildung*. All this forms that concept of (the) age, beginning with the age of the concept (the age of Hegel), whose every term the GREPH would have to deconstruct even as it enlists it for strategic purposes. This is neither primarily nor exclusively a theoretical necessity, but rather the precondition of a political practice that seeks to be as coherent as possible in its successive steps, in the strategy of its alliances and in its discourse.

Let us look more closely and more concretely at the trap this seductive Hegelian reference could become for the GREPH. It appears that Hegel approves a progress and a progression — both qualitative and quantitative — of philosophical teaching in the Gymnasium. In fact, and even if this were actually "progressive" in every sense of the word, in respect to the struggles of the time, today this gesture inaugurates the very structure against which we are struggling. Indeed, one could say that it excludes all access to the practice of philosophy before the University. Hegel proposes the introduction in the Gymnasium of a better *preparation* for the "proper essence of philosophy" (*das eigentliche Wesen der Philosophie*), for example, for its pure contents in the "speculative form." But access to this content remains impossible or forbidden in the Gymnasium. "But I need not add that the exposition of philoso-

phy is still to be excluded from instruction in the Gymnasium and reserved for the University, since the high rescript of the Royal Ministry
has itself already presupposed this exclusion (diese Ausschließung schon
vorausgesetzt)." This *presupposition* functions as do all presuppositions
(*Voraussetzungen*) in Hegelian discourse; furthermore, it situates the
point of contact between a state of political action (philosophy reserved
for the University) and the logic of Hegelian discourse, here exempted
from the need to explain itself. The whole paragraph following the allusion to this exemption makes its consequences explicit. Up to the point
of the strict exclusion of the history of philosophy from the domain of
secondary education. Here is the beginning of the next paragraph:
"With respect to the more defined circle of the fields of knowledge to
which Gymnasium instruction is to be restricted, I would like expressly
to exclude the *history of philosophy*." Now, such an exclusion is justified
by the concept of the presupposition of the Idea (projection or result of
beginning at the end) as it organizes the entire Hegelian systematic, the
entire onto-encyclopedia. And thereby the entire *Universitas*, which
cannot be dissociated from it. The "ministerial" presupposition ade-
quates the Hegelian proposition, both in its principle and in its end:
"But without presupposing the speculative Idea, this history (of philosophy) will often be no more than a simple narrative (*Erzählung*) of
superfluous opinions." In our analysis of this justification of the
exclusion of the history of philosophy from the curriculum of the
Gymnasium, we should not forget that today, in our own Gymnasium,
an allusion to the history of philosophy as such still meets with official
disapproval, especially if it takes the form of an exposé or a narrative.
The "good reasons" invoked to justify this attitude make sense only
within the Hegelian concept of presupposition. It is not a matter here
simply of disputing these reasons, but rather, first of all, of recognizing
their presuppositions, the presupposed logic of presupposition. And
then, another exclusion: metaphysics. "A final consideration has to do
with the higher reasons for excluding metaphysics as such from the
Gymnasium." This exclusion postpones (until the University proper)
access to thought — in its speculative form — of something whose content
is already present, Hegel insists, in secondary education. If metaphysics
as such, in its speculative form, is excluded, we can retaliate by teaching, on the secondary level, that which refers to will, liberty, law, and
duty, everything that would be "all the more called for in that this
teaching would be related to the religious teaching carried out at every
level, at least for eight to ten years." In other words, philosophy proper
is excluded, but its content continues to be taught, albeit in an
improperly philosophical form, in a nonphilosophical manner. Its

content is advocated through the teaching of other disciplines, notably prescriptive and normative teachings such as morals, political morals (the "just concepts of the nature of duty which bind the man and the citizen," for example) or religion. This schema, so familiar by now, is one of the principal targets of the GREPH.

Finally, everything in the letter concerning the extension (*Ausdehnung*) of content and progressivity (*Stufenfolge*) in the acquisition of knowledge refers, on the one hand, to what was said about "religion and morals," and, on the other hand, to a psychology of (the) age (youth being more "docile" and "more teachable" [*folgsamer und gelehriger*]). And the naturalist determination of the different ages recovers, perforce, and according to a profound homology, the entire philosophical teleology of Hegelianism as we find it from the works on Judaism (the Jew is childish — *kindisch* — and not even childlike — *kindlich* — as is the Christian, especially because the Jew appears more docile, more submissive to the heteronomy of his God) to the anthropology of the *Encyclopedia* and the definition of the "natural *course* of the ages of life," the "child," the "young man," the "mature man," the "old man" (§369). The differences of age are the first (and hence the most natural) of the "physical and spiritual" differences of the "natural soul." But this "naturality" is always already the spirituality it has not yet become in the (teleological and encyclopedic) speculative circle that governs this entire discourse.

It has been impossible to read this letter as a "minor" text, alien to the "great" philosophical problematic, addressing itself to ancillary problems and allowing itself to be determined immediately by ecto-philosophical matters, for example, by conjunctions of empirico-political forces. In order to figure out what the (pre-Hegelian) philosopher would have considered secondary, it has been necessary to invoke all the philosophemes of the "great" works as well as the entire so-called "internal" systematic. And this latter comes increasingly to resemble, in every respect, the canonical corpus. Are we dealing here with a reversal with which we can be content? This passage from "minor" to "major" is tautological and reproduces the Hegelian gesture, the heterotautology of the speculative proposition. For Hegel, there is, with respect to the philosophical, no simple exteriority. What other philosophers (the ones I just called pre-Hegelian) would consider — on account of formalism, empiricism, dialectical impotence — to be "everyday," "journalistic" empiricity, accidental contingency, or external particularity is no less alien to the system and to the development (*devenir*) of Reason than, according to Hegel, the morning "gazette" is heterogeneous, insignificant, or illegible from the point of view of the *Greater Logic*.

There is a Hegelian hierarchization, but it is circular, and the minor is always carried, sublated (*relevé*) beyond the opposition, beyond the limit of inside and outside in(to) the major. And inversely. The potency of this age without age derives from this great empirico-philosophical cycle. Hegel does not conceive of the school as the consequence or the image of the system, indeed, as its *pars totalis*: the system itself is an immense school, the thoroughgoing auto-encyclopedia of the absolute spirit in absolute knowledge. And it is a school we never leave, hence an obligatory instruction, which obliges (by) itself, since the necessity can no longer come from without. The Letter—let us not forget this homology—follows closely on the establishment of obligatory schooling. Altenstein was one of its most active advocates. As under Charlemagne, mandatory schooling is extended, and the attempt is made to reduce the Church to a service of the State.

The *Universitas* is that onto- and auto-encyclopedic circle of the State. Whatever the particular forces in civil society may be that dispose over the power of the State, every university, insofar as it is one ("right wing" or "left wing"), depends upon this model. Since this model (which, by definition, claims universality) is always in negotiated compromise with the forces of a particular State (Prussian, Napoleonic—I and II—republican-bourgeois, Nazi, fascist, social democratic, popular democratic, or socialist), the deconstruction of its concepts, of its instruments, of its practices cannot proceed by attacking it *immediately* and attempting to do away with it without risking the *immediate* return of other forces equally capable of adapting to it. *Immediately* to retreat and make way for the "other" of the *Universitas* might represent a welcome invitation to those very determinate and very determined forces, ready and waiting, close by, to take over the State and the University. Whence the necessity for a deconstruction not to abandon the terrain of the University at the very moment when it begins to come to grips with its most powerful foundations. Whence the necessity not to abandon the field to empiricism and thereby to whatever forces are at hand. Whence the political necessity of our alliances, a necessity that must be constantly reevaluated. For the GREPH, as we know, this problem is neither remote nor abstract. If the current French State is afraid of philosophy, it is because its teaching contributes to the progress of *two* types of threatening forces: those wanting to change the State (those, let's say, belonging to the left-wing age of Hegel) and to wrest it from the control of those forces currently in power, and those which, on the other hand or simultaneously, allied or not with the foregoing, tend toward the destruction of the State.[12] These two forces cannot be classified according to the prevailing divisions. They seem to me, for example, to cohabitate today within that theoretical and practical field commonly known as "Marxism."

Charlemagne is dead a second time, but this time it lasts, and a Hegel can always be found to occupy his throne.

In 1822 (the year of our Letter), the beneficiary of Hegel's insurance policy at the University Widows' Fund received another missive: "You see, my dear wife, that I have arrived at the goal of my voyage, which is to say, at its most distant point. . . . We arrived at 10 P.M. At Aix-la-Chapelle. The first thing I saw was the cathedral and I sat down on Charlemagne's throne. . . . One hundred years after his death, Charlemagne was found *seated* upon this throne—by the Emperor Frederic, I believe . . . and his remains were interred. I sat on this throne—on which, as the sacristan assured me, 32 emperors have been crowned—just like any other person, and the entire satisfaction is simply to have been seated there."

NOTES

1. The reference to the texts of the *Philosophy of Right* of Berlin as well as to the political scene of the epoch is a precondition for a minimal intelligibility of this Letter. We should therefore specify it immediately: it is becoming increasingly clear today that it is necessary to speak of the "Philosoph*ies* of Right" of Berlin. This multiplicity is not simply a matter of revisions, of versions, of editions, or of additions. It is part and parcel of the complexity of the political situation in Berlin, of the overdeterminations, stratagems, and occasional secrets of Hegel's political practice or writing. It is certain today that we can no longer simplify this multiplicity—as has often been done to the point of caricature—to reduce it to that of the "Prussian philosopher of the State." As a preface to this Letter, and in view of the reelaboration of all these questions (the "Philosoph*ies* of Right," Marx's and Engel's relations to this entire politico-theoretical aggregate, Hegel's effective political writings, etc.), I will indicate at least two absolutely indispensable discussions: Jacques d'Hondt's *Hegel et son temps* (Berlin, 1818–1831, Editions Sociales, 1968) and Jean-Pierre Lefebvre's preface to his translation of *La société civile bourgeoise* (Paris: Maspero, 1975). See also Eric Weil, *Hegel et l'Etat* (Paris: Vrin, 1970).

It will also be necessary to read two other texts concerning teaching in the Gymnasium and at the University. They are as yet little known and will be translated soon. These are (1) the Report to Niethammer, Inspector General of the Kingdom of Bavaria, on the teaching of the philosophical propaedeutic in the *Gymnasium* (1812). This report constitutes a systematic and important *ensemble* regarding that which is assimilable in one age or another, regarding the necessity of beginning by learning philosophic *content* and not simply "learning to philosophize," regarding the speculative; that is to say, "the philosophical in the form of the concept," which can appear only "discretely" in the Gymnasium. (2) On the teaching of philosophy at the University (text addressed to Prof. von Raumer, Governmental Counsel of the Kingdom of Prussia, 1816).

2. [The ENA (*Ecole normale d'administration*) is the training academy for the French administrative elite. Trans.]

3. Contemporary with the Correspondence between Hegel and Cousin about all these questions (a correspondence reread, after a manner, in *Glas* (Paris: Editions Galilée, 1974); English trans. by John Leavey, Richard Rand, Gregory Ulmer, forthcoming) is my analysis, elsewhere, in the course of work on the teaching body (*le corps enseignant*), of the defense of philosophy, ideology, and the Ideologues, Cousin's famous discourse, its content, and its political inscription. Parts of this work will be published later. The same applies to certain writings from 1975 to 1976 about Nietzsche and teaching, *Ecce homo*, the political heritage of Nietzsche, and — since I allude to it later — the question of the ear.

4. [I leave the word *collèges* untranslated because there is no American English counterpart to the institution. Trans.]

5. [GREPH stands for Groupe de recherches sur l'enseignement philosophique (Research Group on the Teaching of Philosophy). Trans.]

6. [In French, *il se raconte*, literally, "he narrates himself." Trans.]

7. Once again, and in order fully to fathom the complexity of this strategy, all the constraints its ruse had to take into account, I refer to Jacques d'Hondt, *Hegel et son temps*, particularly to the section *Les Démagogues* and to the chapter *Hegel clandestin*.

8. [The German word *Beispiel* is translated as "example," but it is composed of the words *bei* (near, with, among, at, during, *chez*) and *Spiel* (Play, game, etc.) Trans.]

9. [The reference here is to the volume *Qui a peur de la philosophie?* (Paris: Flammarion, 1977), a collection of writings by "members" of the GREPH in which this article was originally published. Trans.]

10. *Hegel et son temps*, p. 9: "That philosophy which he publishes [makes public], which he exposes to the attacks of his enemies, and which surmounts, barely, being barred by censorship; . . . that one his friends and intelligent disciples read between the lines . . . completing with oral indications, and taking into account the inflections imposed upon him by events and incidents, a legislation which they bear as well. And then . . . the philosophy of right whose maxims Hegel actually follows . . . how he treats the positive institutions whose theory he elaborates: production and profit (*métier et gain*), marriage and the family, civil society, administration, the State — and also, how they treat him."

11. The "Haby Reform," named after the then Minister of Education under the Presidency of Valéry Giscard d'Estaing, included among its many provisions the massive reduction of the hours of philosophy previously taught in the final year of the Gymnasium. This was widely interpreted as a move to marginalize, if not to eliminate, the study of philosophy from secondary education, and was one of the events that led to the formation of the GREPH in January 1975.

12. This does not necessarily (or simply) amount to some tendentious movement (via the integral State) toward the "decline" (*dépérissement*) of the State in Engels' "regulated society" or Gramsci's "State without a State." But I will try to return to these difficult "limits" elsewhere . . .

APPENDIX

To the Royal Ministry of Spiritual, Academic, and Medical Affairs

G.W. F. Hegel
Translated by Terry Cochran and Samuel Weber

Berlin, April 16, 1822

In its gracious rescript of November 1 of the preceding year, in which I was given the task of reporting on the lessons held by Dr. von Henning, the Royal Ministry at the same time — in view of the widely held complaint that the student youth generally arrive at the University without the preparation requisite to the study of philosophy — deigned most graciously to take into consideration what I, with the utmost respect, might profer, and to charge me with expressing, in an advisory report, how an adequate preparation in this regard might be organized in the gymnasium.[1]

In this regard, I would first take the liberty of remarking that a reorganization that aims at alleviating this deficiency in the gymnasiums could itself have an effect only on those who have attended those institutions before entering the University. According to existing laws, however, University rectors are required to admit to the University even uneducated and ignorant youths, as long as they are in possession of a diploma attesting to their brilliant immaturity. The former arrangement in the Universities, whereby the Dean of the College to which the prospective student applied, submitted the student to an examination — which, to be sure, had long since sunk to the level of a mere formality — still granted the Universities the possibility and justification of excluding those who were completely uneducated and not yet mature. Although one could cite a provision from the statutes of our University (Chap. VIII, §6, art. 1, p. 43) that appears to contradict both practice and the aforementioned situation, its effect is superseded and annulled (*aufgehoben*) by a more precise provision to be found in the October 12, 1812, edict relative to the examination of gymnasium students applying to the University, and to which actual practice accordingly conforms. As a member of the Scientific Examination Commission, to which the Royal Ministry deigned to name me, I have had occasion to see that the ignorance of those obtaining a diploma to enter the University extends to all levels and that the preparation required by the more or less considerable number of such subjects would at times have to begin with the orthography of their native tongue. Since, at the same time I am also a professor in this University, I cannot but be extremely alarmed for myself and my colleagues in the face of such utterly deficient knowledge and culture in college students, whom we are asked to teach and for whom we must bear responsibility if the aims and expenditures of the Government are not fulfilled: the aim that those leaving the University take with them not merely vocational training, but an educated and cultivated mind. No further elaboration is required to demonstrate that the honor and esteem of the University also do not benefit from the admission of such utterly immature young people.

In this context I would like respectfully to offer the Royal Ministry my own experience stemming from my membership in the Scientific Examination Commission. Namely — insofar as the examinations are designed *to inform* those persons, by ascertaining the extent of their knowledge, who are still thoroughly unprepared for the University, and *to advise* them to postpone entering the University until they have completed their deficient preparation — this aim appears rarely to be attained, since those examinees whose ignorance is thereby revealed learn nothing new; rather, being entirely aware that they know no Latin, no Greek, nothing of mathematics or of history, they have already made their decision to enter the University and hence seek nothing from the Commission but the acquisition of the certificate that allows them to register. They are all the less likely to take such a certificate as advice against entering the University, since, independently of its content, it gives them the possibility of being admitted to the University.

In order now to proceed to the object at hand designated by the Royal Ministry, that is, *preparation in the Gymnasium for speculative thinking and for the study of philosophy,* I find myself compelled to take as my point of departure the difference between a *more material* and a *more formal preparation.* And although the former may be more indirect and less accessible, I believe it should be considered to be the proper foundation of speculative thinking and hence should not be passed over in silence. However, since I would consider studies in the Gymnasium to be the material component of that preparation, I need only name these objects and mention their relation to the end in question.

The first object that I would like to take into account would be the study of the ancients, insofar as through such study the mind and the imagination (*Vorstellung*) of the young are introduced to the great historical and artistic visions (*Anschauungen*) of individuals and of peoples, their deeds and their destinies, as well as their virtues, basic moral principles, and religiosity. But the study of classical literature can only be truly fruitful for the spirit and its more profound activity when, in the higher grades of the Gymnasium, formal linguistic knowledge is seen more as a means, the matter of which, on the contrary, becomes the prime concern, whereas the more scholarly aspects of philology are reserved for the University and for those who want to dedicate themselves exclusively to philology.

The other material, however, does not contain the content of truth only for itself — a content that also constitutes the interest of philosophy, with its characteristic mode of knowledge — but also entails an immediate connection with the formal element of speculative thought. In this regard I would here make mention of the *dogmatic content of our religion*, inasmuch as it does not only contain the truth in and for itself, but rather elevates it so far in the direction of speculative thinking that it simultaneously entails the contradiction of the understanding and the abandonment of rationalization (*Räsonnement*). Whether or not such content, however, will have this exemplary relation in regard to speculative thinking depends on the manner in which Religion is treated: if it is dealt with merely historically, and instead of implanting a veritable and profound respect for it, the main emphasis is placed upon theistic generalities, moral doctrines, or even upon mere subjective feelings, a frame of mind opposed to speculative thought will be inculcated: the idiosyncrasies (*Eigendünkel*) of the understanding and of a certain willfullness are thereby elevated to prominence, which immediately either leads to a simple indifference toward philosophy or succumbs to sophistry.

I would view both of these, classical vision and religious truth — inasmuch as the latter would still constitute the older dogmatic doctrine of the Church — as the substantial portion of the preparation for philosophical studies. If the intellect and spirit of the young have not been imbued with that vision and that truth, the University would be faced with the nearly impossible task of arousing the mind for substantial content and overcoming an already entrenched vanity, with its orientation toward ordinary interests that are all too easily gratified.

The proper essence of philosophy would have to be posed in terms of the process by which that solid, tempered content acquires speculative form. But I need not add that the exposition of philosophy is still to be excluded from instruction in the Gymnasium and to be reserved for the University, since the high edict of the Royal Ministry has itself already presupposed this exclusion.

Thus, what remains for Gymnasium instruction itself is the *intermediary link*, which is to be viewed as the transition from the belief in and representation of that tempered material to philosophical thinking.

This intermediary link would have to be situated in the activity of engaging *in general representations* and, more proximately, in those *forms of thought* common to both philosophical thinking and to mere rationalization. Such activity would entail a closer relation to speculative thinking: in part, insofar as this thinking presupposes exercise in moving about in the medium of abstract thoughts, in and of themselves, without the sensible material that is still present in mathematical contents; in part, however, insofar as the forms of thought, the knowledge of which would be provided by instruction, are subsequently used by philosophy, while also constituting a principal component of the material upon which it works. Precisely this acquaintance and habituation in dealing with formal (*förmlichen*) thoughts, however, should be viewed as the more direct preparation for University studies of philosophy.

With respect to the more defined circle of the fields of knowledge to which, in this regard, gymnasium instruction is to be restricted, I would expressly like to exclude the *history of philosophy*, although it frequently seems to offer itself as suitable for it. But without presupposing the speculative idea, it might well become nothing more than a narrative (*Erzählung*) of contingent and superfluous opinions, this easily leads to a disparaging and contemptible opinion of philosophy — and sometimes such an effect might even be viewed as the purpose behind the history of philosophy and those recommending it — which produces the impression (*Vorstellung*) that all efforts involved with this science have been futile and that it would be an even more fuitle effort for student youth to give themselves over to it.

On the contrary, among the fields of knowledge to be included in the preparational instruction here in question, I would mention the following:

1. So-called *empirical psychology*. Representations of external sensations, imagination, memory, and other psychic faculties are indeed already in themselves something so current that an exposition restricting itself to them would easily be trivial and pedantic. On the one hand, however, such could be all the more easily dispensed with in the University if it were already to be found in the Gymnasium; on the other hand, it could be limited to an introduction to logic, whereby in any event this would have to be preceded by the mention of intellectual activities different in character from thinking as such. Beginning with the external senses, images and representations, then proceeding to their conjunction or so-called association, and from there to the nature of languages, and especially to the distinctions between representations, thoughts, and concepts, much of considerable interest could be adduced, which moreover would be of great use, insofar as the latter

subject matter — once the part that thinking has in intuition (*Anschauungen*) had been rendered apparent — would constitute a more direct introduction to the study of logic.

2. The rudiments of logic, however, would have to be considered to be the main object. Excluding its speculative significance and treatment, instruction could be extended to cover the doctrine of concepts, of judgments, of syllogisms and their modes, and then to the doctrine of definition, division, proof, and the scientific method, in full accordance with already established procedure. Usually, the doctrine of the concept already takes up determinations that more proximately belong to the field of what otherwise is called ontology; a part of this doctrine is also customarily introduced in the form of laws of thought. At this point it would be advantageous to introduce an acquaintance with the Kantian categories as the so-called elementary concepts of understanding, leaving aside, however, the remainder of Kantian metaphysics; yet a mention of the antinomies could still open up at least a negative and formal perspective on reason and the ideas.

What speaks in favor of linking this instruction to Gymnasium education is the fact that no object is less apt to be judged adequately by the young in respect to its importance or utility. If such instruction has gradually been abandoned, it is in all probability primarily because this insight has largely been lost. Besides, such an object is not attractive enough in general to entice the young into studying logic during their stay at the University, where they are in a position to choose those fields of knowledge — outside of their vocational studies — that they want to become involved in. Moreover, it is not unknown for teachers in the positive sciences to advise students against studying philosophy, which they also probably take to include the study of logic. If this instruction is introduced into the Gymnasium, however, pupils will at least for once have the experience of receiving, and thus having, well-formed (*förmliche*) thoughts in their heads. It should be considered a highly significant, subjective effect if the attention of the young can be directed toward a domain of thought for itself, and toward the fact that formed thoughts are themselves an object worthy of consideration — indeed, an object to which public authority itself attaches importance, as indicated by this organization of the curriculum.

The fact that such instruction does not exceed the intellectual capacities of Gymnasium students is attested to by the general experience of the past, and if I may be permitted to evoke my own experience, not only have I daily had before my eyes the ability and receptivity of pupils for such subject matter, since I have been a professor of philosophical propaedeutics for many years, and a Gymnasium rector; in addition, I remember having learned, in my twelfth year — destined as I was to enter the theological seminary of my country — Wolf's definitions of the so-called *idea clara*, and that, in my fourteenth year, I had assimilated all the figures and rules of the syllogisms. And I still know them. Were it not to defy openly contemporary prejudices in favor of "thinking for oneself" and "productive activity," etc., I would not be averse to bringing something of this sort into the proposal for the Gymnasium instruction of this track: for in order to possess knowledge of any sort, including the highest kind, one must have it in memory, whether one begins or ends with this: if one begins with it, one has all the more freedom and occasion to think that knowledge itself. Moreover, in such a way one could most surely counteract the danger that The Royal Ministry rightly seeks to avoid, "That philosophical instruction in the Gymnasium should lose itself in empty formulas or exceed the limits of school instruction.[2]

3. The preceding point joins forces with higher reasons *to exclude metaphysics proper* from the Gymnasium. Yet there is *one* aspect of the previous Wolfian philosophy that could be brought under consideration, what in the *Theologia naturalis* is advanced under the name of *the proofs of the existence of God*. By itself, Gymnasium instruction will be unable to avoid connecting the doctrine of God with the thought of the finitude and the contingency of worldly things, with the purposive relations within them, etc.; however, such a connection will be eternally evident to unbiased human intelligence, no matter what the objects of critical philosophy may be. However, these so-called proofs contain nothing but a formal analysis of the content that has already introduced itself spontaneously into Gymnasium instruction. Of course, they require further correction by means of speculative philosophy so that they in fact correspond to the content accumulated by the unbiased human intelligence along its way. A preliminary acquaintance with the form of that way would be of more immediate interest to all subsequent speculative reflection

4. In a similar manner, certain just and determinate concepts of the nature of volition and of freedom, of law and of duty, can be brought into the Gymnasium instruction concerning *ethics*. This will be all the more feasible in the higher classes, where instruction will be linked to religious instruction, which runs through all classes and which therefore extends over a period of possibly eight to ten years. In our times it could also seem more urgent to work against the shallowness of insight — the results of which, already manifest in the Gymnasiums, have at times attained public notoriety — through correct concepts concerning the nature of the obligations of citizens and of human beings.

This, then, would be my humble opinion concerning *the extension of the contents* of the philosophical preparatory studies in the Gymnasium, an opinion that I most respectfully place before the Royal Ministry. As to what is still at issue concerning the length of time, and likewise the progression to be followed in exposing such knowledge, nothing more need be called to mind than what has been mentioned regarding religion and ethics.[3] With respect to the initiation into the psychological and logical fields of knowledge, it could be specified that, if two hours per week were taken up in one year-long course, the psychological component would be dealt with primarily as an introduction, and hence should be offered before the logical portion. If, keeping the same number of hours, considered as adequate, three or four semiannual courses were devoted to it, more detailed notions about the nature of the spirit, its activities and states, could be taught; in this case it might be more advantageous to begin with instruction in logic, on a level that is simple, abstract, and therefore easy to grasp. This instruction would thereby fall in an earlier period, when the young are more docile and submissive to authority, and are not so infected by the demand that, to merit their attention, the subject matter must conform to their representations (*Vorstellungen*) and to their emotional interests.

The possible difficulty entailed in increasing Gymnasium instruction by two additional hours might best be avoided by reducing the so-called instruction in German and in German literature by one or two hours, or, even more appropriately, by canceling the lectures dealing with the legal encyclopedia, where these occur in the Gymnasium, and replacing them with lectures on logic; all the more so, in order that the *general* formation of the spirit in the Gymnasium — an institution which can be considered as being exclusively devoted to this kind of formation — not continue its apparent decline in favor of a training oriented toward vocational service and alimentary studies.

Finally, concerning the textbooks that can be recommended to teachers for such preparatory instructionn, of those with which I am acquainted I would not know which to indicate as preferable[4]; the material, however, can possibly be found more or less in any textbook, but in the older ones it is more complete and defined, and less contaminated with heterogeneous ingredients; an ultimate instruction from the Royal Ministry could put forth the directives designating which materials should be selected.

Reaffirming my beholden respect
and obedience to the high Royal Ministry

Hegel
Prof. at the Royal University

NOTES

1. The English translation of this letter is based on G. W. F. Hegel, *Berliner Schriften, 1818–1831*, ed. J. Hoffmeister (Hamburg: F. Meiner, 1956), pp. 543–553.

2. *Addendum from the rough draft*: The knowledge of logical forms would be expedient not only in the aforementioned respect, insofar as the treatment of such forms entails an exercise that also includes the treatment of abstract thoughts themselves — but also insofar as these logical forms are themselves already presupposed as the material that then is treated by speculative thinking in its own way. Speculative philosophy's dual task — on the one hand, bringing its material, the general determinations of thoughts, to consciousness and raising it to a level of familiarity; and, on the other, linking this material to the higher idea — is limited to this latter aspect by the fact that knowledge of the forms is presupposed. Anyone who is so prepared and then moves into philosophy proper finds himself on familiar grounds.

3. *Variant in the rough draft*: As to what merely concerns the older Natural Theology, its exposition would be entirely taken up in the instruction of religion, where the matter will already appear for itself and only its formal aspect need be added; but this knowledge would have to be given only in a wholly historical manner, rather than projecting a modern contempt upon forms that (since Anselmus — *deleted*) come from Catholic Theology and from even ancient times, and which have always been venerated . . .

4. *Addendum from the Rough draft*: Not as if I held none of the present textbooks to be suitable, but because every book fair presents us with new compendia and I am not in the habit of following up this literature; in my experience those that I have seen are nothing more than more or less elaborate repetitions of the older manuals, augmented with useless innovations. Without attempting to anticipate, in my view the entire aim and mode of this instruction would require teachers to refer to previous textbooks, on the whole to those belonging to the Wolfian School, with perhaps the single modification of replacing the Aristotelian category-table by the Kantian . . .

2

INSTITUTIONALIZING TRANSLATION
On Florio's Montaigne

Tom Conley

The apex of American letters has often been said to be the department of comparative literature. And for good reason: the native
student is asked to read and write fluently in three or four languages
after having spent at least twenty-odd years of training in the fiercely
monolingual setting of the United States. For Americans, preparation
involves reading an immense volume of major classics that have to be
assimilated in translation before originals can be tackled. We are asked
to acquire the taste or effect of a foreign master — on a basis of theme,
narrative structure, genre, or other issues that often depend only mar-
ginally on the physical substance of language — before we can proceed
to a closer reading of the tongue in which it is written. This implies that
the position of the comparative institution is betrayed by its own appeal
to translation. Ideally, it seems, comparative literature would really be
most effective by leading students back through the national departments of language and literature whence it had taken them in the first
place. The double bind is overwhelming in its sway between national
and international orientations at work in the American university.

We have seen comparative literature face two major problems in its
recent history, especially what happens when a body of modern classics
is translated and edited in paperback for courses that could virtually be
taught in any department in the humanities. Like the spoils of fishing
rights, we have seen fratricide, feud, and war declared over who can
be allowed to teach what: can the octopus of letters in America, the re-
doubtable English department, stake claim to Proust next to Henry
James? Should History teach Simone de Beauvoir to import a flavor of
postwar France next to the hard facts of archives, while Anthropology
reads an English Rousseau as founder of the nostalgia of its discipline?

Ought French steal Freud from the psychologists and German letters to whet its thirst for lines of speculation its literature had never entirely possessed? Or better, should comparative literature outlaw all regional use of literary translation so that, to keep itself in the black, it can attract credit-hours from other departments to avoid its demise in the academy that must produce optimum credit-hours for the deans who patrol the faculties?

And, too, the discipline of comparative literature — and by "discipline" we can suggest the self-authorized surveillance over what its members consider to be worthy of the designation *modern master* — has mediated the problem of translation by turning inward, by teaching its history in programmed readings moving from Schlegel to Walter Benjamin. In a powerful way the institution theorizes its basis of existence, justifying well that comparatism indeed serves a pluralizing influence and maintains, as it thinks it should, a hard-fought liberal stance. It is here, in its attention to its own history, that comparative literature politicizes its place in the liberal arts far more directly and cogently than many other disciplines in the humanities.

The pages that follow aim at cutting a wedge through these two problems: (a) We would like to suggest that the comparative institution is born at the time Weber — at least in *The Protestant Ethic and the Spirit of Capitalism* — envisages the Reform and expansion as part of possessive individualism. We can surmise that the ideology of translation — or the ethic of an international pantheon of a timeless nation of "modern masters" in leather on a long bookshelf — finds its origin in this current. For translation was obviously the agent that precipitated a nationalizing of the university, allowing the frame of *translatio studii* in medieval centers to be oriented toward new generations of scholars who speculated not only upon the style but directly on the international sales of original works.

If we reflect on the Tudor program of translation in Elizabethan England, the effect of erosion would be neither less disquieting nor enthralling. That comparative literature has depended on its role as a go-between among "translations" and "originals" seems to be one of its historical *raisons d'être*. To sketch how speculation on two languages functions in John Florio's work is at the center of the following analysis. Remembered primarily as the first translator of Montaigne, Florio was also author of Anglo-Italian dialogues, the *First Fruites*. These bear analogy with the modern textbook. Although the latter diagrams grammatical paradigms into practice drills which become increasingly complicated as more elements are explicated, the former resembles a Berlitz guide of expressions needed for the traveler to effectuate daily

duties in foreign lands or appear civil and decorous in the theater or in
hotel lobbies and restaurants. The *First Fruites* are not unlike the dialogues that initiate chapters of textbooks. They also resemble the inten-
sified French courses taught to recruits by the American Army in the
1940s. These are what Professors Julian Harris and André Lévêque
remodeled a decade later to implement stupendous royalties from textbooks for the first and second year of the college curriculum. Florio
made the most of English taste for things Italian, just as Harris and
Lévêque (and myriad other authors in more recent editions) reaped
profits by combining tourism with the academy of letters. As we shall
observe, with Florio the profit motive invested into translation is more
overt and hilariously outrageous than in the case of Harris and Lévêque
or the contemporary textbook business.

(b) In following his rendering of Montaigne, we shall locate where
the capital of translation cannot so easily be cast as an alibi of "learning
a foreign language for fun and profit." We shall see where the rendering
of an English version "faithful" to Montaigne succeeds best when it
fails, that is, in brief, where French and English derive their common
force from each being self-identical, where they depend on each other
in identities of material figures that coagulate both tongues at once, in
letters that are no longer unilaterally or polyvalently meaningful signs,
but where each language is visibly embedded in the other in a way that
both lose their properly semantic order and accede to limitless power
of poetic extension.

It is at these points, too, where any institution of letters would be
hard put to valorize either Montaigne or Florio (or other translations)
through modes of comparative evaluation. Florio is one shape of poetry,
and the *Essais* are identically another. These points of stress determine
how the syntactical resilience of a discourse — both Florio's and Montaigne's collision of English and French — has, because of the "discipline" of translation, virtually been lost in every rendering of the *Essais*
since the beginning of the seventeenth century. To retrieve their time-
liness, that is to say, their graphic disposition that allows signs to regress
to hieroglyphics and become no more than letters floating as self-made
emblems, is the end of this essay. In effect, the position assumed here
is one that endeavors to make both Florio and Montaigne of institu-
tionally questionable worth. In order to do so, we must insist on the
similarity — if not the identity — of the traditions of allegory and translation by the end of the 1500s.

From that standpoint Florio's may remain the "best" translation of
Montaigne. Even if, in Frances Yates's opinion, the *Essayes* are so bad
a rendering that they become a truly original work, the text under

Florio's name is the closest to the Gascon poet. All translations since
have reflected the limits of the discourses of their epoch, and their fantasms of controlled meaning. Where Florio makes for a bombastic Montaigne, he still writes with the view that translation entails first and
foremost a problem of allegory, of turning away, of distorting, of ex-
ceeding, and not exactly of reproducing an original, or even respecting
the existence of an original.

Only since the advent of a respectable tradition of translation could
evaluative readings of Florio and Montaigne be hazarded, for when
critics look to see how the meaning of the original is generated in terms
of its luster in a different tongue, they no more than institute a gap that
figures its own enigma. They insert a loss, not a pluralizing process of
the reading of two versions on the border of a broader plain of all
languages. They occlude all possibility of the existence of an unconscious *langue* formed of many tongues visibly embedded in both texts.
They fix the text, indeed, they ossify it when they evaluate its translation. Not by chance, most professional students of Montaigne have de-
liberated over the worth and fortune of Montaigne in England and
America without looking to the more urgent problem of why they do
it in the first place. The critics fabricate "something [to be] lost in translation" at the very instant they place their eyes between two versions of
a canonical text.

Not only did the already translated status of Montaigne's *Essais* — at
best a macaronic plate of quotations and exempla taken from moralia
and early modern encyclopedias — disallow such a romantic retrieval to
take place in post-Elizabethan English; but also, and more ironically,
the critics have demonstrated how the allegorical mode promotes every
translation to make "identically different" points of stress and paradox
across the surface of Montaigne's page. This is because the strength of
the allegorical tradition in which Montaigne writes is so pervasive and
thorough that the graphemes, seemingly neutral conveyers or arbitrary
vehicles of meaning, turn out to assume pivotal functions. Only an allegory of writing allows for a supple violence of discourse to take place
in both French and English versions. Historically then, Florio's can be
the *only* translation of Montaigne.

Three or four examples can provide a backdrop to our task of com-
plicating what is entailed in evaluating an original and its copy. Most
comparative readers would necessarily place Montaigne in a position
anterior to Florio, therefore in a platonically superior rank; for in an
ideology of copying, the original text would constitute the model for
ulterior imitations. In this light, it would be impossible to believe that
a copy could ever be finer than the original. But no: if we recall how

certain translators have displaced this underlying concept of idealizing difference and have regressed to fabricating renderings far more exemplary and, finally, destructively faithful to the originals than the originals were to themselves. Here the issue of translation loses historical bearing. Baudelaire's imitations of Longfellow and translations of Poe at once reproduce and explicate the American models far more broadly and limpidly than often either poet can do in his own tongue. Baudelaire uncovers systems of specular association in French that require the French and English to be read in the language of each other.[1]

Marcel Duchamp's titling of his ready-mades follows Baudelaire to the letter. He requires multilingual decipherment where the sameness of "French" and "English" reduces all differences that art needs for its transcendentalization in the form of cult objects put forward by a vanguard. When he places in subscription to the moustached copy of the Mona Lisa "L. H. O. O. Q.," Duchamp theorizes the scopic drive at the basis of the visual arts in having us read the script of our will to look; and he glosses the lady with the erotic drive behind the drive, marking the folds that reveal a landscape and screens of veils — of visual shadowing, of scumble — in a verbal reading of the graphemes

elle L a chaud H O au O cul Q.

All gap between an authentic voice or image and a tarnished copy is allayed in the laughter of the copy itself, in the graffito of the signature seizing difference in the perfect identity of French and English.

Were we to posit that the strategy of all of Jacques Derrida's writings uses simultaneous translation to recover a tradition of *translatio studii* which antedates the philosophical traditions he sets forth to fracture, we would still be foregrounding Florio. For when Derrida transliterates his titles in order to make derisory *all* voice heard behind them, he happens upon the aspect of *langue* or a terribly violent indifference common to a few Western writers whose words fold into an unconscious mass of half-formed letters forever circulating between meaning and force. His titles make any "translation" from speech into writing — or vice versa — all but impossible. "Legs de Freud" can mark Freud's familial heritage, his translator's legs (as *Übersetzer*) and a forgotten American slur of *legs* (or *lace, laisse*, etc.) *deferred*. The acronym SEC he chooses to use in agglutinating and economizing "Signature événement contexte" transpires, in an American reading, to deny all metaphysics ascribing a "place" to any enunciation outside of its writing. We read: *est-ce* S *i* E *ci* C, that is, *is it here?*[2] And in *Limited Inc*, he demonstrates graphically how all organizational, institutional differences — whether of speech acts, a bona fide theory, of the university as a corporation, and the like — copyright in-c. In doing so they imitate, limit, and incorporate themselves in passing slyly from a first to a third person, in being *limité, l'imité*. Such a forever-parceling enunciation indebts itself by giving itself a need that becomes economized, therefore set into a relation of institutional obligation and power. Autotranslation all but arrests this capital act of language, as the epithet Derrida stole from John Searle reproduces so coyly. Whereas Searle, Hubert Dreyfus, and their associates note that Derrida has *not quite* understood the subtleties of their own vocabularies and modes of argumentation, in the text of *Limited Inc*, Derrida's rendering of the syntagm *pas quitte* turns Searle and company against themselves. They are neither "quite," "quiet," nor really off the hook, acquitted or *quitte* in the economy of a confrontation by which the Johns Hopkins University Press had stood to gain philosophical prestige.

If each of the examples were to be drawn to a broader conclusion, we would see how the inscription of a self-canceling difference in an "original" discourse (that difference being no more than the quotation marks in the preceding example that contours of parenthesis serve to explicate) depends on two or more languages slipping over each other in order to open upon an infinite multitude of virtual meaning. This is precisely the violence contained in originals that take themselves to be translations already: Baudelaire, Duchamp, Derrida, and, of course, Florio's Montaigne. When each of the texts is read from the optic of discourse reflecting itself and which it binds to its typographical aspect, it accedes to an allegorical status.

Thus Florio must be read neither as a writer transporting ideas of skepticism, pyrrhonism, or the epicurean ideal to England at the turn of the sixteenth century, nor as a figure imitating in Tudor prose the doubt of self-erasure in Montaigne's nascent autobiography. Rather, attention has to be focused on the diagrammatical patterns in the prose, in the differences they chart among themselves and beyond any exact transfer of Montaigne's alliterations, sentences, or stylistic turns. The *Essais* were already copies cheap enough in their borrowings of style. The *Essais*, which contained pastiches of Cicero, Tacitus, Lucretius, and others, also stole entire passages of Plutarch — less from Latin than from Jacques Amyot's French translation. Montaigne's lure of Latin is often centered on a bogus ellipsis between ancient dicta and a vulgar tongue of Gasconized French. That the *Essais* resemble modern novels that have no distinctive syntactical gaps in paragraphs is not surprising, as only a foreign mark or proper name — a chapter heading, a number, an incised quotation — opens up the text and provides syntactical gaps that confer other layers of meaning upon those in the semantic levels. Since Florio, almost every modern edition of the *Essays* has shown an indifference to its textual flow by assuming that a thread of sense can be distinguished by means of division into paragraphs. Now Florio's *Essayes*, historically and typographically more aware of the allegorical underpinning that dispenses with extratextual markings, simply underlines English maxims and rhymed couplets. These approximate the patterns of clichés that so often form the metaphorical substance of Montaigne.

In the French and Florio's English we discover a glyphic sense of the page. When indentations are used to translate shifts and developments in the abstract domain of thought, the eye is deterred from making associations of letters that emerge from combinations of printed characters and which can give validly multiple meanings to the reading. One instant, the eye will catch graphemes of one contour and give literal worth to them as the grammar does not; in another, different sets will promote other readings of the same sort. Only because the figural tradition is so strongly embedded in the literal sensibility, seemingly in the materiality of the renascent body, can we imagine that infinite essays can be produced through the signs that the book promotes the reader to visualize. The failure (or success) in writing devoid of paragraphs demonstrates how allegory always turns us away from mimesis to the emblematic designs of typography. From a sea and froth of letters the essays are written to be translated. Speaking of Montaigne's deplorable confusion in his refusal to divide the chapters into paragraphs, E. J. Trechmann inadvertently tells us why allegory may well be the reason why the paragraph is not a logical principle of sixteenth-century writing:

> In any case it seems a pity that Florio has never been subjected to a little "editing." His numerous elementary blunders (e.g., *poisson*: poison), inaccuracies and misrepresentations (he makes Montaigne say that he was "altogether ignorant in the holy Scripture," whereas Montaigne in the same essay quotes the Bible at least sixteen times) must be very perplexing to the reader. He is besides generally published in a very unattractive form. Like the earliest edition of the French original, Florio's work, as it is still repeatedly issued, flows on in one continuous stream, with no breaks except where the poetical quotations occur. Every chapter is a paragraph. In an author like Montaigne, who digresses on every page, this is a great disadvantage, and leaves the reader very much at sea.[3]

Obviously, Montaigne and Florio *saw* language. The verbal history of words shined through graphemes that they could touch, fondle, caress, and sniff. A dominant set of terms would emerge from the mass on one occasion, and another on another.

The strategy of an allegory of graphics is evinced already in the dialogue of title and text. Montaigne had taken care to let his titles float in the gap between a cypher and a script. The position of a chapter heading was set in rapport with its number in order to imply a tension of word and image in an evanescent emblem, between the super- and subscription of the former and following chapters. The title would have to be deciphered *as if* it were a foreign tongue, translated into its identity. Thus, in Book 3, Chapter 3, "De trois commerces," Montaigne exacts a resemblance of III, iii to the title before offsetting the obvious symmetries in a sentence that complicates the triadic aspect of perfection. He puts a cadre of four within three. "Il ne faut pas se clouër si fort à ses humeurs et complexions."[4] It is graphically obvious that a double symmetry of threes cannot be nailed to (four) humors and (four) complexions. Two sets of odd digits in the titular number are dyssymetrical in relation to the ostensible ensemble of events. The title and incipit force us to visualize an ever-bifurcating sum which will multiply through the discourse. *Si fort* echoes the homonym *ci-fort*, here and now, on the page, in a figure of *four* forking out of *forche* and *furca*, what later in the chapter he will call a forever extravagant discourse, both blind and lusty, when he sets out to "parler tousjours bandé, *favellar in punta di forchetta*" (799), "to speak curiously," or "to speak on the point of a pitchfork." With the half-reference to the quadrature of a Christian cross on which the typographical nails (*il ne faut pas se clouër si fort*) of the title would be driven, a figure is set in the frame of simultaneously literal and figurative readings of the emblem-title and the initial sentence in subscription. Simply by following the typeface of Angelier or any other early edition of the *Essais*, Florio's text respects the play of force between a purely visual and intellective reading.

In making Montaigne both more and less than he is, Florio apprehends the power of allegory as translation. More often than not, modern editors read the English for points of rift that betray how anything other than the original is lacking. What avers to be overaffected, bombastic, euphuistic, or merely stupid is summarily put forward. As we have seen, Frances Yates has unearthed many of the most flagrant errors.[5] Yet, like more modern translators, many editors do not see where the text establishes firm allegorical bindings between the two languages, when a simple cognate or other ploy of identity gives resonance to the discourse. In the first sentence of the third volume, the writer decries—

but also tells how to read—the inanities that follow for the next two hundred pages. Thus Montaigne (1592):

> Personne n'est exempt de dire des fadaises. Le malheur est de les dire curieusement.

A brief historical profile of all English renderings might indicate how the irony of the beginning gets lost in common sense.

> Florio (1603):
> No man living is free from speaking foolish things; the ill luck is, to speake them curiously.

> Cotton (1686):
> No man is free from speaking foolish things; but the worst on't is, when a man labours to play the fool.

> The Younger Hazlitt (1842):
> No man is free from saying silly things; but the misfortune is when we endeavor to give them an air of importance.

> Ives (1925):
> No one is exempt from saying foolish things; the misfortune is to say them intentionally.

> Trechmann (1927):
> No man is exempt from saying silly things; the mischief is to say them deliberately.

> Zeitlin (1936):
> No man is exempt from saying foolish things. The misfortune is to say them in a studied manner.

> Frame (1948):
> No one is exempt from saying silly things. The misfortune is to say them with earnest effort.[6]

Where most of the translators find it necessary to metaphorize *curieusement* in words that properly reflect a condition of calculated expenditure and effort, Florio sticks to *curiously*. No doubt the force of the word was strong enough in the early seventeenth century to evoke things "curious," of "difficult beauty," things overtly wrought with care, thus of sibylline, protean aspect—also born in *malheur* as *ill luck*—to merit reprinting of the cognate. Its multiple iconic sense is lost in the elegance and affected polish of later renderings. When Randle Cotgrave's French-English dictionary of 1611 registered *curieusement* as "curiously, precisely, nicely, quaintly, daintily, scrupulously; carefully, heedfully, busily, too too diligently," he was not thinking of anything so chimerical as a "mot juste." No word could justly render such a daimonic adverb; better, Cotgrave implies, to multiply meanings than to control them. Likewise, Florio's *curiously* lets the swarm of meanings float beneath a term so charged that its nine graphemes allow a grand verbal history to cast light from them. For Montaigne could have quite carefully wrought *soigneusement* in its place, but, in insisting on *curieux*, on the one hand he harks back to *curiosus* and *curiositas*, inflecting "care" with "need" and vice versa. On the other hand, he alludes to a distinctly styleless style of writing, a *style curial* that has to do with the banalities of papal dicta, or Roman curia, or a paternal voice that has absolutely no place in the written text. To utter like an official bull connotes already an inverting, in the manner of the *topos* of the world upside down, of the mouth from the head to the rectum — or from the voice into print. For the "right" way of banalizing — of making discourse proper — involves officious petulance that the graphics of *curieusement* renders as hilarious, since *cu[l]rieux* is ass-laughing, indeed Nietzschean in the derision of truth repeated in characters, ultimately self-maculated by replication and re-edition. By letting the word's own attributes play on its surface, the allegorical force of the adverb allows Florio to translate into English its own circularity. (The expulsive dimension of *curiosité* surfaces in many verbal tricks in "De la vanité.")

In one of the most difficult openings of the later essays, Montaigne brings into a cliché myriad cycles of meaning supported by figural traditions. Anticipating a discussion of the *Aeneid* at the outset of "Sur des vers de Virgile," we read:

Chapitre V
Sur des vers de Virgile

A mesure que les pensemens utiles sont plus plains et solides, ils sont aussi plus empeschans et plus onereux. Le vice, la mort, la pauvreté, les maladies, sont subjets graves et qui grevent. Il faut avoir l'ame instruite des moyens de soustenir et combatre les maux, et instruite des reigles de bien vivre et de bien croire, et souvent l'esveiller et exercer en cette belle estude; mais à une ame de commune sorte il faut que ce soit avec reláche et moderation: elle s'affole d'estre trop continuellement bandée. (818)

Chapter V
Upon Some Verses of Virgil

Profitable thoughts, the more full and solide they are, the more cumbersome and heavy are they; vice, death, poverty and disease are subjects that waigh and grieve. We must have our minde instructed with meanes to sustaine and combat mischiefes, and furnished with rules how to live well and believe right: and often rouze and exercise it in this goodly study. But to a mind of the common stampe; it must be with intermission and moderation; it groweth weake, by being continually overwrested.[7]

Evidently the text invokes the topic of the melancholy of love to center on a writing about sexual indifference. The old man must have a paper Venus to sustain the most prickling sallies of thought. An aged writer must copulate the paginal beauty of his masters—he must translate them—to forge a stronger writing that will tarnish their luster; he must become the verbal embodiment of the Lady of Lucretius and Virgile, both an earthly and a heavenly goddess of love. Montaigne's passage depends on two unstable terms apprehended across the flow of text. *Pensemens* evokes at once meditation, bleeding, and menstrual cycles. Hygienic ideas of sorts, these "thoughts" project words into an indeterminate sexuality opened in anagram in the title, in the *nerge* and its *revers*. Mensual and mental conditions are struck in -*mens* which recasts the mind of the Latin *mens* and the *mes* of *mesure*. Now *bandée* elucidates the portmanteau *pensemens* in oblique reference to Cupid-*cum*-Montaigne "blinded" and erect. In effect, the cycles thinking are all that can distinguish one sexual "code" from another; in a prototypically Freudian light, writing and anatomy aver to be indifferent signs of the same things in the course of *écriture* that knows neither season nor reason—so the subject of the clause *elle s'affole d'estre trop continuellement bandée* can refer at once to an innocuous *ame* "of common stamp," Montaigne in drag of Venus, and to difference itself (*relâche et moderation*).

If *pensemens* grow increasingly hard with the difficulties of old age, it is because they do not anoint themselves with menstrual blood. The erotic circularity of the passage is all but written out of modern translations. The erection of blindness in *bandée* is rendered effetely as *intent* (Younger Hazlitt), *strained* (Ives), *deranged* (Trechmann), *strained* (Zeitlin), *tense* (Frame). Florio's *overwrested* locks the violence of maddening desire and its sleepy obverse within the unvoiced grapheme *w*. All other renderings translate the contradiction out of the text and into an area of unilateral meaning.

In coining *profitable thoughts* to convert *pensemens utiles*, Florio indicates a discourse of exaggeration. *Pro-* of the PROFITABLE makes for a "vertugalle" (as Cotgrave puts it) of thinking, a mannered codpiece extending — as Montaigne later notes of Lucretius's description of Venus, "sortablement" — or "able to fit forward." The rest of the sentence merely backgrounds the thrust of the opening when `it completes a euphuistic balance in the chiasm of "they are . . . are they." That turn of calm might well tell us how Montaigne's *onereux* is both onerous and *oneiric* in the difference between the mask of the letters and the platitude of the page. Some subsequent translations (Cotton, Hazlitt, Ives, Zeitlin) stick to *profitable* but do not let the face of a supple allegory smile through the letters. When Trechmann ("edifying") and Frame ("useful") orient "profitable" toward the use-value of *utile*, they unwittingly make us remark, in effect, that the thrust of the essay is to put all self-possessive utility into question; that the allegorical dimension in the original and first English translation is what makes for a happy vanity of writing as an allegory, of old age blindfolded before Eros or Beauty.

Apart from Florio, then — and perhaps his eminence in these pages has nothing to do with him or his name, but with a process of reading and transcription of such great calligraphical dexterity that all modern literature tends only to discover it over and again in literal *allegories of writing* — no other translation allows single words to deploy and fold over their own contradictions. Two speculative conclusions may serve to resolve the issue. Through the first, we can project how allegory is no doubt a term that delineates the difference between a line of type and a meaning beyond it. In the tradition of nominalism, which seems to underpin all discourse that deals with the sign, in which the enigma of meaning is a "third term," a term that mediates or cuts a path between two others,[8] literal and figurative shadings of words move according to the will of the writerly reader. Where a meaning can be arrested or subverted by another sign within it, it is syntax that allows one sense to be displaced into another and back again. The writers of the sixteenth century saw the grand face of the page in terms of the space of syntax, as a physiognomy of allegory, as a place where typographical chance forces all meanings to acquire various meanings by diverse manners of reading. In a quite different way, Walter Benjamin hits the point when he notes that "real translations" are achieved by a "literal rendering of the syntax which proves words rather than sentences to be the primary element of the translator."[9] Attention to the duplicities of a single word fractures and congeals sense, violates it, and renders it curiously precious. So, when Benjamin also notes in the context of his translation of Baudelaire that "the intention of the poet is spontaneous, primary, graphic; that of the translator is derivative, ultimate, ideational,"[10] he tells us that, like Florio, he must translate his intentions into those of the poet by virtue of having single words retrieve their allegorical shine through their graphic and emblematic shapes. This he attains only when he dares to cross over, to become the poet in the full sense of the urgency of writing literally and even catachrestically.

A second conclusion may serve to historicize the import of the single words we have taken from Florio and the passing remarks of Benjamin. The indeterminate similarities of allegory and translation pinpoint how the Tudor campaigns of converting great authors of all time into a pantheon of "modern masters" accessible to a monolingual readership were based on a comparative tradition that later had to be modified and repressed. Translating involves keeping to a double discourse, thus having various traits of language converge into one shape and relegate the material substance or graphic force of discourse to a background—unless, as in Florio's case, alternate shapes come to the fore and play a diagrammatical role coextensive with those figures of the untranslated original. But generally, this amounts to a naturalizing, not a materializing, of the difference of the translation. It dissimulates the other tongue within the decorous effect of the secondary discourse. So the double play of meaning and figure has to recede to invisibility, but only in order that the literary or institutional value of the translation can be centered on that recession. This is why, as a second conclusion, we can note that Florio had to preface his text with the ironic reminder that, as translation, "such conversion is the subversion of our universities." By that he adduces how the great figural tradition of *translatio studii* finally came to a halt when the Tudor translators instituted the beginnings of what we might call a modern tradition in comparative literatures, where the lure of a master text should lead the students to learn another language through the existential desire to know and to historicize the foreign text they have read in a falsely "natural" tongue. Florio also discloses that the ethic of the plenary individual has no better sign of its strategies in early modern Europe than through the mediation of translating. By making an allegorical mode useful and profitable—and not excessive or exaggerated—a translator can dissimulate the money of graphics in the folds and illusion of voice, in the repression of one tongue behind another. Such a naturalization of an obvious cultural difference is what emerges from translations after Florio's. In aspect they are all too proper, too useful, too profitable. The element of profit remains too in his *Essayes*—and he admits it in his apologia—but there is also to be found residue of what generates not a loss but a crusty performance of letters. This is what conveys the precious brutality of the *Essais*; the graphics of translation are a literal allegory at a graphic limit. Here and there they come across Florio in single words in ways they never have since the end of the sixteenth century. That this remainder scatters all over his sloppy conceits and florid turns in the 1603 rendering may be the most elegant heritage of Montaigne in English.

If the institutions of comparative studies are to capitalize on the history of translation, they may well begin with Florio's curious reversal of Montaigne. Curious, we note, in its bizarre curiosity, in its way of dislodging the truth of anteriority and putting forward in simultaneity a virtual, vain curiosity. For like many moderns, Florio succeeds in *dispensing with* the original to the extent that both model and copy cohere as a hieroglyph.

In a certain manner Florio and his avatars would assume roles in another "daimonic agency" of allegory where in the going between, the buyer of the book is lured to think that an original foregrounds its translation; to believe in a better form and shape of truth; to feel that the strange cast of letters in a foreign language — because they are strange, impalpable, of wondrous enigma — confers more worth upon the platitude of recognition, that is, upon meaning. The shuffle of difference in the graphic configurations of letters does not allow the institution of originality to be taught or bought so easily. If anarchy of the same sort is carried out methodically — within the frame of a curriculum — then the inauspicious canon of *other* translations will have to be studied. It will have also to count, as we have already listed, Baudelaire's Poe, Duchamp, and Derrida, and also include, beyond Florio, Beckett and Freud.

NOTES

1. In his translation of Poe's "The Gold Bug" ("Le Scarabée d'or"), Baudelaire notes that he *cannot* translate Jupiter's remark "I nose," but in an addendum, he substitutes an explanation of his own doctrine of *correspondances* of languages and aromas, writing of his need to combine thinking and smelling in *"je le sens* pour *je le sais."* His footnote underscores the graphics of synesthesia, which is based less on conflicting odors than on conflations of irremediably different pronouns and homonyms, in *Oeuvres complètes* (Paris: Conard, 1932), 6:87.

2. Jacques Derrida's "Legs de Freud" first appeared in the *Etudes freudiennes*, no. 13–14 (1978), but has since been reprinted in *La Carte postale* (Paris: Flammarion, 1980). *Limited Inc* was published in French by the Johns Hopkins University Press in 1978.

3. Preface to E. J. Trechmann, *Essays of Montaigne* (New York: Oxford University Press, 1927), p. xii.

4. Montaigne, *Essais*, in *Oeuvres complètes*, ed. Albert Thibaudet and Maurice Rat (Paris: Gallimard, 1962). All other reference to the *Essais* will be made to this edi-

tion. We also refer to the J. M. Dent & Sons reprint of Florio's *Essayes of Montaigne* in three volumes (London, 1919).

At the end of the first chapter of his *Allegory: Theory of a Symbolical Mode* (Ithaca: Cornell University Press, 1964), Angus Fletcher noted that allegory always tends toward the geometrical and diagrammatical dimensions of language, toward a duplicitous writing that calls for two different and simultaneous modes of apprehension. Substitution of different typeface in modern editions all but obliterates this will-to-diagram the printed word. Obviously the fifth chapter of the third volume, "Sur des vers de Virgile," requires that "V" hang over the contents "like" both a cutting blade and a monogram for the female pudenda; the letter synthesizes sexual difference, which the long essay takes such pain to suggest in discursive ellipsis. Frame's edition — among others uses the "5" to signal what Florio's word apprehended immediately with its use of "V." On typographical grounds alone, it can be argued that Florio's is the only possible translation of Montaigne.

Similarly, when Frances Yates metaphorizes the visible and diagrammatical side of the essays, she does so far less innocently than she would like. In summing up her evaluation, by calling Montaigne the "picture" and Florio the "curiously wrought frame" (*John Florio* [Cambridge: At the University Press, 1934], p. 240), she uses the age-old distinction of form-content and substance-decor that allegory had already questioned when it equated each as a dynamic function of the other.

5. Yates, *John Florio*.

6. Charles Cotton, *Essays of Montaigne*, ed. William Carew Hazlitt (London: Reeves & Turner, 1902), 3:225; (the younger) William Hazlitt, *Essays of Montaigne* (Philadelphia: J. W. Moore, 1850), p. 390; George B. Ives, *Essays of Montaigne* (Cambridge: Harvard University Press, 1925), 3:235; Trechmann, *Essays of Montaigne*, p. 241; Jacob Zeitlin, *Essays of Montaigne* (New York: Knopf, 1936), 3:1; Donald M. Frame, *Essays of Montaigne* (New York: Doubleday, 1960), 3:1.

7. Exception must be made for Cotton's translation of this passage. He apprehends the aspect of bodily cycles in "it will otherwise grow *besotted* if continually intent."

8. This tradition Antoine Compagnon has studied well in a book on William of Ockham entitled *Nous Michel de Montaigne* (Paris: Seuil, 1980).

9. Walter Benjamin, "The Task of the Translator," in *Illuminations*, trans. Harry Zohn (New York: Schocken, 1969), p. 79.

10. Ibid., pp. 76–77. We must recall that translation involves money. By the sixteenth century poets had imagined that the Latins, ages before, had been enriching their tongue by *imitating* Greek orators, but only in the illusion that they were balancing their words in the two pans of a scale. The model of an inaccessible beauty had to be advanced in order to mask the money involved in the rights of translation. Coins were exchanged for words. In articulating "la loy de traduyre," Joachim du Bellay, in his *Deffence et illustration de la langue françoyse*, notes very graphically how the task is one of *spacing*, "qui est n'espacier point hors des limites de l'auteur" (Book 1, Chapter 5; Paris: Didier [STFM], 1948, p. 36). Like Benjamin, Du Bellay insists that an ideal translation works only when it is graphic, or syntactic rather than semantic; by implication, it is ideal when it no longer has to involve an institution that would serve as its final reference and significance. "What I say," he adds, "is not addressed to those who, by command of princes and great lords, translate the most celebrated Greek and Latin poets." He says this by liberally cribbing Sperone, Cicero, and Quintilian. It is "pour ce que l'obeissance qu'on doit à telz personnages ne reçoit aucune excuse en cet endroit: mais bien, j'entens parler à ceux qui de gayeté de coeur (comme on dict) entreprenant telles choses legerement, & s'en *aquitent* de mesmes" (our stress: "because obligation one owes to such characters has

no excuse in this spot: but rather, I prefer to speak to those of a gay heart (as they say) undertaking such tasks lightly, and acquitting themselves from them in the same fashion"). The crux is one of removing all labor from the "task of the translator," which indeed involves writing a piece of literature, a work that affords royalties only when it is placed in a curriculum. With neither labor lost nor money gained, source and origin are no longer contained in the translation, but, more violently and more incestuously, or more marvelously, they are once again original together. There we have neither surplus nor deficit, a condition too good to be true.

3

ASTERION'S DOOR

Truth's True Contents in Shakespeare, Nietzsche, Artaud, the Reverend A. E. Sims . . .

Malcolm Evans

I. THE BARD AND THE *DOXA*

There is a proverb, about a cat who wanted fish but was not prepared to get her feet wet, that was sufficiently well known in 1606 to be referred to metonymically in the popular theater. Lady Macbeth, goading her hesitant husband to murder Duncan, asks:

> Wouldst thou have that
> Which thou esteem'st the ornament of life,
> And live a coward in thine own esteem,
> Letting 'I dare not' wait upon 'I would',
> Like the poor cat i' th'adage?
> (*Macbeth*, 1.7.41–44)[1]

Proverbs and *sententiae* usually work in Shakespeare's plays to express, or conceal, a devious or misguided purpose.[2] But such implicit warnings about the treacheries of received wisdom do nothing to deter the modern discourse that mines the Shakespearean text for proverbs and then reappropriates them to the received ideas of the *doxa*, adding double validation through the mark of that most potent of cultural signifiers, the Bard. This is the work of the "collective and anonymous voice originating in traditional human experience" which Roland Barthes called the Gnomic Code, the distillate of practices wherein 'Life', seen as the transcendent reality to which all language refers, is concocted from the detritus of language itself — "a nauseating mixture of common opinions, a smothering layer of received ideas."[3] In relation to Shakespeare, its products can be sometimes disconcerting. Visitors to the Exxon/Folger Shakespeare Library exhibition that toured the United States in 1980 were sprayed with a prophylactic shower of adages, emanating from speakers concealed at the entrance, before proceeding to the model of the Globe Theatre, the costumes, Elizabethan printed books, and other cult objects housed in the sacred space within. But even this onslaught of roses by any other name glistering in the winter of our discontent is outdone by *A Shakespeare Birthday Book* compiled by the Reverend A. E. Sims.[4] This volume comprises 365 eternal verities and moral injunctions culled from the plays and poems, each headed by a day of the year, with ornamental borders and occasional color plates commemorating such characters as Falstaff and Mistress Quickly, Romeo and Juliet, Shylock and Jessica, Perdita, perhaps even Lady Macbeth herself. The improving sentiment it offers to Christian boys and girls born on March 15, in a bizarre transformation of something like "he who hesitates is lost," is — complete with the poor cat — Lady Macbeth's incitement to regicide.

At first glance, the Shakespeares of Exxon and the Reverend Sims both appear to be located in the discourse that spans birthday books, calendars, dictionaries of quotations, programs on BBC Radio 4 in celebration of Shakespeare's birthday, and ashtrays on sale at Stratford-upon-Avon. But the fifteenth *is* the Ides of March, and this, combined with the choice of quotation, interrupts the 'finish' of the appropriation that acts as an ideological commentary on the texts. This is the fissure that reveals, beneath the hallmarked platitudes, a shadow text of cabbalism, conspiracy, and assassination. Even the ontological comfort of an author is denied as "A. E. Sims" becomes the function of the *Birthday Book* that fractures and diffuses its anagram "is same" to deny the work its univocity, identity, and self-presence. The publisher's imprint gives no date, but one would imagine Sims a contemporary of Borges, Nabokov, Pynchon, and Barthes himself, for whom "the work of the commentary, once it is separated from any ideology of totality," consists "precisely in *manhandling* the text and *interrupting* it," thereby denying not "the *quality* of the text . . . but its 'naturalness.' "[5]

II. SIGNIFYING NOTHING

One step up from the fragmentary "wisdom of the Bard" subverted by Sims is the speech so well known that the actor in the modern theater is compelled to adopt the most irritating mannerisms to rescue it from an inaudible familiarity. If the 'vulgar' still attended the theater as they did in the Elizabethan and Jacobean age,[6] this type of speech would provoke a reaction comparable to that which greets the opening bars of "My Way" or "Strangers in the Night" at a Frank Sinatra farewell concert. But the modern audience gets excited less by dint of passionate involvement in a popular tradition than the intervention of the educational apparatus, with its fondness in the past for the discipline of rote-learning. "To be or not to be," "The quality of mercy," "All the world's a stage," "Out, out, brief candle," and the like have all been staple tests of memory that confirm, on a larger scale, those eternal verities and felicities of expression that contribute to a cultural gold reserve and manifest the wisdom of the mythic Shakespeare. These speeches — Shakespeare's greatest hits — can sidestep their context even in performance, hijacked by the codes of received ideas and smothered by the notion that they are in some sense *true* or that they at least represent what Shakespeare, with his unique insight into an abiding 'human nature', *thought*.

A quick, somewhat enigmatic, antidote to these practices emerges from a statement by one of Shakespeare's contemporaries, Sir Philip Sidney: "Now, for the poet, he *nothing* affirms, and therefore never lieth."[7] Traditional Shakespeare criticism would also take issue with received wisdom in this matter, stressing the importance of context and reassimilating what may or may not be affirmed to the *doxa* at a higher level by fixing the analysis on the complexities of 'character', thus affirming in a more subtle way the merely *mimetic* relationship of the language of drama to 'Life'.[8] But the Shakespearean text itself interrogates the discourses that rework it in a much more radical way. In our brief extract from *Macbeth*, for example, signifiers pertaining to language ("I dare not," "I would," "adage") displace the concrete register of proverbial lore ("cat," "fish," "wet feet") to cut loose, and *make present* the materials of discourse *absented* by the naive, self-naturalizing, and speciously 'given' idiom of the proverb. To read this simply in terms of a reference to the motives of Lady Macbeth would be to reproduce the erasures of proverbial language in a deletion of the productivity of the linguistic and theatrical signifiers that constitute 'character'.

The issues at stake become clearer in Macbeth's "Out, out, brief candle" speech. According to the "wisdom of the Bard," the author here affirms, through a dramatic character and the medium of exquisitely fine and appropriate language, some such universal truth as "life is merely a play." A traditional critical interpretation, on the other hand, would use the speech to mark a stage in Macbeth's spiritual journey, discovering in it some intimations of self-knowledge and a poetic evocation of despair which is connected with other aspects of the play's imagery —a Macbeth who cannot effectively perform his role being dressed as he is in the ill-fitting robes of kingship, to give just one example — to create a unified, and perhaps tragic, 'vision' of life. But in both cases it is certain key constitutents of 'life', transcendentally signified and beyond the play of signs, that are being recovered from a speech that unravels the category of 'character' and defamiliarizes the apparently natural signifying practices within which it is constructed both in and outside the theater.

"Life," says Macbeth, is:

> but a walking shadow, a poor player,
> That struts and frets his hour upon the stage,
> And then is heard no more; it is a tale
> Told by an idiot, full of sound and fury,
> Signifying nothing.
>
> (5.5.24–28)

Here, as in Jaques's "All the world's a stage" speech in *As You Like It*, a medieval commonplace about the futility of life — the world is *merely* a play, men and women *merely* actors[9] — is transformed by the fact that it is spoken from the stage by an actor. The actor who speaks, or at least the actor he acts — Macbeth overparted as king — *is* the poor player whose incompetence blocks any smooth passage to what is being represented and, like the language of madness, foregrounds the very materials of signification in signifying nothing. The stage, then, can in no way be simply the means for *expressing* this commonplace. Shadows cast no light, except in a text where language is no longer permitted to function "naturally," where "Fair is foul and foul is fair" (1.1.10) and "nothing is but what is not" (1.3.139–140). The "nothing" signified is not the futility of life alone nor a mere absence of meaning. It is the play of a semiotic space anterior to the closures in language that construct the Life which language is then seen to merely reflect. It is the signifier always in excess, not yet connected to, and therefore undermining, the stable signified — like the "written troubles of the brain" (5.3.42) that emanate from Lady Macbeth between sleep and waking, madness and reason. The transgression cuts across the unity of the sign, thereby unhinging the structures of Life itself. Darkness strangles the day, mousing owls hunt falcons, and the king's horses break loose and devour one another (2.4.1–39) according to the credulous choric observations of Ross and an old man, but what regicide has brought about is a breech in a *symbolic* order, effected by the equivocal discourse of Macbeth and the witches, in whose cauldron the syntax of nature is disrupted and reconstituted: "Eye for newt, and toe of frog,/ Wool of bat, and tongue of dog,/ Adder's fork . . . " (4.1.13–15). Their "double, double" doggerel, enacting the pleasure in sound of nursery rhyme and nonsense, works with their self-contradictory pronouncements, Macbeth's sound, fury, strutting, and fretting, and the written troubles of Lady Macbeth's brain to counter the mimetic reference to a hypostasized Life with the opaque materiality of its constituent codes. All are "imperfect speakers" (1.3.70).

The symbolic order disclosed in *Macbeth* constitutes not only the 'real world' but the *subjects* who exist for and in it. In response to his wife's incitement to murder, Macbeth insists: "I dare all that may become a man;/ Who dares do more is none" (1.7.46–47). In daring to do more and becoming one with the witches, Macbeth not only shakes the state and ceases to be a good subject of the king but cracks open his own "single state of man" (1.3.139) and literally ceases, in his sound and fury, to be a *coherent* subject in the Lacanian sense. Catherine Belsey develops a persuasive analysis of *Macbeth* along these lines and shows how the metaphor of the shaken state of man points out a parallel "between crisis in the social formation and the subject in crisis" in a text that gives "glimpses in discursive practice of the subject as a process rather than a fixity."[10] But if Macbeth's "signifying nothing" implies that "he has refused the subject-positions offered him by the symbolic order and in consequence meaning eludes him, he has fallen into non-meaning,"[11] the problematization of the whole context of his utterance, in which the sound and the strutting traverse the 'meaning' of the speech itself, puts the unity of 'Macbeth' as character under erasure and constructs for the audience subject positions unlike those of a purely mimetic drama or a language that affects easy access to its signifieds. When he does more than may become a *man*, and is consequently *none*, 'Macbeth' is united with his unsexed wife. They share with the sexless witches the movement of the text that permits sound a separate existence from sense, that allows opposites to be identical and Life to be no longer articulated even into woman-man, sleep-waking, illusion-reality, let alone the intricate hierarchies of absolutist notions of kingship and its place in "nature." When the text signifies "signifying nothing," it does so by displaying its own materiality — the residue of actors, characters, verbal and linguistic signs that will never be fully absorbed in symbolic meanings. This "nothing" is the ground of the multifarious "somethings" of the "real world," to which the text can no longer innocently refer. From within the unperceived closures of the signified — sublime confidence in an unshakeable truth — the new voice of kingship and the symbolic order at the end of the play constricts these limitless transformations of "nothing" into the most complacent and parsimonious of definitions: "this dead butcher, and his fiend-like queen" (5.8.79). 'Character' may be reaffirmed here, not as an absolute subjectivity so much as an *inscription*, the mark of a limited discursive practice. 'Macbeth' has seen more—enough to cease being Macbeth and to become coterminous with the text, which incorporates a position adjacent to the signified and the subject in which the raveled sleeve of language is never conclusively knit.

"First of all we must recognize that the theater, like the plague, is a delirium and is communicative."[12] Artaud's observation has a special relevance to *Macbeth*, in which the subject positions provided for the audience put in crisis the unity of both the sign and the self who purports to use signs to communicate with others about the world. Delirium takes priority—in the insistence of madness, dream, the unconscious, the insoluble signifier—to affirm a play *reduced* in the construction of subjects and signs, and woefully attenuated in the metaphysics of the 'communicative' symbolic order as 'sin', 'evil', 'chaos', and so on. Yet Artaud could regard Shakespeare as the antithesis of the drama he himself advocated, presenting his work as the source of a modern theater of "falsehood and illusion":

> We have been accustomed to four hundred years, that is since the Renaissance, to a purely descriptive and narrative theater-—storytelling psychology . . . every possible ingenuity has been exerted in bringing to life on the stage plausible but detached beings, with the spectacle on one side, the public on the other.
>
> Shakespeare himself is responsible for this aberration and decline.[13]

But Artaud's conception is very much the Shakespeare of the *doxa* and of traditional criticism, the text which, in Macherey's terms, can never simply be itself, crossed as it is by "everything which has been written about it, everything which has been collected on it, become attached to it—like shells on a rock by the seashore forming a whole incrustation."[14] In this respect the dominant tradition in criticism, for all its apparent distance from the popular signifier of the Bard, has stood at the up-market end of the *doxa*, taking its place in the same culture industry[15] and, based as it so firmly is in the education system, establishing its distance in the context of the reproduction of existing relations of production and specifically the perpetuation of a class whose accomplishments must surpass a certain minimal theshold in the 'liberal arts'—a process re-presented in the strictly personal and humane jargon of the business as 'refining the sensibilities' or 'enhancing the critical awareness'.[16] This is the tradition that assiduously underplays its own theory and status as discourse, holding sacred what it chooses to call a unique, imaginative response of individual to work of art. It is the

Shakespeare incrusted with this discourse that is inserted into Artaud's origin myth of a drama that tells stories, creates characters, and "wishes to leave the public intact".[17] This Shakespeare, in spite of the strictures of L. C. Knights first published as long ago as 1933,[18] still deals in character, and the increasing interest since that time in the poetic language, theatrical conventions, and use of the stage has been primarily formalistic and devoted to an interpretation of what the play communicates about Life *sub specie aeternatis*. Modes of production and signifying practices are largely overlooked in the incrusted Shakespeare except where a knowledge of the appropriate conventions or historical 'background' are seen to be useful in facilitating access to the signified and in showing *how* it is transmitted. The criticism absents the process in which the oral performance of a *play*, regarded by many Elizabethans and Jacobeans as antithetical to the literary *work*,[19] before an audience drawn from a cross-section of society[20] *becomes* the work contained in the printed text, which, in turn, is inserted into the educational apparatus and the subsidized bourgeois theater in which Shakespearean drama is, in Artaud's terms, the enervating *mise en scène* of a canonized written document.[21] Thus the insistently *present* discursive construct 'Shakespeare' is systematically misrecognized and naturalized as a cultural monument of the past whose very monumentality vouches for its universal reference to the 'realities' that precede discourse.[22]

The incrusted Shakespeare of the *doxa*, which incorporates the bulk of academic criticism, sustains such transcendental *givens* as *subject* ('author', 'reader'/'spectator'), the unity of which is mirrored in character; *object* ('reality', 'nature', 'life'), of which the text, viewed as a fixed and concrete commodity, becomes a constituent part; and the *essence* or *meaning* ('truth', 'nature'), discovered by the subject in contemplation of the object, or the reader in the interpretation of what the writer has encoded into the text. The status of these signifieds is threatened by the unraveling of signifiers even when constituted in abstract, denotative language. 'Nature' spans 'essence' and 'raw reality' in a potentially volatile ambiguity that is put to play in *King Lear*. 'Subject' connotes at once the consistent self-present individual consciousness conjured by the signifier from the contradictory processes of the unconscious and the symbolic order *and* the main concern that centers a text. The pun on 'subject' deconstructs both of its signifieds into the *process* of the subject of Lacan, always other than itself, an effect of the signifier that has discovered its unity in the text of the mirror image and remains split from this 'subject' of the symbolic order, doomed to 'suture', in imaginary centered structures, the gap between itself and its 'self'.[23] The problems present even in abstraction are compounded in the

67

Shakespearean text, and not in *Macbeth* alone, which intimates the 'splitting' and 'suture' to achieve precisely the effect denied by Artaud to the Shakespeare who leaves his audience intact, "without setting off one image that will shake the organism to its foundations and leave an ineffaceable scar."[24]

In a paradoxical transference, this type of text 'reads' traditional criticism — which is inscribed in the closures the text itself precedes and manifests — and unmoors it from its signifieds. Duke Senior's speech on nature and self-knowledge, a minor example of the classic Shakespearean set-piece, works in this way:

> *Duke S.*   Now, my co-mates and brothers in exile,
> Hath not old custom made this life more sweet
> Than that of painted pomp? Are not these woods
> More free from peril than the envious court?
> Here feel we not the penalty of Adam,
> The seasons' difference; as the icy fang
> And churlish chiding of the winter's wind,
> Which even when it bites and blows upon my body,
> Even till I shrink with cold, I smile and say
> 'This is no flattery; these are counsellors
> That feelingly persuade me what I am'.
> Sweet are the uses of adversity;
> Which, like the toad, ugly and venomous,
> Wears yet a precious jewel in his head;
> And this our life, exempt from public haunt,
> Finds tongues in trees, books in the running brooks,
> Sermons in stones, and good in everything.
> I would not change it.
>
> *Amiens*   Happy is your Grace,
> That can translate the stubbornness of fortune
> Into so quiet and so sweet a style.
>   (*As You Like It*, 2.1.1–20)

The critical problem here has traditionally been cast in terms of *interpretation*. What does Duke Senior's speech *mean* in terms of affirmations about life, the presentation of character, and the development of theme? One approach takes this as a central statement of the play as a whole about the redemptive and educative power of nature, seen as an abiding theme in Shakespeare. The Duke's rejection of courtly sophistication and acceptance of natural "counsellors" "is a foretaste of Lear upon the heath, and a development of the princess's advice to the king in *Love's Labour's Lost.*"[25] Nature enhances self-knowledge where court flattery stands in its way. Another view of the problem sustains the notion of Duke Senior being an admirable man — "the play invites us to honour him"[26] — but detaches the play from any necessary affirmation of the good in nature and emphasizes the transformative power of his imaginative perceptions, indicated by the reference to *translation* in Amiens's response. The focus moves, in this account, from nature, artifice, and self-knowledge to character: "It is characteristic of the Duke . . . that he should make a disadvantage appear advantageous."[27] The third main approach offers an urbane riposte to the first two, in the liberal spirit of "Yes, but . . . ," and interprets the speech as presenting a more complex, ironic view of character. The contrivance of the speech is seen to undermine its rejection of artifice. The claim to self-knowledge is contradicted by the Duke's smugness and credulity. His view of nature — "good in everything" — is ultimately closer than it may at first seem to the pastoral fantasies expressed at court, in which the Duke and his merry men "live like the old Robin Hood of England" (1.1.106–107) [28] The three interpretations differ, but show a common gratitude to the more fundamental level of scholarship that establishes the meaning of specific words and phrases and the importance of conventional dramatic and rhetorical forms. It is comforting, for example, that the text can be helped along to yield the author's sense where it becomes a little ragged. "Here *feel we not* the penalty of Adam" introduces the possiblity of a self-contradiction until it is recuperated as "we are none the worse for," or the poor punctuation of the text is corrected to make this the third in a series of rhetorical questions.[29] It is helpful to know that "old custom" means "prolonged experience," although an ambiguity here introduces another possible sense — having to do with the classical conventions of literary pastoral — in which case the irony would confirm a dominance of artifice in the speech. The same issue, with its implications for the interpretation of character, arises in the image of the toad[30] with a precious jewel in his head. The fact that the image occurs in Pliny and Lyly[31] and that the imaginary jewel is an antidote to the imaginary venom either enhances the Duke's presentation of the joy and wisdom gained from a nature at once hostile and healing, or further compromises his rhetoric by contact with the fanciful natural history that is one mark of the artifice of euphuism, another being a routine fondness for antithesis which begins to insinuate itself in "tongues in trees, books in running brooks,/ Sermons in stones, and good in everything." The footnote, even when it permits a limited plural, is circumscribed by debates centered on character, form, and interpretation.

The problem with this formalistic and interpretive discourse, which prides itself in its empiricism and its 'close reading', is that it does not read closely enough. For all its apparent pluralism and accommodation of differences in the pursuit of meaning, its undisclosed metaphysical assumptions constitute a dogma that the text itself can read back. What is remarkable about Duke Senior's speech is the way in which its transcendent 'givens'—the natural world, "life" (l. 9), and the "body" (l. 2)—set apart as they are from the culture and artifice of the court, are themselves artifices constituted by an ostentatious textuality: "churlish *chiding*," "no *flattery*," "counsellors/That feelingly *persuade* me," "*tongues* in trees," "*books* in running brooks," "*sermons in stones*," and, in Amiens's reaction, "*translate*" and "so quiet and so sweet a *style*." To simply call this an extended conceit will not put it to rest. The 'natural world' is itself constituted as a *text*, in a weave of voices which perpetually defers the unmediated felt presence of a signified *reality* that can establish a firm structural opposition to courtly *illusion*.

The language resists any denotation of the "natural" but also deflects any attempt to reduce its play of affirmation and deconstruction to an analysis of Duke Senior by enacting a fading of the subject in its interrogation of the very category of 'character'. When Amiens reinterprets Duke Senior's natural communion as a translation of the stubborn into the sweet, the pun on "your Grace" (title and spiritual quality), unavoidable in performance, instigates a play of subject, attribute, title reflecting status and in this case title "genuinely" reflecting attribute. In the motion of the signifier the character as subject, already compromised by the name "Senior," is subsumed into an effect of signifying practice in the text—into some such actantial function as the space occupied by "the wisdom of age," to which Amiens, ample testimony to the flattery that does exist in the forest, actantially signals his "Amens."[32]

The text itself becomes no less a weave of voices, a space traversed by codes, than are the terms—'life', 'nature'—it recovers from their privileged place beyond the pale. Where the world is so much constituted and mediated by the signifier, the whole issue of the presence or absence of *self-knowledge* in "Senior"/"Grace," the preposterous notion of a real unified subject's unmediated knowledge of itself,[33] becomes another absolute to dissolve in the cauldron. The "poor" (disruptive) syntax of lines 6–10, in which "*I*" jostles and supplants the substantive "*wind*" as the subject of the subordinate clause,[34] slashes that space in which the transcendental ego is constituted.[35] The critical practice that corrects or explains away such rough edges and indiscretions in language, *enabling* the access to a "true sense," minimizes the play of a process that has cut itself loose from the signifieds endorsed by that practice. The contradiction introduced by "Here feel we not the penalty of Adam" is not to be smoothed over, but allowed its disconcerting presence along with what may be considered preferable meanings. The play on "old custom," which jolts the nature-culture axis of the speech by affirming experience and the artifice of writing as *one*, can only be halted by a reductive intervention. As the signified progressively loses ground, the text has no source or meaning to absolutely prohibit any extrapolation of free-associations and puns—"grace" as "grays" (mark of seniority, balance, compromise, tedium, the avoidance of extremes). The subject position adopted by traditional criticism sustains closures that the text resists by offering a position in process, ranging from the closed/mimetic/affirmative to a psychotic delirium. The question is not *what*, but *how* it signifies, and its meanings and foreclosures, in the face of all interpretation, are as you like it. Its discursive mode is not the affirmation of truths that cannot be remade, but the deconstruction of carnival and saturnalia, in which the signifying practices that make up the real world are momentarily viewed as arbitrary and beyond enforcement.[36]

"Texts," according to Macherey, "are constantly rewritten, their effects are altered," and the interpretations attached to them are part of their material history, "finally incorporated *into* them.[37] As Borges's Pierre Menard writes *Don Quixote*, without changing a word, so the perspectives of contemporary critical theory propose a rewriting of Shakespeare. Cracks also appear in another site of the *doxa*, the 'legitimate' theater. Under the threat of general cuts in British government subsidies to the arts in 1980, Peter O'Toole strutted and fretted a delirious Old Vic *Macbeth* that interrogated the incrusted Shakespeare sufficiently to bring back some of the 'vulgar' and threaten to make the theater a self-financing place of resort. The production extended its crisis of subject, actor, and signifier into other areas of the mode of production, to be derided by critics and ultimately disowned by its own theatrical administration. The Bard in process leaves only the birthday book to be rewritten, with proverbs of the signifier rather than the signified—like "nothing is but what is not"; Touchstone's "the truest poetry is the most feigning" (*As You Like It*, 3.3.16–17); the immortal words of the old hermit of Prague to a niece of King Gorboduc: "'That that is is' . . . for what is 'that' but that, and 'is' but is?" (*Twelfth Night*, 4.2.14–16); "Richard loves Richard; that is I am I" (*Richard III*, 5.3.183); "Oschorbilducos volivorco" (*All's Well That Ends Well*,

4.1.76); "Comparisons are odorous" (*Much Ado About Nothing*, 3.5.15); "Pillicock sat on Pillicock hill/ Alow, alow, loo, loo" (*King Lear*, 3.4.74–75); and, for those born on March 15, Hymen's "*If* truth holds true contents."

III. TRUTH'S TRUE CONTENTS

The NOTHING affirmed by Sir Philip Sidney's poet and signified by the language of madness and the poor player in *Macbeth* is the ground and negation of the symbolic order, the subject, the truth. Leakage from this semiotic site — like the puns and slips of the tongue that bedevil communication generally[38] — warps any text's mimetic affirmation of a world. Shakesepare's language opens the floodgates and derides any insertion of critical digits in dykes, so much so that the text is less an utterance to be interpreted, with its origin in "Shakespeare," than a space that is the crisis of discourses and subject positions — those of the Elizabethan social formation *and* of later interpretive practices. This is a far cry from what Morris Weitz, in his case study of the in-crusted *Hamlet*, calls the assumed "*logical univocity* of the language of *Hamlet* criticism," in which the construction of the text as an enigma is a strategy for disclosing some stable "truth" about the *text*, seen as its container, and the '*world*', to which it refers:

> The critics of *Hamlet* assume that their utterance and argu-ment are true (or false) in relation to an objectively existing set of facts in *Hamlet* or the world. They agree that there is the real *Hamlet* . . . and that tragedy, drama, aesthetic comprehen-sion or response, and dramatic and artistic greatness or merit are also facts in the world which are (ideally) definable in terms of their essences. The aim of the critic, thus, is presumed to be the making of true statements about the nature of *Hamlet* . . . and its relation to life and the world.[39]

The critical discourse writes the text, as the text writes 'life and the world', leaving on its 'object' indelible traces of a constitutive inscrip-tion. To cut across this recession of inscriptions by interpreting the truth beyond play is to embrace the doctrine of Touchstone's heathen philos-opher, who,

> when he had a desire to eat a grape, would open his lips when he put it into his mouth; meaning thereby that grapes were made to eat and lips to open. (*As You Like It*, 5.1.30–33)

The tautologous self-justifications of interpretation are nowhere clearer than in *As You Like It*, which maintains, as a condition of its own closure, that the contents of *truth* should be *true*. The masque of Hymen, which brings the play to its conclusion, has long been a topic of controversy. Some commentators dismiss it as unworthy of Shakespeare, there being "no dramatic necessity for this masque business,"[40] and invoke the shade of some Jacobean actor or hack who has mangled the text. Others strenuously defend it as a solemn and fitting resolution of some central themes of the play which is in keeping with the pastoral convention.[41] It is Hymen who stipulates that the truth should be true, having first announced the reconciliation in an epithalamium:

> Then is there mirth in heaven,
> When earthly things made even
>   Atone together.
> Good Duke, receive they daughter;
> Hymen from heaven brought her.
>   Yea, brought her hither,
> That thou mightst join her hand with his,
> Whose heart within his bosom is.
> (5.1.102–109)

A proliferation of words threatens this newly achieved "atonement":

> *Duke S.* If there be truth in sight, you are my daughter.
> *Orlando* If there be truth in sight, you are my Rosalind.
> *Phebe* If sight and shape be true,
>   Why then, my love adieu!
> (ll. 112–115)

Hymen intervenes, cutting across this multiplication of conditionals, appearances, and "truths," and invites those assembled on stage to put the matter to rest by acceding to the tautology:

> Peace, ho! I bar confusion;
> 'Tis I must make conclusion
> Of these most strange events.
> Here's eight must take hands,
> To join in Hymen's bands,
> *If truth holds true contents.*
> (ll. 119–124)

This is the climatic precondition for marriage, festivity, the conventional ending of romantic comedy. As a stipulation that truth be true, it compounds the transgression in the Hymen sequence as a whole and has proved a matter of some embarrassment to guardians of the mythical Swan of Avon.[42] It adds to the sense that we are dealing here with something "not in the least Shakespearean,"[43] at least according to one, immediately recognizable construction of Shakespeare. But if the play is read along the lines of a standard interpretive schema that preserves intact the unity of the subject and the sign, Hymen's injunction can be recuperated to common sense by reference to some of the major preoccupations of the play as a whole. In the language of flatterers, for example, and in the authoritative utterance of state and domestic power at the court of Duke Frederick, what is held to be "truth" clearly contains falsehood. The "gentle" and "noble" Orlando (1.1.150–151) is branded "villainous contriver against . . . his natural brother"(ll. 132–133). Rosalind's innocence is misrepresented as treachery, and in this inverted order her "very *silence* and her patience" are seen to "*speak* to the people" (1.3.74–75). In contrast to this version of "truth," Duke Senior's self-knowledge gained in contact with natural counsellors — the central concern of a schematic reading of the opening speech in Act 2 — may seem legitimate, true in its contents. By the same sort of structural opposition, this version of nature — fallen yet truthful — may set up a contrast with the idealized illusions of court pastoral, which constructs a fiction in which the Duke and his entourage "fleet the time carelessly, as they did in the golden world" (1.1.208–209).

Once the play of Duke Senior's first speech has been arrested, and attached to a signified "truth" that is *true* — nature, the subject's self-awareness — other oppositions follow. While the Duke hears the voice of nature ("Tongues in trees" [2.1.10]), Orlando insulates himself against its force ("Tongues *I'll hang* on every tree" [3.2.117]) with his love poems, inserting the willful absolutes of a debased petrarchism between himself and the realities that serve notice of the finite, the imperfect, and of mortality. Thus the first instance of distortion, in the "truth" of the court, gives way to a second — in a literal adherence of youth to the literary conventions of romantic love. Silvius and Phebe, unknowingly, enact their "pageant truly play'd/ Between the pale complexion of true love/ And the red glow of scorn and proud disdain" (3.4.47–49), while Orlando reproduces the same pastoral and petrarchian scenario of "love *in vacuo*,"[44] languishing in solitude for the distant, deified Rosalind. Touchstone, confronted with the woes of true love as exemplified by Silvius, recalls his own idolatrous passion for the personified rustic come-on, Jane Smile, and remembers "the wooing of a peascod instead of her" (2.4.47). As a reference to fetishism or masturbation ("peascod"-"codpiece"), the Fool's comment punctures the complacent "truth" of romance. Love in the forest is, at best, a solitary vice devoid of the reciprocity and the dialectic Touchstone restores with his obscene parodies and commentaries on the bland, idealistic love lyrics he encounters. The disguised 'Ganymede', delivered from the identity of the goddess Rosalind, can work in a comparable way on Orlando's limited repertoire of platitudes. S/he challenges his stereotyped divine lady with another Rosalind, who will laugh when he is sad, weep when he is happy, and sleep with his neighbor. When he protests that he will die for love, s/he dismantles the literary models that validate such ridiculous protestations:

> Troilus had his brains dashed out with a Grecian club; yet he did what he could to die before, and he is one of the patterns of love. Leander, he . . . went but forth to wash himself in the Hellespont, and being taken with a cramp, was drown'd; and the foolish chroniclers of the age found it was — Hero of Sestos. But these are all lies; men have died from time to time, and worms have eaten them, but not for love.
>
> (4.1.85–95)

"All writing is Pig-Shit."[45] Artaud's image of the conventional, of a 'truth' always already-written, would incorporate his view of the modern theatrical production of Shakespeare. But the Shakespearean text itself alludes to this very traditional concept of writing, of a 'dead letter' cut off from the 'spirit', or full presence, in speech.[46] Pastoralism, petrarchism, and classical romance write 'love' in *As You Like It*, and these discourses encounter other instances of the already-written. Corin's rustic home-truths concerning the realities of court and country life are countered by a *tour de force* of sophistic argument from Touchstone, who proves the shepherd to be, like the lovers, half-baked, like an "ill-roasted egg, all on one side" (3.1.35). The trite generalizations of Jaques, who is written by the Gnomic Code, are likewise dislodged from within their own, self-naturalizing idiom — on this occasion by Touchstone's parody:

> It is ten o'clock;
> Thus we may see . . . how the world wags;
> 'Tis but an hour ago since it was nine;
> And after one hour more 'twill be eleven;
> And so, from hour to hour, we ripe and ripe,
> And then, from hour to hour, we rot and rot;
> And thereby hangs a tale . . .
>
> (2.7.22–28)

Jaques misses the point of this acute anticipation of Eliot's *Four Quartets* — an indication of just how far gone he is. Nor does he respond to the attentions of 'Ganymede'. Here the text offers its closest parallels to Artaud's image of writing and the references in Barthes to "the quintessence, the residual condensate of what cannot be re-written" as a staling, a rotting, or as vomit.[47] When Touchstone euphemistically addresses Jaques as "good master What-ye-call't" (3.3.63), the text names its actantial function "jakes," shithouse of language. Duke Senior's allusion to the "embossed sores and headed evils" that Jaques would "disgorge into the general world" (2.7.67–69) brings out the wordplay in the melancholic's relentless pursuit of matter which represents, at once, a truth beyond the play of language and a linguistic pus. Jaques is beyond redemption. In his conversation with Orlando, it becomes clear that both speak the already-written — the lover has taken his lines from mottoes engraved on love-tokens, while Jaques speaks the "right painted cloth" (3.2.258) of cheap didactic wall hangings — but Orlando shows the *humility* that, according to the constructions of a more subtle didacticism, would be the basis of self-knowledge, in his refusal to join Jaques in railing and generalizing about the world: "I will chide no breather . . . but myself, against whom I know most faults" (1. 363–364).[48] If Ganymede's advice to Phebe, "know yourself" (3.5.57), resounds behind the play's scrutiny of simpleminded adherence to the already-written, Orlando's reaction anticipates his ultimate inclusion in the renewed order in which self-awareness and experiential wisdom, as opposed to conventional belief, may seem to guarantee that "truth holds true contents" at last. Jaques, in contrast, will exclude himself and remain the creature of received ideas, seeking at the end the repentant Duke Frederick and the "much *matter* to be heard and learn'd" from him (5.4.179).[49]

When Duke Senior speaks of natural " 'counsellors/ That feelingly persuade me what I am' " (2.1.10–11), the fact that he is quoting *himself* compounds the implacable textuality of a speech which postulates an *immediate* knowledge of the subject and the object in language that discloses an interplay of constitutive inscriptions. The erasure of discourse in an affirmation of "nature" and "self-knowledge" can only be provisional, contingent on a suspension of the text's crossing of these signifieds with *writing* — "books in the running brooks," "sermons in stones," and so on. But this strategic interpretive myopia will deliver, at the end of the play, a new dispensation headed by the restored patriarch in which the wisdom he embodies has displaced the various manifestations of the already-written, and in which "truth" *is* true. This is confirmed by a phonocentrism implicit elsewhere in the play. Lovers are symptomatically silent — "What passion hangs these weights upon my tongue?" (1.2.256) — or garrulous, wearying the hearer with a "tedious homily of love" (3.2.145). Their isolation, or verbal insulation, sets them aside from an experiential, communicative practice in language and constitutes the space of a written, monolithic discourse. This contravenes an ethic of reciprocation and self-revelation given authoritative utterance in Cicero and the Renaissance courtesy books,[50] and implicit in Ben Jonson's "speake that I may see thee" — an injunction based on an anecdote in which Socrates challenges a coy and beautiful youth who trades more on looks than on dialectic.[51] Touchstone and "Ganymede" deliver the characters they encounter in the forest from "singleness," not only in the Elizabethan sense of simplemindedness[52] but also in the concrete sense of their separation from the society of which, in another commonplace recorded by Ben Jonson in *Timber*, language is the major instrument.[53] The fleeting stuff of 'life' is, in Shakespeare, also the material of speech — in *Love's Labour's Lost*, for example, conversation is the "converse of *breath*" (5.2.723) — and it is no accident that, at the moment of his incipient self-awareness, the Orlando who wrote sonnets on trees has become a *breather*. Redeemed from writing by speech, restored to the *presence* of 'nature' and other 'selves', the lovers can form the heart of a new order. The truth that has been *true* all along, or at least since the first appearance of Duke Senior, need no longer be obliterated by writing. It can be embraced now happily, and the pun facilitated by the Elizabethan pronunciation con-*tents* for both "that which is contained" and "pleasures" (*O.E.D.*)[54] enacts, at the level of the sign, the 'atonement' and 'making even' of earthly things which, according to Hymen, provoke "mirth in heaven." Reality and desire achieve a comic harmony, "*If* truth holds true con-*tents*," under the aegis of the divine and the patriarchal.

"Much virtue in If," says Touchstone immediately before Hymen appears on stage with Rosalind and Celia — "Your If is the only peacemaker" (5.4.96–97). It is Hymen's *If*, with its rhetorical invitation to consent, that invokes the paradoxical freedom in subjection accorded to those who would become subjects of Duke Senior's renewed symbolic order, in which signifier is tautologously pinned to signifier — 'truth' to 'truth' — in order to affirm the transcendental, unmediated signified The second sense of 'contents' as 'pleasures', which reinforces the importance of consent, is adumbrated earlier in the play. Rosalind leaves the court for the forest "in content" (1.3.133), while Orlando and Adam escape to "light upon some settled low content" (2.3.68) and Touchstone, footsore in Arden, consoles himself with the gnomic observation that "travellers must be content" (2.4.14–15). Before 'Ganymede' exits for

the last time s/he promises the lovers "magic" and the Word that re-
solves perplexities, adding "I will content you if what pleases you contents you, and you shall be married tomorrow" (5.3.107–109). Duke
Senior, finally, announces the marriages and the dance in terms that recapitulate this sense of Hymen's "true contents": "Proceed, proceed. We
will begin these rites,/ As we do trust they'll end, in *true delights*"
(5.4.191–192). This insistence on consent to *truth's truth* is, however,
the unraveling of the very possibility of such a signified. The pun on
'contents' works with the disconcerting circularity of Hymen's formulation to pry open the "natural" unity of the sign. Syllepsis, like condensation in the dream-work, short-circuits the track of desire in waking,
public discourse — the "serious use of words" — but also puts the signifier
forward in place of the signified, by "focusing our psychical attitude
upon the *sound* of a word instead of upon its *meaning* — in making the
(acoustic) word-presentation itself take the place of its significance as
given by its relation to thing-presentations".[55]

If the full presence of *truth* is deferred by the play on 'contents', its
case is rendered more critical still by the pun on 'truth' itself, as "that
which is true" in an abstract or general sense, and 'fidelity', specifically
the 'troth' plighted in marriage vows (*O.E.D.*). Following a conventional reading, the latter sense would give "If truth holds true contents"
a climactic position in regard to the play's treatment of love. Young
lovers have been 'educated' out of youthful idealism and reached a position in which 'self-knowledge' and a regenerative exposure to 'nature',
with all its connotations of limitation and mortality, add up to an
achieved adulthood, in which a commitment to wedding vows is the
'atonement' and 'making even' of the conflicting perspectives of the 'car-
nal', given rein in the speeches of Touchstone and 'Ganymede', and the
'spiritual', taken to a debilitating extreme in the conventions of romantic love. Thus Hymen requires that fidelity be a realistic proposition and
that marriage should hold true pleasures. By this point, however, the
hope of ever achieving a stable signified is being left behind by the cu-
mulative play of the signifier, which takes on dizzying proportions
when the play on 'truth' extends itself, inevitably, to 'true', and
Hymen's cacography assumes a density that surpasses even that of the
weave of voices and texts that constitutes, and undermines, Duke
Senior's initial affirmation of the givenness of nature. The god now
speaks of marriage containing faithfulness and chaste pleasures, but
speaking *anything* has become profoundly problematic. The "mirth in
heaven" at this attempt to resolve perplexity is clearly derived from the
pleasure of the text and, at the same time, the ludicrous activity of

atoning and making even that is the unity of the sign and the affirmation of anything beyond it.[56]

The three puns give rise to eight separate chains of meaning in Hymen's condition for the marriages, festivity and an ending to the play, "If *truth* holds *true contents*" (see accompanying diagram). Paraphrase

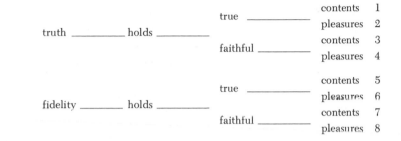

may assist a clearer reference to what has gone before and a centering of a unified structure imposed on the text. Thus chain 1 is Dr. Johnson's gloss "if there be truth in truth"; 5, "If fidelity is a realistic proposition"; 2, "if the truth can be accepted contentedly"; 6, "if there can be true pleasure in marriage"; 8, "if that pleasure can be sustained by remaining faithful". Chains 1 and 7 are tautologies, 3 an enigma that probably means very little—"if the truth is chaste."[57] Like Touchstone's philosophized grapes, they are the negation of an illusory center, fracturing the imaginary unity of structures, signs, and any metaphysical or empirical truth. The signified recedes further if "contents" means "contented people" (cognate to "malcontents") and four new chains are added. The connotations of "holds" as "maintains" and "restrains" double the number of permutations to give 24 in all, including such interesting variants as "if marriage restrains, or impedes genuine pleasure" and "if 'truth' is constituted by a coercion, rather than an upholding, of what is real." Here Hymen's brief text enters the sphere of self-contradiction which, like tautology, is assigned to philosophy. On the question of the shepherd's life, Touchstone tells Corin:

> In respect of itself, it is a good life; but in respect that it is a shepherd's life, it is nought. In respect that it is solitary, I like it very well; but in respect that it is private, it is a very vile life. . . . As it is a spare life, look you, it fits my humour well; but as there is no more plenty in it, it goes much against my stomach. Hast any philosophy in *thee*, shepherd?
>
> (3.1.13–21)

Again the signifier moves on, crossing any possibility of an affirmative or mimetic mode. Hymen's contradictions extend the play of his text even as far as the 'peacemaker', *If*. The marriages shall proceed whether fidelity sustains or holds back contentment. The new order of the patriarch, Duke Senior — to be inaugurated with this sacrament — will be installed whether the "truth" it sustains is a valid container of the "real" or a limit imposed arbitrarily on its play. The "if," then, is both the conditional which implies an *invitation* to consent, and a fiction belied by the fact that marriages, new dispensation, and ending will proceed regardless. This fissured "if" is the mark of the contradictory subject of humanism — "the totality of discourse through which Western man is told: 'Even though you don't exercise power, you can still be a ruler. Better yet, the more you deny yourself the exercise of power, the more you submit to those in power, then the more this increases your sovereignty.' "[58] Hymen's "if" indicates, at once, the *active* subject of grammar and *subjection* to the father and legitimate soveriegn, Duke Senior, whose voice is amplified in that of the god.[59]

These are all effects of the signifier, however, whose delirium now extends to 48 separate conditional clauses at play in "If truth holds true contents" — the "feeble line" which, according to Dover Wilson, serves only to provide "a rhyme for 'events.' " But the function of the classic footnote has been to limit polysemy, to construct a Shakespearean text that affirms the unity of the subject and the sign in a 'serious', communicative use of words. The current *Arden* edition, for example, limits the line to one narrow contextual reference: "If you are still contented with your marriage partners now that disguises are cast off and you know the truth about them".[60] The unwitting effect of this denotative straitjacket, however, is to liberate yet another dimension of Hymen's utterance, in which "truth" refers to the immediate presence of 'characters' — theatrical signifiers — on stage. While this reading takes "contents" to mean "contentment," it opens up another sense of "contents" as "that which is contained," in which Hymen is saying of the transformation of 'Ganymede', "If we can believe our eyes" or "If this is *truly* Rosalind." The permutations of signification by this time, to quote the immortal words of Hamlet, would truly "dozy th' arithmetic of memory" without recourse to a mathematical model. If the five words of the clause are *a*, *b*, *c*, *d*, and *e*, respectively, and if each is accorded the appropriate number of significations, as outlined above, the resulting set $\{a_{1-2}b_{1-3}c_{1-2}d_{1-2}e_{1-3}\}$ has 72 values — the number of signifying chains at work in "If truth holds true contents." The attempt to pin down a definitive "truth" has been confounded by the infinite[61] play of language. Even 72 is an arbitrary limit. Once this process is in motion, additional

paraphrases, puns, free associations, and slips of the tongue can constitute in Hymen's words a dictionary or thesaurus in which signifiers refer
perpetually to each other and the self-present truth is indefinitely
barred. On the level of the theatrical signifier, the 'real' Rosalind,
whose emergence from 'Ganymede' is the immediate contextual reference for Hymen's words, is rapidly transformed into the boy actor
whose Epilogue ushers the audience from the pleasure of play to the
limit of subjectivity, subjection, and discourse in the 'real world'. But
the subject, and the signifier, will remain in process. When the Epilogue says "*If* I were a woman . . . " (1. 21), it affirms a content that
is unconditionally true—that truth is, as ever, other than itself, always
already somewhere else.

Where the play ends, another play continues indefinitely. With the
removal of Hymen's 'resolution', the other main support of an affirmative and mimetic reading of the text as a reference to 'life' may be allowed its problematic scope, and the textual compromising of Duke
Senior's affirmation of an immediate knowledge of self and nature can
be embraced in all its decentered, contradictory *jouissance*. This makes
the general text something of a minefield for one particular interpretation of interpretation, the traditional critical practice that, in the words
of Derrida, "seeks to decipher, dreams of deciphering a truth or an origin which escapes play and the order of the sign."[62] The best this tradition can muster is a somewhat bewildered vision of play: "One must not
say that Shakespeare never judges, but one judgement is always being
modified by another. Opposite views may contradict one another, but
of course they do not cancel out."[63] One revealing strategy has been to
associate *As You Like It* with that distinctively twentieth-century category, the "problem play,"[64] which makes the problem of the interpretation of Shakespeare generally disappear in the creation of an extraneous
generic space occupied by a small minority of plays that not only offer
the disturbing luxury of situations "admitting of *different* ethical interpretations,"[65] but may even go to the outrageous extreme of freeing the
audience from the paternalistic norms of critical discourse itself—
"uncertain and divided responses . . . in the minds of the audience
are possible and *even probable*."[66]

The "problem play," like L. C. Knights's attack on character in
"How Many Children had Lady Macbeth?" is the site of a potential
epistemological break, ultimately recuperated as a form of tokenism by
a dominant critical discourse that still speaks of characters and interpretations. The true break comes with a different view of interpretation
itself, which brings onto the stage an actant whose remarks from the
tiring-house have ranged from the helpful to the inaudible. Nietzsche's

interpretation banishes the source, the center, the retrievable origin. All are lost in the discursive operations of the Nietzschean subject, the will to power:

> The actual causes of a thing's origins and its eventual uses, the manner of its incorporation into a system of purposes, are worlds apart . . . everything that exists, no matter what its origin, is periodically reinterpreted by those in power in terms of fresh intentions.[67]

Derrida and Barthes elaborate, from this absent center, a different practice of interpretation associated by both with Nietzsche. This embraces the "play of the world" and is "the affirmation of a world of signs which has no truth, no origin, no nostalgic guilt, and is proffered for active interpretation."[68] It views the text as "a galaxy of signifiers, not a structure of signifieds," and in this sense "interpretation" is not to give the text "a (more or less justified, more or less free) meaning, but on the contrary to appreciate what *plural* constitutes it," and to posit "the image of a triumphant plural, unimpoverished by any constraint of representation (of imitation)."[69]

The triumphant plural of *As You Like It* incorporates simultaneously all the reductive interpretations of critical tradition. Unhampered by a metaphysic of 'truth', it proffers a 'nature' that is at once constructed and unmediated, 'character' and its impossibility, and a blank check for the distribution of ironies, or not, as you like it. Orlando is the callow youth educated in love, and the true lover whose passion survives all obstacles and tests and emerges, unchanged, to project love at first sight into a happily ever after. He is also subsumed in a play of actants, as "Signior Love" to Jaques's "Monsieur Melancholy" (3.2.275–277), to "Patriarchal Wisdom" in Senior — wise and legitimate leader, pompous buffoon, usurper and murderer of the forest's natural lords. Jaques is at once "jakes" and the function of the text that resists the hopelessly compromised closures of Senior's new symbolic order in a heroic quest for the "matter" of the full Word. His fate, in resisting the Lacanian Name-of-the-Father[70] that inaugurates Law and the signified, is to be 'cut off' in, and from, the new order. The dangers in his possession of the phallus have already been outlined by the patriarch in his warning about the revenges that visit libertines who roam the world "with licence of free foot" (2.7.68). His final excision is his failure to negotiate access to the symbolic via the Oedipal stage.[71] Senior, who institutes his own language, does so as a sort of Absolute Subject, supported by the gods, who has won the Oedipal struggle by a symbolic castration of the Father and the murder of grammar. When he speaks of the "churlish chiding of the *winter's wind*,/ Which when it bites and blows upon my body,/Even till I shrink with cold, *I* smile and say . . . ," his modest shrinkage is less striking than the violent displacement from its *subjecting* position in the clause of the biting winter wind, authoritative breath of the father, by the "I" of Duke Senior as "little me" — the biter bit. The theatrical actant that begins as a woman, who disguises herself as 'Ganymede', who pretends for the benefit of Orlando to be Rosalind, who becomes "Ganymede" again, then, climactically, the "real" Rosalind, then almost immediately the boy actor s/h/s/h/s/he was, apparently, all along, resists the whole sorry business of the signifying phallus and its seminal role in the creation of symbolic orders by summarily slipping from the until-death contract of sexed individuals and reaffirming its own final location in play, in the theater.

The play and *frayage* of actants, their splitting and overlapping, at once constitute and deconstruct the mirage of unique and complex character — imbued with the spark of 'life'. The semiotic crises that write these theatrical signifiers — bodies on the stage — also rend their language. Long before the climactic nonsense with Hymen, the discretely obscene and transgressive Touchstone, with his puns and solecisms, is saying the unsayable, effing the ineffable, refusing to acknowledge even his own wit — "till I break my shins against it" (2.4.55). Throughout the text the materiality of language exacts its dues from the simple and univocal. A lyric of Orlando's ends "Run, run, Orlando; carve on every tree,/The fair, the chaste, and *unexpressive she*" (3.2.9 – 10). Editors invariably gloss his "unexpressive" as "inexpressible" or something equivalent,[72] thus assisting Orlando's conventionally petrarchan sense. But the text indicates that the semi-deified lady, the object of a lover's idolatry, is "speechless" or "dead" — a face like the death's head in Walter Benjamin: "total expressionlessness — the black of the eye-sockets — coupled to the most unbridled expression — the grinning rows of teeth."[73] Both of these additional connotations are a commentary on the 'dead letter' of debased petrarchism. When Jaques describes the uniqueness of his melancholy, "compounded of many simples, extracted from many objects, and, indeed, the sundry contemplation of my travels" (4.1.15–17), the pun on "simples" points to the naive commonplaces of received wisdom that constitute this "unique" and narcissistic humor, while enacting a complexity in language that denies these "simples" their undivided simplicity. "Travels," as "travails," points out the laborious seriousness of the whole business, and 'Ganymede' makes the *asteismus* explicit when s/he responds "I had rather have a foole to make me merrie, then experience to make me sad, and to *travaile* for it too."[74] Such "travails" belong to the "serious use of words," which Freud contrasts with the pleasure of turning meaning away. The puns in *As You Like It* do not merely correct, or install ironies in the 'single' utterance, but dismantle it altogether. The "galaxy of signifiers" envisaged by Barthes is constituted in the text by the periodic explosions of wordplay — in "bills" and "presents" (1.2.109), "hem" (1.3.18), "feet" (3.2.157), and "stairs" (5.2.34), all in the speeches of Rosalind/'Ganymede', and in Touchstone's "rank" (1.2.95), "cross" (2.4.10), "manners" (3.2.37–38), "lin'd" and "prick" (3.2.95, 102) "capricious" and "Goths" (3.3.5–6), "honest" (3.3.22), and "Jaques" (3.3.63). When the Duke and his men sing "The horn, the horn, the lusty horn,/ Is not a thing to laugh to scorn" (4.2.17–18), the signifier they celebrate takes up the quarry hunted by these merry usurpers, the sound that heralds the pursuit,[75] the phallus, and the crest of the cuckold. "Horn" itself constitutes a minor galaxy whose elements escape, by an accident of sound, the categories of the signified, throwing into new and gratuitous combinations the disparate elements of the text — from wedded love to the "brutish sting" and "headed evils" (2.7.66 − 67) of veneral disease, from Machiaveliian intrigue to a raw nature. The differences that establish structure here dissolve in the signifier, to be precipitated again at random. The galaxy of the text is stretched to infinity between the vagaries of sound and its own "unconscious" — the ideological traces left by the muddy feet of the sign. The pun remains the *bête noire* of discursive closures, throwing the naturalizations of ideology into delirious crisis: "Here's a billiard-room where Prince Charles can entertain his friends while Lady Diana's *beavering* away in the kitchen."[76] The unctuous TV commentator's evocation of the natural world betrays his routine chauvinism and sets up a deconstructive intertext of cheap romantic fiction, hardcore pornography, the rhetoric of conservationism, and the domesticity of rakish princes and sequestered maidens soon to be wed. Much virtue in "beaver."[77]

As You Like It is itself an intertext, a field mined with puns, tautologies, and other devices, crossed by discourses that erase their own productivity in the affirmation of truths beyond play. Here the codes of pastoralism and petrarchanism inscribed in 'nature' and 'true love' — a staple of the publishing industry in the 1580s and 1590s — collide with the Gnomic Code and the nostrums of rustic lore. Duke Senior and Duke Frederick are contrasting instances of the larger closures of subjection. The didactic operations of satiric comedy also come into play in Jaques's attempt to usurp Touchstone as Fool. Delighted by Touchstone's banal meditation on time, and missing altogether the point of the parody, Jaques covets the motley in order to persist in his own humor of tedious melancholy generalization. He will "anatomize" folly,

and administer "medicine" that will "cleanse the foul body of th' infected world" (2.7.56, 60.61). In *Every Man Out of his Humour*, a play
first staged, at the Globe, a year or two before *As You Like It* in 1598,
Asper, who is described as being privy to the thoughts of the author,
speaks of his self-appointed task as being to administer "physic of the
mind" to those who are "sick in taste," to:

> scourge those apes,
> And to these courteous eyes oppose a mirror,
> As large as the stage whereon we act;
> Where they shall see the time's deformity
> *Anatomized* in every nerve and sinew.[78]

Satiric comedy too speaks Jaques, then, and a 'truth' located beyond
play in an ethical absolutism. "Touchstone" and "Rosalind" mark the
space where all such absolutisms fall apart, where the intertextual fragmentation of discourses and signs is accelerated. This is the space of the
play itself, of actors and of Fools — "the constant, accredited representa-
tives of the carnival spirit in everyday life out of Carnival Season."[79]
The text here again signifies *nothing* and, in Sidney's terms, "nothing
affirms." The self-contradiction, and the foregrounding in wordplay,
recapitulate the process of the play when Touchstone says "the truest
poetry is the most *feigning*" (3.3.16–17). Sincerity and insincerity clash
in a signifier cut loose from its moorings. A mimetic mode by which *As
You Like It* might be forced to "fain" say something about "life" is tra-
duced by the 'feigning' of this most outrageous of fictions.[80] The last
word is, again, Touchstone's, whose "*natural*" (3.1.29) is at once "given
by nature" and, as all things given by nature are, "foolish." The
materiality of this pun is the last resting place of the signified and its
discourses.

Theatrical signifiers lie as thick on the ground as the debris of the
fractured linguistic sign in this ostentatious fabrication. Jolly foresters
in green lights sing "hey nonino" at the drop of a leaf, while the boy
disguised as a woman disguised as a boy pretends to be a woman, and
malefactors undergo perfunctory conversions that pick at a threadbare
convention. Recurrent theatrical imagery and Jaques's "All the world's
a stage" (2.7.139f) — like "Out, out, brief candle" an unraveling of stage
pointing out the pointless stage — locate the audience in the text as co-
sharers, more aware of a specific social transaction in the theater than
any mimetic action. The cat is out of the adage long before Hymen
enters for the extreme disclosures of play-within-play and his own, em-
barrassing function as *deus ex machina* with nothing to do, no probabil-

ity to save in the nick of time—the classic spare willy at a wedding. There is no "willing *suspension* of disbelief" here but a reveling in it. It is little wonder that the traditional commentary is torn between excision and an outlandish special pleading for the convention against a moment that tears it apart.[81] Hymen's talk of truth's true contents functions in two contexts, constructing subjects not only on the stage (S) but also in the audience (A), who confront in the theater, as on an agenda, the discourses and signifieds that constitute the world outside. Marriage, nature, self-knowledge are not so much endorsed in the play as reconstructed, as if in quotation marks, with ideology and the subject in process. The play ends "If truth holds true contents" for and in the audience. But only the most jejune, or devious, of critical rewritings would construct for itself a subject position within an unproblematized sign and read off from the text a center, a unity, an affirmation, or a meaning. Hymen's precondition carries for the audience yet another set of significations arising from the 'truth'—always radically other than itself—paradoxically present, if so wished, in the most "feigning" of confections. Romantic comedy is not the *form* or *convention* that assists the 'sense' of *As You Like It*, but another aesthetic ideology, placed with the sonnet, satire, and the pastoral romance on its agenda. In this case the "If" signals what may be a true choice, to leave early with Jaques—a very tempting proposition—or to join in the conclusion and finally, at the margin of the text, respond to the boy actor's request, "bid me farewell." The audience's "farewell," the last word of the play, is also the first word of communicative utterance back in the real world, the site of coherent subjects. It is a word absented by the text, whose play continues undeterred. Those who agree that the play signifies some *truth* are Touchstone's "*natural* philosophers." With the dual context of stage and audience, and the additional reference to the "truth" of the play, Hymen's attempt to make the truth present to itself now spawns 168 separate meanings: $S\{a_{1\text{-}2}b_{1\text{-}3}c_{1\text{-}2}d_{1\text{-}2}e_{1\text{-}3}\} + A\{a_{1\text{-}2}b_{1\text{-}4}c_{1\text{-}2}d_{1\text{-}2}e_{1\text{-}3}\} = 168.$[82]

In "The Theater of Cruelty and the Closure of Representation," Derrida writes of Artaud's drama as one that has done away with the differences that constitute a centered structure, and which attacks, like Nietzsche, "the *imitative* concept of art, with the Aristotelian aesthetics in which the metaphysics of Western art comes into its own."[83] Artaud was misled by an Aristotelianized Shakespeare to the extent of setting it up as the Law, or the Letter, to be deconstructed in his own practice. But the Shakespearean text proposes a theater, like Artaud's, that "like the plague, is a delirium and is communicative,"[84] and Hymen's invitation to a defense of its multiple truth and its pleasure works *for* this delirium and *against* the hostility it provoked from Puritans, civic authorities, and members of an intellectual elite.[85] The Puritan polemicist Philip Stubbes railed against actors as *"doble dealing ambodexters,"*[86] pointing to the very plurality that — combined in the theater with poetic language, which exceeds "the limits of common utterance" and draws speech "from plainnesse and simplicitie to a certain *doublenesse"*[87] — confounds the 'single' in its various manifestations. To Artaud, Shakespeare *was* the 'single', the dominance of the already-written. But Shakespeare's theater, to the Puritans, was the site of physical and moral plague, of idolatry, transvestism, idleness, and sexual license,[88] and if the plague is to be for Artaud the antithesis of the "Pig-Shit" of writing, his placing of Shakespeare is complicated by the fact that only "Venus and Adonis" and "The Rape of Lucrece," both written in 1592–94 when the theaters were closed by plague, show evidence of having been prepared by their author for dissemination in *print*. But this is merely a footnote to another 'writing' in the Shakespearean text, the *écriture* characterized by Barthes and Derrida that is cut free from any origin and continually defers or deflects any statement of unitary meaning. The already-written, in *As You Like It*, is juxtaposed to forms of the 'natural' or 'immediate', which then reveal themselves to be other instances of writing. The structural differences accomplished thus — youth/age, nature/culture, illusion/self-knowledge — are momentary deferments of a free play that is reasserted in a perpetual pushing back of the horizon of the signified. The role of Shakespeare's Hymen in this is not that accorded to the god in such medieval sources as Martianus Capella's *De Nuptiis Philologiae et Mercurii*, where he presides over a "marriage" of words and wisdom,[89] but closer to Derrida's "hymen," which marks the edge of the symbolic order and the interpretable — "describes a margin where the control over meaning or code is without recourse, poses the limit to the relevance of the hermeneutic or systematic question."[90] The sex of the deity, traditionally male although feminized in name, is unmarked in the text of *As You Like It*. S/he, with Rosalind/'Ganymede', presides over the anarchic semiotic space also associated with the unsexed witches and Macbeths — a process named "holiday humour" here (4 1 61) and, in the later play, "equivocation," "evil," "blight." The "plague," in all senses, is closer to home here than in the doodlings addressed to an infinitely more hygienic audience by Artaud, who extracts from Shakespeare a logocentrism which is the truth that contents *him*. Artaud's critique of Shakespeare is, ultimately, at the service of metaphysics, working in the interest of transcendental signifieds that the Shakespearean text would put in crisis — the "thought-energy" or "life force" petrified in the written, "the *presence of mind*," the need to "break through language in order to touch *life*."[91] The text, meanwhile, works on the signifier like the plague, "takes images that are dormant, a latent disorder, and suddenly extends them in the most extreme gestures" and gives words "approximately the importance they have in dreams."[92] Shakespeare is Artaud, Artaud Shakespeare.

NOTES

1. All citations, unless otherwise stated, are to the *Complete Works*, ed. P. Alexander London: Collins, 1951), and refer to act, scene, and line.

2. See Katherine Lever, "Proverbs and *Sententiae* in the plays of Shakespeare," *Shakespeare Association Bulletin* 12 (1938): 173–183, 224–239.

3. *S/Z*, trans. R. Hiller (New York: Hill & Wang, 1974), pp. 18, 206.

4. London: Harrap, n.d.

5. *S/Z*, p. 15. The apparent exclusion of women from this activity in "*man*handling" (*malmener*) is the work of the translator, not Barthes. That the hesitant cat should be female is the sexism of the Gnomic Code: "The cate would eate fyshe, and would not wet *her* feete" (*Macbeth*, ed. K. Muir, *The Arden Shakespeare* [London: Methuen, 1964,] p. 41n.) The authority on this subject is Flaubert, whose *Dictionnaire des idées recues* includes "BLONDES. Hotter than brunettes (See BRUNETTES)," "BRUNETTES. Hotter than blondes (See Blondes)," "NEGRESSES. Hotter than white women (See BLONDES, BRUNETTES)," and "REDHEADS. See BLONDES, BRUNETTES and NEGRESSES." (*Flaubert's Dictionary of Accepted Ideas*, trans. J. Barzun [London: Max Reinhardt, 1954], pp. 20, 21, 62, 71).

6. "With Shakespeare . . . we accept precisely the confusion of colours, this medley of the most delicate, the coarsest and most artificial, with a secure confidence and cordiality, we enjoy him as an artistic refinement reserved precisely for us and allow ourselves to be as little disturbed by the repellent fumes and proximity of the English rabble in which Shakespeare's art and taste live as we do on the Chiaja of Naples, where we go on our way enchanted and willing with all our senses alert, however much the sewers of the plebeian quarters may fill the air." (Friedrich Nietzsche, *Beyond Good and Evil*, trans. R. J. Hollingdale [Harmondsworth: Penguin, 1973], pp. 134–135.)

7. *A Defence of Poetry*, ed. J. A. Van Dorsten (London: Oxford University Press, 1966), p. 52.

8. See Lever, "Proverbs and *Sententiae*."

9. See John of Salisbury, *Policraticus*, trans. J. B. Pike (Minneapolis: University of Minnesota Press, 1938), pp. 171–173.

10. *Critical Practice* (London: Methuen, 1980), p. 90.

11. Ibid., p. 89.

12. Antonin Artaud, *The Theater and Its Double*, trans. M. C. Richards (New York: Grove, 1958), p. 27.

13. Ibid. p. 76.

14. "An Interview with Pierre Macherey," ed. C. Mercer and J. Radford, *Red Letters* 5 (1977): 7.

15. See T. W. Adorno and M. Horkheimer, *Dialectic of Enlightenment*, trans. J. Cumming (London: NLB, 1979), pp. 134f.

16. C. B. Cox and A. E. Dyson, having strongly recommended that teachers disclose

their political stance to avoid an insidious coloring of discussion, put forward as models of a good "practical critic" the Connoisseur, for example a connoisseur of wine, and the orchestral conductor, interpreting the established score and bringing it to life. (*The Practical Criticism of Poetry* [London: Arnold, 1965], pp. 29.30.) In spite of current reappraisals, the most useful and accessible brief clarification of these and allied notions in relation to ideology and the subject is in Louis Althusser's "Ideology and Ideological State Apparatuses," *Lenin and Philosophy*, trans. Ben Brewster (London: NLB, 1977).

17. *The Theater and Its Double*, p. 76.

18. "How Many Children had Lady Macbeth?" repr. in *Explorations* (London: Chatto and Windus, 1946).

19. See Stanley Wells, *Literature and Drama* (London: Routledge and Kegan Paul, 1970), pp. 25–55.

20. See Alfred Harbage, *Shakespeare's Audience* (New York: Columbia University Press, 1941), pp. 11–14.

21. *The Theater and Its Double*, p. 68.

22. It is impossible to footnote the major trend in Shakespeare criticism, but the outline of its major preoccupations is visible in the useful summaries in *Shakespeare: Select Bibliographical Guides*, ed. Stanley Wells (London: Oxford University Press, 1973).

23. See Jacques Lacan, *Écrits*, trans. A. Sheridan (London: Tavistock, 1977), pp. 1–7, 164–165, 200, R. Coward and J. Ellis, *Language and Materialism* (London: Routledge and Kegan Paul, 1977), pp. 93–94, 100, 105, 109–112; J-A. Miller, "Suture," *Screen* 18 (1977–78): 24–34.

24. *The Theater and Its Double*, pp. 76–77.

25. J. R. Brown, *Shakespeare and His Comedies* (London: Methuen, 1957), p. 145.

26. *As You Like It*, ed. A. Latham, *The Arden Shakespeare* (London: Methuen, 1975), p. 29n.

27. Ibid.

28. See R. B. Pierce, "The Moral Language of Rosalynde and As You Like It," *Studies in Philology* 68 (1971): 73–74; and A. Latham's survey of the negative responses to Duke Senior, *As You Like It*, edition cited above, p. lxix.

29. See *As You Like It*, ed. Latham, pp. 29–30n.

30. "FROG. Female of the toad." (*Flaubert's Dictionary of Accepted Ideas*, p. 41.)

31. *As You Like It*, ed. Latham, p. 30n.

32. For the actantial model, see Terence Hawkes, *Structuralism and Semiotics* (London: Methuen, 1977), pp. 89–95.

33. "I have always thought little of and about myself, only in very rare instances have I done so, only when compelled, always without wanting to 'go in for it,' liable to digress from 'myself,' never with any faith in the outcome, thanks to an unconquerable mistrust of the very *possibility* of self-knowledge which has led me so far as to sense a *contradictio in adjecto* even in the concept 'immediate knowledge' . . . this whole fact is almost the most certain thing I know about myself." (Nietzsche, *Beyond Good and Evil*, p. 193.) Nietzsche also refers to the concept of unmediated knowledge as "the dogma of the Immaculate Perception."

34. Duke Senior talks about the changes the seasons bring, "such as the *wind* which, even when *it* blows, even when I shrink with cold, *I* say 'This is no flattery . . . . ' "

35. "In its origin language belongs to an age of the most rudimentary forms of psychology . . . for here the doer and his deed are seen in all circumstances . . . the ego is taken for granted, the ego is Being, and as substance, and the faith in the ego as substance is projected into all things — in this way, alone, the concept 'thing' is created. Being is thought into and insinuated into everything as cause. . . . I fear we shall never be

rid of God, so long as we still believe in grammar." (Nietzsche, *Twilight of the Idols*, trans. O. Levy [London: T. N. Foulis, 1911], pp. 21–22.)

36. See Mikhail Bakhtin, *Rabelais and His World* (Cambridge, Mass.: M.I.T. Press, 1968), pp. 1–75; C. L. Barber, *Shakespeare's Festive Comedy* (Princeton: Princeton University Press, 1959), *passim*.

37. Macherey, "Interview," p. 7.

38. Discussed by Freud in *The Psychopathology of Everyday Life* and *Jokes and Their Relation to the Unconscious* (*Complete Psychological Works*, [London: Hogarth Press, 1953–74], vols. 6, 8.)

39. Morris Weitz, *Hamlet and the Philosophy of Literary Criticism* (London: Faber, 1972), pp. 212–213.

40. *As You Like It*, ed. Sir A. Quiller-Couch and J. D. Wilson (Cambridge: Cambridge University Press, 1926), p. 163n. See also *As You Like It*, ed. H. H. Furness, *New Varicrum Shakespeare* (Philadelphia: J. B. Lippincott, 1896), pp. 277n, 280n.

41. See G. K. Hunter, *The Late Comedies* (London: Longmans, 1962), p. 41; M. L. Williamson, "The Masque of Hymen," *Comparative Drama* 2 (1967): 257; R. Knowles, "Myth and Type in *As You Like It*," *ELH* 33 (1966): 13–14; J. R. Brown, *Shakespeare and His Comedies*, pp. 141–142; *As You Like It*, ed. latham, pp. xxii–xxiii.

42. "Johnson. 'That is, if there be truth in truth, unless truth fails of veracity.' Wright. 'This appears to be the only sense of which this poor phrase is capable.' It is merely a strong asseveration, stronger, perhaps (since there is no contradiction) than the occasion demands; but then, what of that? Hymen is *always* a little incomprehensible." (*As You Like It*, ed. Furness, p. 280n.) "The only point of this feeble line seems to be that it provides a rhyme for 'events.' " (*As You Like It*, ed. Quiller-Couch and Wilson, p. 167n.)

43. *As You Like It*, ed. Quiller-Couch and Wilson, p. 163n.

44. R. B. Young, "English Petrarke," *Yale Studies in English* 138 (1958): 12.

45. Gilles Deleuze, "The Schizophrenic and Language," *Textual Strategies*, ed. J. V. Harari (London: Methuen, 1980), p. 287. Cf. *The Theater and Its Double*, p. 151.

46. For an outline and critique of this tradition, see Jacques Derrida, *Of Grammatology*, trans. G. C. Spivak (Baltimore: Johns Hopkins University Press, 1976), *passim*.

47. *S/Z*, pp. 21, 98, 206.

48. "The trodden worm curls up. This testifies to its caution. It thus reduces its chance of being trodden upon again. In the language of morality: Humility." (Nietzsche, *Twilight of the Idols*, pp. 5–6.)

49. "The character of Jaques is natural and well preserved. . . . By hastening to the end of his work, Shakespeare suppressed the dialogue between the usurper and the hermit and lost an opportunity of exhibiting a moral lesson in which he might have found matter worthy of his highest powers." (*Dr. Johnson on Shakespeare*, ed. W. K. Wimsatt [Harmondsworth: Penguin, 1969], p. 107.)

50. See Cicero, *De Oratore*, 1: 32–34 and *De Officilis*, 1: 134–137; B. Castiglione, *The Book of the Courtier*, ed. W. E. Henley (London: David Nutt, 1900), pp. 70, 123–124, 140; G. Della Casa, *Galateo*, trans. R. Peterson (1576), repr. with introduction by J. E. Spingarn (London: Grant Richards, 1914), pp. 35f.; S. Guazzo, *The Civile Conversation*, ed. C. Whibley (London: Constable, 1925), 1: 72, 78–79.

51. *The Works of Ben Jonson*, ed. C. H. Herford, P. Simpson, and E. Simpson (Oxford: Clarendon Press, 1925–52), 8: 625; J. L. Vives, *On Education*, trans. F. Watson (Cambridge: Cambridge University Press, 1913), pp. 14, 90–91. Cf. Nietzsche: "The anthropologists among the criminal specialists declare that the typical criminal is ugly. . . . While on his way through Athens a certain foreigner who was no fool at

judging by looks, told Socrates to his face that he was a monster, that his body harboured all the worst vices and passions. And Socrates replied simply: 'You know me, sir!' " (*Twilight of the Idols*, p. 11.)

52. See *Romeo and Juliet*, 2.4.64–65; *2 Henry IV*, 1.2.172–173.

53. *Works*, 8: 621.

54. H. Kökeritz, *Shakespeare's Pronunciation* (New Haven: Yale University Press, 1953), pp. 335, 397.

55. Freud, *Complete Psychological Works*, 8: 119.

56. "And if the gods too philosophize, as many an inference has driven me to suppose — I do not doubt that while doing so they also know how to laugh in a new and superhuman way — and at the expense of all serious things! Gods are fond of mockery; it seems they cannot refrain from laughter even when sacraments are in progress." (Nietzsche, *Beyond Good and Evil*, p. 199.)

57. Possibly an allusion to Nietzsche's "dogma of the immaculate perception."

58. Michel Foucault, *Language, Counter-Memory, Practice*, trans. D. F. Bouchard and S. Simon (Oxford: Blackwell, 1977), p. 221.

59. "Humanism invented a whole series of subjected sovereignties: the soul (ruling the body, but subjected to God), consciousness (sovereign in a context of judgement, but subjected to the necessities of truth), the individual (a titular control of personal rights subjected by the laws of nature and society), basic freedom (sovereign within, but accepting the demands of an outside world and 'aligned with destiny'). In short, humanism is everything in Western civilization that restricts *the desire for power*: it . . . excludes the possibility of power being seized. The theory of the subject (in the double sense of the word) is at the heart of humanism and this is why our culture has tenaciously rejected anything that could weaken its hold upon us. But it can be attacked in two ways: either by a 'desubjectification' of the will to power (that is, through political struggle in the context of class warfare) or by the destruction of the subject as a pseudosovereign (that is, through an attack on 'culture': the suppression of taboos and the limitations and divisions imposed upon the sexes . . . the breaking of all the prohibitions that form and guide the development of a normal individual." (Foucault, *Language, Counter-Memory, Practice*, pp. 221–222.)

60. *As You Like It*, ed. Latham, pp. 127–128n.

61. To avoid the exaggerations of a particular type of poststructuralist criticism and the typographical pretensions of the *sous rature*, I use "infinite" in a sense employed by Borges in "The House of Asterion." The eponymous protagonist, the Minotaur, thinks "like the philosopher . . . that nothing is communicable by the art of writing," and has never retained the difference between one letter and another." When he speaks of his home as having an "infinite" number of doors, a footnote explains: "The original says *fourteen* but there is ample reason to infer that, as used by Asterion, this numeral stands for *infinite*." (*Labyrinths*, ed. D. A. Yates and J. E. Irby [New York: New Directions, 1964], pp. 138–139). Thus for "*infinite* play," here and elsewhere, read also "14 play," "4 play," etc.

62. *Writing and Difference*, trans. A. Bass (London: Routledge and Kegan Paul, 1978), p. 292.

63. Harold Jenkins, "*As You Like It*," *Shakespeare Survey* 8 (1955): 45.

64. See J. Smith, "*As You Like It*," *Scrutiny* 9 (1940).

65. W. W. Lawrence, *Shakespeare's Problem Comedies* (New York: Frederick Ungar, [1931] 1960), p. 4.

66. Ernest Schanzer, *The Problem Plays of Shakespeare* (London, Routledge and Kegan Paul, 1963), p. 6.

67. *The Birth of Tragedy and The Genealogy of Morals* trans. F. Golffing (New York: Doubleday, 1956), p. 201.

68. *Writing and Difference*, p. 292.

69. *S/Z*, p. 5.

70. *Ecrits*, pp. 67, 99, 310.

71. See Lacan, *Écrits*, pp. 5–6, 20–25.

72. See *As You Like It*, ed. Latham, p. 61n; cf. Alexander's "beyond all praise" and Dr. Johnson's "inexpressible."

73. Terry Eagleton, *Walter Benjamin* (London: NLB, 1981), p. 20.

74. *The Norton Facsimile: The First Folio of Shakespeare*, ed. C. Hindman (New York: Norton, 1968), p. 218.

75. "HORN (HUNTING). Lovely effect in the woods, and at night across the water." (*Flaubert's Dictionary of Accepted Ideas*, p. 48.)

76. Hugh Scully, on BBC1 "Nationwide," 22 July 1981.

77. On the semiotics of the beaver, see Kurt Vonnegut, Jr., *Breakfast of Champions* (London: Cape, 1973), pp. 30–31.

78. Jonson *Works*, 3: 432–433.

79. Bakhtin, *Rabelais and His World*, p. 8.

80. On this pun, see William Empson, *Some Versions of Pastoral* (London: Chatto and Windus, 1935), pp. 136–138.

81. See *As You Like It*, ed. Latham, pp. xxii–xxiii; and above, n. 41.

82. The set S (stage) applies to the *enoncé* and the presence/absence of choices that confront(s) characters on the edge of Duke Senior's new social and symbolic order. The letter b here is 'truth' (1. in a general sense, 2. as 'fidelity', and 3. as the immediate contextual 'truth' of this being 'really' Rosalind); c is 'true' (1. 'genuine', 2. 'faithful'); d is 'holds' (1. 'sustains' and 2. 'restrains' or 'impedes'); e is 'contents' (1. 'that which is contained', 2. 'joys' or 'delights', and 3. 'contented people'); a then becomes the compromised 'if' that at once signals a need for consent and, in the light of the second meaning of d, the fact that the implied request for consent is only a token 'peacemaker'. The 'play', in all senses, is about to end in any case. The set A (audience) applies to the *enonciation*, and the various 'truths' — love, legitimacy, nature, education, communication, etc. — that are naturalized in ideology but made visible in the text. These are, in a sense, the same signifying chains that appear in set S, except that here they are as if in quotation marks, and framed by the different language-game of self-acknowledged theatrical performance. In this second frame, b ("truth") takes on an additional, fourth, connotation that marks off *enonciation* from *enoncé* by pointing to the paradoxical "truth" of this most extreme and most feigning of fictions, which affirms nothing and yet charts the ground of all constructions and attributions of truth-value. This (S) plural is even more triumphant than that bound by the context of the action. It is the impossibility of the sign and the subject.

83. *Writing and Difference*, p. 234.

84. *The Theater and Its Double*, p. 27.

85. See J. B. Leishman, ed., *The Three Parnassus Plays, 1598–1601* (London: Ivor Nicholson & Watson, 1949), pp. 337–350.

86. Philip Stubbes, *Anatomy of Abuses* (London: Richard Jones, 1595), p. 102.

87. G. Puttenham, *The Arte of English Poesie, 1589*, ed. G. D. Willcock and A. Walker (Cambridge: University Press, 1936), p. 154.

88. See Stubbes, *Anatomy*, pp. 54, 101f.; Stephen Gosson, *The Schoole of Abuse, 1579*, ed. E. Arber (London: English Reprints, 1869), pp. 34–44; John Northbrooke, *A*

Treatise against Dicing, Dancing, Plays and Interludes, ed. J. P. Collier (London: Shakespeare Society Reprint, 1843), pp. 87f.

89. See E. R. Curtius, *European Literature and the Latin Middle Ages*, trans. W. R. Trask (London: Routledge and Kegan Paul, 1953), p. 38.

90. B. Harlow *Spurs*, (Chicago: University of Chicago Press, 1979), p. 99. Cf. Derrida, "Living On: Border Lines," H. Bloom et al., *Deconstruction and Criticism* (London, Routledge and Kegan Paul, 1979), pp. 92, 138.

91. *The Theater and Its Double*, pp. 8, 10, 13, 78.

92. Ibid., p. 94.

4

SHAKESPEARE IN THE WILDERNESS; or, DECONSTRUCTION IN THE CLASSROOM

Ruth Salvaggio

Since everyone nowadays is blaming something or other on the New Criticism, I hate to throw in yet another complaint. But I do believe that the New Criticism has generated, refined, and ultimately killed the undergraduate literary paper. They all sound the same. Considering the kinds of critical methods that confront a typical undergraduate, and considering the fact that most English professors rely primarily on a formalistic approach in their teaching (seconded by historical fill-in), most students will inevitably produce some kind of formal critique—color imagery in this, structural motifs in that, narrative style in the other. And although I am new at the professoring profession, I have to admit that I am getting tired of reading the same old kinds of undergraduate literary criticism. I also happen to feel guilty about my boredom, because deep down inside I believe that the approach is sound, especially for undergraduates at the survey level. Many of them will never take another English course, and it would be a shame to fail to expose them to the subtleties and complexities of literary form. Carefully written critiques are also easy to evaluate: they correspond nicely to the structure of the classroom, which calls for order, clarity, and objectivity. Still, the papers do all sound the same.

So whenever I receive an essay that sounds conspicuously different from the regular critique, I immediately become suspicious. I am suspicious, first, because the paper might be plagiarized. If it isn't, I am suspicious because I wonder where the student ever got the idea from. That is exactly what I thought when I received from one of my sophormore survey students a literary analysis that sounded like deconstruction.

I do not teach deconstruction, but I know what it is, and sometimes

I bring it up — as theory — in the class discussion. I talk about the loose-ness of language, its inability to escape the muddle of meanings. I talk about the absence of structure, the possible absence of the text itself — and how we might create a structure that is not really inherent in the work. But for all such talk, the truth is that sophomore survey students do not buy the theory. They don't trust ambiguity or relativity or nihi-lism, because we teach them not to. They believe in final exams and grades because that's what we give them. And they will call a grade a grade because we do the same thing. When they write their papers, even on the most complex of subjects, they at least aim to practice the kind of clarity that we taught them in freshman composition. To them, deconstruction of a text sounds all too much like deconstruction of the very classroom.

But if this one particular student of mine had not in fact written a piece of deconstructive criticism, he was certainly headed in that direc-tion. His critique of Shakespeare's sonnet 104 has all the characteristics of formalist criticism: well-defined thesis, painstaking close analysis, and a final explanation of what the sonnet is "ultimately" about — what holds it all together. The problem was that, according to his analysis, the sonnet is "ultimately" about nothing, and that it holds together only if we supply the glue. Instead of producing a well-wrought urn, my stu-dent made the poem into a heap of broken glass. He postulated a formu-la (constructed the poem), worked through the formula (analyzed the poem), and then had it all add up to zero (deconstructed the poem).

My first response was pleasure: I found the essay well written and the topic interesting. It entertained me in a way that few student papers do. But my second response was worry: how had this sort of thing gotten into the classroom? More puzzling was the question of how I should evaluate an essay that seemed to be generated from class discus-sion and lecture, but which clearly reflected a kind of criticism that I was not consciously teaching. Let me reprint the sonnet and the student paper. I want then simply to respond — to try to identify what makes the analysis different, and to discuss the situation that we, as professors, might find ourselves in if and when the New Criticism loses its hold on the critical methodology of undergraduates.

104

To me, fair friend, you never can be old,
For as you were when first your eye I eyed,
Such seems your beauty still. Three winters cold
Have from the forests shook three summer's pride,

Three beauteous springs to yellow autumn turned
In process of the seasons have I seen,
Three April perfumes in three hot Junes burned,
Since first I saw you fresh, which yet are green.
Ah, yet doth beauty, like a dial-hand,
Steal from his figure, and no pace perceived;
So your sweet hue, which methinks still doth stand,
Hath motion, and mine eye may be deceived:
For fear of which, hear this, thou age unbred:
Ere you were born was beauty's summer dead.[1]

"Shakespeare's Formula: $i + i + i = \pm 0$"
by
Andrew Scott Jennings

In his sonnet "To Me Fair Friend You Never Can Be Old,"
Shakespeare continually repeats three words: "I," "eye," and
"three." (From now on, I will refer to "eye" and "I" as his "i's.")
He invites his readers to make sense of the various combinations
of these "I's" and "three's." For example, he sets up his triple
beam scales in the second line by saying, "when first your eye
I eyed." Some critics consider this construction unnecessary and
awkward. To the contrary, I have eyed this clause with a third
and more critical eye. Shakespeare uses his "i's" in three different ways to reveal a message only to those who can see it. Once
revealed, the insight fits perfectly into his theme of opposites.

The first of the three "i's" refers to the object, the eye itself.
"First," Shakespeare tells us, "your eye I eyed." He thus paints
a picture of one porthole of human anatomy meeting another,
figure to figure, eye to eye. But later he warns us that what we
see with this "eye" is not reliable, since "mine eye may be deceived." Thus the eye as part of the body simply will not do.

The second of the three "i's" describes the poet himself, in
the process of viewing: "I eyed," "have I seen," and "I saw."
Here again Shakespeare gives us the same warning about the
possibility of deception, but the meaning moves off in a
different direction. It is not an eye looking outward that
deceives him, but an eye looking inward. In this sense, when
he says "mine eye may be deceived," he really means "I" may
be deceived — "I," "me," the poet.

The most important of the "i's" is the third and critical eye

97

Shakespeare wants us to use. It goes beyond what he himself ("I"), and what his physical sight ("eye"), can see. It is a disrobing eye which sees more clearly what it looks at. It can't be deceived. How do we know that this third "i" exists? It's a mathematical formula: Shakespeare uses the first "i" ("eye") exactly three times in the sonnet; he uses the second "i" ("I") exactly three times in the sonnet; and then he uses the word "three" five times in the sonnet.

Why use the word "three" five times? A possible explanation is the notion of using the critical eye as a sixth sense. Three plus three does not equal five (five senses), but it does equal six (a possible sixth sense). It is interesting that Shakespeare uses "three" as an adjective in front of months or seasons of the year, and that all of these months or seasons are surrounded by words that allude to our five senses. For example, "three winters cold" and "three hot Junes burned" appeal to our sense of touch. "Three April perfumes" appeals to our sense of smell. "Three beauteous springs to yellow autumn turned" appeals to our sense of sight, and the fact that autumn is also harvest time may make that season also appeal to our sense of taste.

Shakespeare connects almost all the senses to almost all the seasons in the five lines immediately following the construction of "i's": "when first your eye I eyed." He failed, however, to associate summer with one of the senses. And he also failed to allude to the sense of hearing. But he mentions both summer and hearing in the couplet which concludes the sonnet: "Hear this, thou age unbred: / Ere you were born was beauty's summer dead." The missing sense is now heard. In summer, or summary, Shakespeare tells us that what we finally have, after achieving the sense of the third and critical "i," is death, or nothing.

Here is the genius of Shakespeare's opposites. He has made us, as readers of his sonnets, grow into a critical "i" only after making us function as a merely physical "eye" and then a personal "I." Once we have played this silly game, disrobed his poem, and found the hidden and complex meanings with our own insight (death or nothing), we can then take it or leave it for what it is worth. He has manipulated our minds with "i's" and "three's" and then led us into a senseless sixth sense state of confusion. "Sense" has in fact been defined this way in Webster's dictionary: "one of two opposite directions of motion."

Give birth to a new sense or kill it. Find meaning in the sonnet or nothing in the sonnet. Shakespeare again wants us "to be or not to be," to see or not to see. We have that third "i" to choose our direction, and Shakespeare bids us to open it — or close it.[2]

I

I am convinced that this student essay contains at least five distinctive features of deconstructive criticism.

1. *Playful Tone*. The deconstructionist explores a text, works through its language with his or her language, plays metaphor upon metaphor. When I encountered the phrase "triple beam scales," I thought my student simply had a tendency to use metaphors. But then came "I have eyed this clause with a third and more critical eye." Here it hit me: this student-critic was punning while engaged in the very act of criticizing Shakespeare's puns. I was thus prepared for "In summer, or summary," for by this time the author and critic had clearly merged: both the poem and the critique had become "a silly game," and both poet and critic were engaged in the same kind of endeavor. My student's tone is not the tone of a conventional critic. It is a different tone, one which vies with the poet's for attention and which relies on the poet's for connections. The tone, in short, is playfully creative — not analytical, and surely not objective. It establishes a totally different role for the critic.

2. *The Critic as Creator*. Poststructuralists have generally assumed that the critic does not nor should not take second place to the author. Criticism is itself an art, a creative effort. Geoffrey Hartman can explain the situation much better than I can, and indeed does elaborate on this issue in his *Criticism in the Wilderness*.[3] What sticks in my mind about the issue is once having heard Stanley Fish reprimand a professor for "bowing down" in front of a piece of literature as if a literary work were something sacred. Language is language.[4] So with my student's approach: he may describe "the genius of Shakespeare's opposites," but he quickly admits that we can "take it or leave it." Acceptance or rejection is our creative option as a reader, and was surely his creative option as a critic. The deconstructive critic, almost ironically, always creates. And clearly my student felt no inhibition about creating elements that were missing from the poem. If there are only five senses suggested in the poem, why not create a sixth? And why not make that extra sense all the more important and conspicuous for the very reason that it is not actually there in the poem? Indeed, why not make this sixth sense into the "third and critical eye" because the number three is not a multiple of five (five senses), but is a multiple of six (the pivotal sixth sense)? My student had to create his text so that his argument would work. Had he

not created the text, such criticism would be impossible, for there would be no text to support his reading.

3. *There Is No Text*. What the poet gives us is not a text, but an opportunity. As critics, we jump at that opportunity. There are two ways in which my student has done exactly that. First, he has in fact reconstructed Shakespeare's sonnet by framing it within his own reading of the poem. Second, he has included as part of his interpretation a "critical eye" which is, at the most, postulated by the sonnet, and without which the sonnet falls apart. This "critical eye" must therefore, in Derridian terms, be the infamous lever which, once manipulated, disassembles the entire poem. Take it away and there is no text, for the poem leaves us with nothing. Leave it there and you have a text, for you have created one. Again, we can "take it or leave it. . . . Find meaning in the sonnet or nothing in the sonnet." Yet the poem still equals zero. Even with the recognition made possible by the "critical eye," the sonnet is still about death, about nothing, about the oblivion even of memory. We must make the poem into something more; we must create the "critical eye"—even though we realize that the minute we remove our creation, the poem deconstructs.

4. *Constructed for Deconstruction*. I'm not quite sure why deconstructive criticism tends to be so negative, but it does. That the New Criticism stressed the indisputable autonomy of the text and Deconstruction now stresses the very absence of the text may simply reflect a drastic swing of the pendulum. But whatever the reason, poststructuralist critics have denied rather than affirmed, and when they have attempted to find meaning (if that is the word to use), this meaning hinges tightly on the power of denial. I think that my student's "critical eye" functions as an instrument of both vision and denial. He has taken pains, with his "critical eye," to construct and create the sonnet. But the lever that allows us to "see" the truth also happens to be the very same lever that allows the poem to deconstruct. The situation is paradoxical.

5. *There Is No Answer*. We, as critics, should never presume that there is an answer, something that the poem is "finally" about. We should stop asking "What is the theme?" We should stop asking "How do all the images merge?" They do not merge—they only give us different perspectives: physical perception, the poet's vision, the critical insight. And once we have these perspectives, we do not sit back content and convinced—unless we are satisfied with the knowledge that there can be no answer, no final meaning. I liked it very much when my student ended his critique with " 'to be or not to be,' to see or not to see"— because that kind of statement sounds much like Derrida's notion of *differance*: we know something only by knowing what it is not, what

it differs from. In this case, we know the meaning of the sonnet only by knowing what it does not mean. It does not mean "seeing," so it must mean "not seeing," unless we achieve the "critical eye" that allows us to "see" what it means "not to see." A play of differences, a "theme of opposites."

II

You may argue that a good essay is simply a good essay no matter what the particular critical angle. And indeed you may very well think that this student essay is no good. I myself like its style and appreciate its ingenuity. More than that, I think this student managed to uncover (retrieve, break open, disrobe) a theme in Shakespeare's sonnet 104 that is actually not a theme at all. It is not something we would be interested in if we were taking the poem apart only to discover its "ultimate" design and symmetry. Instead, this student has taken the poem apart only to leave it dismantled. There is the possibility of vision, but the inevitability of zero. He has, I think, truly deconstructed the sonnet — and all in the guise of formalism.

But should students write this way? Should they arrive at such conclusions? As a professor who teaches the undergraduate British survey, I feel at least somewhat justified in asking such a practical question, because the very practical structure of the classroom seems to demand a "saner" and more reasonable approach to literature. Can we really teach literature and literary criticism as if it were all a game of make-believe? I think of parents wondering why they bring up their children to believe in ethics and morality if a college education is going to expose them to Sartre and Camus. And I also wonder if English courses will suffer an identity crisis: composition teaches directness and clarity, while literature denies the ability of language to clarify anything.

Two colleagues of mine walked into my office while I was reworking a draft of this article. Both asked to see the student essay. I found each of their responses interesting, each for a different reason. One of them, after glancing at the critique, asked: "What level is this student?" Sophomore-survey, I replied. His remark: "The tone just doesn't sound like an undergraduate's or even a graduate's." The second individual, a person accustomed to orthodox Shakespeare criticism, commented: "It's cute, but also pert. I'd tell the student to shape up."

Such responses might very well indicate a range of professional reaction to out-of-the-line undergraduate writing. From one perspective, sophomore writing doesn't seem to be the place for this sort of criticism ("isn't this territory just for the advanced folk?"). From an entirely different perspective, there seems to be *no* place for this sort of criticism ("why isn't he serious and scholarly, like a real critic?"). As for my response — and it has passed through several stages of development — I am not convinced that either the tone or the message of the critique is inappropriate. Indeed, I am shocked at just how apropos the whole thing sounds. Perhaps my response can best be described as the literary version of future shock: what happens when critical assumptions about negation and deconstruction jar with classroom assumptions about well-designed syllabi, final exams, and grades? Maybe we can structure the class without structuring the poetry — leave Shakespeare in the wilderness and bring deconstruction into the classroom. Maybe we will have to, since the wilderness seems to be creeping in anyway. Clearly something has happened to the New Criticism, and sooner or later, we are going to see the results in the classroom. I wasn't quite prepared. But I am now moving toward acceptance, maybe even welcome. And I am changing many of my assumptions.

NOTES

1. I follow the text from *The Norton Anthology of English Literature*, 3rd ed., Major Authors Edition, ed. M. H. Abrams et al. (New York: Norton, 1975), since this is the text we used in the class.

2. Jennings wrote this paper as a requirement for English 2121 ("Masterpieces of British Literature"), November 1980.

3. *Criticism in the Wilderness: The Study of Literature Today* (New Haven: Yale University Press, 1980).

4. Commentary following presentation on "Is There A Text in this Class?" Colloquium on Contemporary Literary Criticism, Rice University, Houston, Texas, April 1978.

5

"FOR THOU WERT THERE"
History, Erasure, and Superscription in
The Prelude

Robert Young

I

In Coleridge's account of *The Prelude* Wordsworth's involvement in the French Revolution is crucial:

> For thou wert there, thine own brows garlanded,
> Amid the tremor of a realm aglow,
> Amid a mighty nation jubilant,
> When from the general heart of human kind
> Hope sprang forth like a full-born Deity![1]

But what does it mean to be in history? What is the relation of a text to history, or of history to a text? What is the relation of history to the history of a text? These questions have recently begun to be asked with increasing urgency, and involve not only the question of history and text but also, necessarily, that of politics and text, as well as the relation of the text to the institution. If texts are no longer considered to have intrinsic meanings, does this also mean that they no longer have intrinsic politics, or an intrinsic relation to history? And what is the history to which a text can relate?

In 1949 René Wellek and Austin Warren defined the three main branches of literary study as criticism, theory, and literary history, and argued that "they implicate each other so thoroughly as to make inconceivable literary theory without criticism or history, or history without theory and criticism."[2] The critical debates of more recent years continue to circulate around this triad: criticism without theory claims that theory is without criticism, that it does not address the text, and that it neglects the question of history. Deconstruction, it is argued, is a mere

textual aestheticism, a parasite upon the real scholarly work of historical criticism.[3] Or, in a recent Marxist variant from the side of history,
deconstruction is both "the death drive at the level of theory" and a
"desperate last-ditch strategy" to salvage "some of the dominant themes
of traditional bourgeois liberalism" and its criticism.[4] Yet deconstruction, with its critique of presence and the possibility of a pure present,
necessarily invokes the question of history, even though it is not prepared to take "history" as such on trust.[5] Orthodox historical criticism,
on the other hand, although historical in approach, in fact only
introduces history in order to erase it, to affirm the function of art as
the bearer of a transhistorical truth:

> Ultimately literature . . . is a chorus of voices — articulate
> throughout the ages — which asserts man's defiance of time and
> destiny, his victory over impermanence, relativity, and
> history.[6]

Voice over writing, life over death.

In this context Wordsworth's *Prelude* is a key text, both because it
has a particularly interesting history in its relation to the institution and
because the poem itself raises the question of its own relation to history.
The Prelude is a history that is about history — Wordsworth's own and
the political history of his time — and it explores their articulation. And
the poem itself now has a history, a doubled one of its text and its criticism. Yet it is history that criticism of the poem most conspicuously refuses to take seriously. History, if invoked, is invoked only to be obliterated, a process which appears to mime the text's own treatment of it.
But if history can be neither present nor absent, if it appears only as
effects, then equally it can never be erased. Its place must always be
filled, if only by a blank, and even the blank will be the white ink of
a superscription. Superscription: a piece of writing or an inscription
upon or above a line of writing, a piece of writing at the head or the
beginning of a document, the address or direction on a letter (to Coleridge?), and a name signed, a signature.

Criticism is itself a form of superscription that writes above different lines, attaches its own signature to particular figurations to direct
them to the reader. *The Prelude* has given rise to a particularly interesting form of superscription, insofar as the signature is attached to differ-
ing elements in the poem, elements that differ only from each other but
which the critical superscription seeks to transform into positive terms,
particular critical values and the identity of the poem. And when the
text on which the superscription takes place is itself a superscription, a
piece of writing at the head of a poem (*The Recluse*) that was never

completed, the play of inscription begins to reveal itself as a play over the "blank abyss," a self-duplicating process of inscription and erasure within and without a poem that was to be Wordsworth's shrine, his "monument and arbitrary sign," and his epitaph: a writing that remains.

Unpublished and unread except by a few before Wordsworth's death, even after publication the epitaph remained a blank, written off the page of literary history. Arnold's famous preface to his selection of Wordsworth's poetry alludes to it only to remove it: "*The Excursion* and *The Prelude*, his poems of greatest bulk, are by no means Wordsworth's best work. His best work is in his shorter pieces."[7] *The Prelude*'s absence is followed by an erasure. The poem's reception in 1850, however, was not quite as bleak as is usually suggested: in fact many of the reviewers were enthusiastic and gave the poem the highest praise.[8] The poem's publication was, in a political sense, remarkably timely, providing a subscription to two contemporary events: the Royal Commission on the universities of Oxford and Cambridge, and the 1848 revolutions. The *Examiner* applauded Wordsworth's "discriminating, yet resolute exposure, of the hollowness and deadness of our English university training at the period of his youth, unaltered to that of his age" ("Decency and Custom starving Truth,/And blind Authority beating with his staff/The child that might have led him"), and concluded:

> These remarkable passages are singularly apposite at the present time; and we can imagine the stupified surprise with which not a few of the dull defenders of old routine will read such writing from one whom they have been taught to regard as wholly theirs.[9]

Curiously, then, part of the poem's immediate impact was upon nothing less than the academic institution itself; its subsequent eclipse in the realm of the institution suggests the power of the poem's rebuke and blow. Perhaps significantly, the critical reappropriation of *The Prelude* began not in Oxford or Cambridge but in Glasgow with the lectures of A. C. Bradley, and has been developed most powerfully in the twentieth century in the academic institutions of the U.S.A. Even so, *The Prelude*'s subsequent career in the institution testifies to its continuing ability to surprise those who had regarded it as wholly theirs. the "Limits of Pluralism" debate, for instance, was conducted around a critical work that centers on *The Prelude*, espouses its values, and reduplicates its form.

The poem's treatment of the French Revolution was also opportune in another age of revolutions. Here again, however, the 1850 reaction was not entirely one of comfort. Much emphasis was placed on Wordsworth's sympathy with the Revolution, the crucial role in the poem of the crisis of his apostacy, and the fact that he came to believe "that he might perhaps have formed an erroneous estimate of man and his political rights."[10] But as Lindenberger points out, the reaction against the Revolution was noticed far less than the surprising "extent of Wordsworth's involvement in revolutionary activities. . . . The *British Quarterly Review* and the *Athenaeum* both assumed that Wordsworth withheld publication of the poem because of his revolutionary opinions. . . . Macaulay, writing in his journal, stated the case bluntly: 'The poem is to the last degree Jacobinical, indeed Socialist.' "[11] Once again, the *Examiner* reviewer took a searching view of the poem's political significance:

> Wordsworth's muse was essentially liberal — one may say, Jacobinical. [Yet, after his change of politics] it was Wordsworth's wayward fate to be patronised and puffed into notice by the champions of old abuses, by the advocates of the pedantry of Oxford, and by the maintainers of the despotism not even of Pitt but of Castlereagh. It is already felt, however, that the poet whom these men were mainly instrumental in bringing into notice, will live in men's memories by exactly those of his writings most powerful to undermine and overthrow their dull and faded bigotries. Despite his own efforts, Wordsworth (as has been said of Napoleon) is the child and champion of Jacobinism. . . . Even in the ranks of our opponents Wordsworth has been labouring in our behalf.[12]

From the very first then, *The Prelude* has been framed and appropriated by opposing political and critical factions. An unresolved ambivalence in the poem had been identified many years before David Ferry and later critics were to suggest that there was a duplicity and instability in the poem toward those values that it seemed most conspicuously to advance. In 1850 the crisis of the French Revolution in *The Prelude*, and Wordsworth's turn to conservatism, were not steady enough. The poem failed to reassure another age living in the fear of revolution: its articulations with contemporary history were too unsettling. Why?

A third and no doubt major reason for the poem's neglect in the nineteenth century was that it was too philosophical. When the 1850 reviewers did criticize the poem, it was largely because it was, as Coleridge put it, a "philosophico-biographical Poem." For De Quincey it was a "great philosophical poem . . . absolutely unique in its class";

in 1850 the *Spectator* commented that the poem contained "criticism, reflection, politics, metaphysics, and reverie, rather than occurrences" and suggested that these "metaphysico-critical disquisitions" lacked interest and should have been omitted. Similarly, *Graham's* declared that the poem included "a more constant use of analysis and reflection, and a greater substitution of the metaphysical for the poetic process, than poetry is willing to admit." Poetry and philosophy are considered incompatible: Wordsworth presents "truth often as a clear-headed, earnest-hearted metaphysician would, rather than as a poet." *The Prelude*'s "old crazy mystical metaphysics," as Macaulay put it, had already caused discomfort before Arnold, in 1879, was to draw his distinction between the poetry and the philosophy, and suggest that the philosophy was an illusion.[13]

This distrust of *The Prelude*'s philosophy can be related to the ever increasing dominance of empiricism during the course of the nineteenth century, and the consequent eclipse of the philosophical form of criticism that Coleridge had initiated. Clough's comments in 1869 highlight the clash between an idealist poem and its empiricist readers:

> What is meant when people complain of him as mawkish, is a different matter. It is, I believe, that instead of looking directly at an object, and considering it as a thing in itself, he takes the sentiment produced by it in his own mind, as the thing, as the important and really real fact. The real things cease to be real; the world no longer exists; all that exists is the feeling, somehow generated in the poet's sensibility.[14]

Clough's assumption that there is no philosophical problem involved in perception and cognition, that we can know things in themselves, "the really real fact," is also implicit in Arnold's desire to look at the object "as it really is." But as R. H. Hutton was to point out in 1871, the philosophical differences implied in Clough's remark are in fact differences already contained within Wordsworth's poetry:

> The commonplace modern criticism on Wordsworth is that he is too transcendental. On the other hand the criticism with which he was first assailed . . . was that he was ridiculously simple.[15]

It is generally agreed among critics that Wordsworth's poetry oscillates between the "simple" and the transcendental. *The Prelude* itself, in its expansion from 1799 to 1805, can be seen to trace a movement away from a sensationalist or empiricist position toward an idealist or transcendental one. With the notable exception of Pater, criticism of

Wordsworth tends to subscribe to, and thus validate, one of the polarities rather than the restlessness between them. As has been often pointed out, Wordsworth criticism has divided according to the antitheses within the poetry itself.[16] The empiricist strain has tended to be associated with British criticism, the idealist with American. The first follows a line that stems from Arnold, the second from the neo-Hegelian Bradley.

Thus *The Prelude* is intimately involved with those issues that criticism itself is now in the continued process of debating: empiricism/idealism, criticism/theory. These controversies themselves reduplicate the philosophical positions of the antithetical political views present in the poem, the radical philosophical ideals of the Jacobins and the conservative common-sense regard for tradition, "with high disdain,/Exploding upstart Theory" (1850, 7.528–529), of Burke. If the Bradleian strain has been conspicuously more successful in influencing critical opinion about the poem, the Arnoldian strain has replied not merely by emphasizing Wordsworth's simplicity, but also by producing a "new" *Prelude* — the Two-Part *Prelude* of 1799. The differences within the poem multiply into the institutional production of three or four different texts, the supremacy of each of them being successively proclaimed and denied by its adherents. But though the effect of editing is to make each version look like a discrete poem, a glance at Wordsworth's manuscripts reveals instead a *composition*, a dense layering of inscriptions superscribed upon and even across earlier inscriptions and transcriptions, cancellations and deletions that do not obliterate the traces of now illegible writing.[17]

The poem remains a critical scandal, from which criticism dare not advert its eyes. The scandal itself repeats the poem's own moral lapse and intense crisis at the time of the French Revolution. While criticism repeats the conflicting "contrarieties" of that period, it remains curiously blind to the question that this raises about the effect of history in the poem. In general the Bradleians tend to ignore history. Hartman, if we may take him as the greatest exponent of this school, gives an interesting though brief treatment of the French Revolution, turning it toward his theme of the consciousness of consciousness. The Revolution is identified with Wordsworth's recognition of "the apocalyptic implication of his break with nature." With the shock of the English declaration of war, Wordsworth "begins to glimpse the fact that the French Revolution may be a work of the apocalyptic imagination."[18] He thus suggests that imagination makes history, but doesn't pursue the possibility that it *is* history. The Arnoldians, on the other hand, claim history as their own, but only to endorse the poem's turning away from history as a self-evident process that involves no complexities and needs no investigation. M. H. Abrams, who represents the Arnoldian view most forcibly, certainly emphasizes the centrality of the French Revolution to _The Prelude_, but at the same time consistently valorizes the success and necessity of the recourse "from mass action to individual quietism, and from outer revolution to a revolutionary mode of imaginative perception." The revolution is "translated" to the values of the individual mind, and the effect of this translation from the political to the personal is, unsurprisingly, the erasure of history:

> The burden of what they had to say was that contemporary man can redeem himself and his world, and that his only way to this end is to reclaim and to bring to realization the great positives of the Western past. When, therefore, they assumed the visionary persona, they spoke as members of what Wordsworth called the "One great Society . . . / The noble Living and the noble Dead," whose mission was to assure the continuance of civilization by reinterpreting to their drastically altered condition the enduring humane values.[19]

Abrams thus endorses the supposedly perfect translation of the actual history of the Revolution to the timeless truths of what George Eliot called the "choir invisible." The poem's translation of the political to the private, of the exterior to the interior, is complete. But what if there is no such thing as a perfect translation? If the etching of what Abrams calls the "acid bath of counter-evidence in personal experience, human history," remained?

The role of inscription and residual figuration in the poem have been the subject of a number of recent deconstructive readings. The most remarkable of these, Cynthia Chase's "The Accidents of Disfiguration," shows how Book 5, the book of Books, "succumbs to a peculiar subversion of intentionality, its effects produced through a process at once overdetermined and accidental, keyed to repetition rather than recovery."[20] Chase focuses on the way in which the "accidental" slippage from literal to figural (and vice versa) in the poem, which occurs through "the coincidences and collusion of meaning" through "a non-progressive, atemporal repetition of _wording_ from one passage to another," leads to an inevitable difficulty of reading:

> The difficulty in interpreting [the Drowned Man episode] chances to exemplify a general predicament of the reader of Romantic texts: an erosion of the distinction between literal and figurative modes on which recovery of meaning depends. The

text both requires to be read literally and thwarts attempts to fix its referential status. Trying to retrace Wordsworth's effaced figure discloses the limits of rhetorical categories. (548)

The subtlety of Chase's analysis cannot be briefly summarized, but for present purposes it is enough to note that the slides between literal and figural, and the consequent impossibility of reading with which she concludes, are a form of the kind of deconstructive analysis most vulnerable to the accusations that have already been cited. Chase's account, however, makes possible a different kind of deconstructive practice that attends to the question of history, and the relation of texts to it, through an analysis of inscription as a historical marking rather than as the irrecuperable movement of figuration and disfiguration per se.

II

If history is constantly repeated by criticism even as it repeats its exclusion, then perhaps the poem's own relation to it is one of incorporation as well as extirpation. At a number of different levels the poem comprehends the question of history: it is, of course, a history of Wordsworth himself, a personal history that he articulates with a historical event, the French Revolution. History is inscribed in a historical text, which suggests that it is unlikely that once inscribed it could be entirely erased. At the very least, it will be a lurking, "efficacious spirit" with continuing effects. Eagleton suggests something like this when he describes the poem as "creased and haunted by the ideological ambiguities of its moment." But his specification of this, which points to the rupture of the "official" "organicist evolutionary" ideology by the "starkly epiphanic" spots of time, is hardly adequate to the complexities of the text.[21] In broad terms, the poem involves the ideologies of both Jacobinism and conservatism, Rousseau and Burke, interlaced within each other. These competing ideologies ought to mean that the poem presents antithetical forms of history, and we might expect that during the progress of the poem the second will supervene upon the first. The radical view of nature as the innocent state of man free from the oppression of society and its institutions would be replaced by the conservative interpretation of nature as the timeless spirit that has ensured the historical evolution of the present, producing permanent and universal values. Wordsworth does indeed begin the poem with the first view, proclaiming at Cambridge, for instance, "what majestic sway we have,/As natural beings in the strength of Nature" (3.193–194), and he ends with the second, seeking in man "permanence, the gifts divine/And universal, the pervading grace/That hath been, is, and shall be" (12.42–44). But the articulation of history in the poem is far more intricate. As the *Examiner* reviewer noted, history and politics in *The Prelude* are duplicitous, undermining the possibility of a simple change of position. The poem involves structures more like those suggested by the deconstructive view of history as a "conceptual chain . . . a 'monumental, stratified, contradictory' history; a history that also implies a new logic of *repetition* and the *trace*." History is not presented as a unitary phenomenon, nor merely as a disrupted one, but rather as *histories* "*different* in their type, rhythm, mode of inscription — intervallic, differentiated histories."[22] *The Prelude* does not *reflect* the ideology of its "moment" in any straightforward way. Although the contradictory positions of the different ideologies of its period are inscribed in the text, their multiple conjuncture develops according to a specific textual logic that is its own.

The difficulty with which the poem deals is the contamination of individual and political history. Up to and including the Five-Book *Prelude* of early spring 1804 the poem dealt only with the former. In order to account for it adequately, however, Wordsworth felt obliged to expand the poem and include his experiences during the French Revolution. In the thirteen book version of 1805 Wordsworth does deal with the Revolution and its political history if only to exclude it again in favor of personal history by the end of the poem. Inside to outside, then back to inside — except that by the third stage the inside has discovered that it must include the outside in order to constitute itself as inside, and indeed that it has always been constituted by this now familiar logic from the very first. The best model of this structure is given by De Quincey in his description of the mind as a palimpsest of the inscriptions of history:

> Yes, reader, countless are the mysterious handwritings of grief or joy which have inscribed themselves successively upon the palimpsest of your brain; and, like the annual leaves of aboriginal forests or the undissolving snows on the Himalaya or light falling upon light, the endless strata have covered each other in forgetfulness. But by the hour of death, but by fever, but by the searchings of opium, all these can revive in strength. They are not dead, but sleeping. In the illustration imagined by myself, from the case of some individual palimpsest, the Grecian tragedy had seemed to be displaced but was *not* displaced by the monkish legend; and the monkish legend had seemed to be dis-

placed but was *not* displaced by the knightly romance. In some
potent convulsion of the system, all wheels back into its earliest
elementary stage.[23]

The exterior convulsion calls up the interior inscription, except that that
very inscription is the imprint of some previous convulsion. When De
Quincey wrote of Wordsworth's experience of the French Revolution,
he remarked on "its appalling effects — its convulsing, revolutionary
effects upon Wordsworth's heart and soul. . . . Mighty was the transformation which it wrought in the whole economy of his thoughts"
(*Recollections*, 174). If, as in Wordsworth's case, an interior inscription
is called up to repair the shock of the exterior convulsion of the Revolution, it can only do so by repeating the inscription of an earlier convulsion. This is the structure of the spots of time, memories as disturbing
as they are renovative, which almost seem to be the wounds that they
come to heal. The structure of the spots cuts indifferently across all the
tropologies of history, beneficent and malevolent, radical and conservative, interior and exterior, private and public, that the poem proposes.
The spots are a form of history in which these oppositions are dissolved
and redeployed, which might suggest that history becomes imagination, or that imagination is nothing less than historical determination.
Like imagination, history itself has no history: it is *sui generis* ("un-
fathered"), an effect that reveals itself only in its disappearance, an
insensible power.

III

The "exterior" political history of the French Revolution begins
with Book 9, which, in its invocation, presents itself self-consciously as
a repetition of the opening of Book 9 of *Paradise Lost*. The Fall, with
which history may be said to have begun, repeats itself:

> breach
> Disloyal on the part of man, revolt,
> And disobedience: on the part of heaven
> Now alienated, distance and distaste.
> (*Paradise Lost*, 9.6–9)

Book 9 of *The Prelude* is from the first superscribed upon the texts of
Genesis and *Paradise Lost*, an eschatalogical or teleological structure of
history that has been repeated from the Bible to Marx. But though we
might expect the "breach" to be identified with the Revolution, as it is
in Burke, this is not to be the case. The breach is displaced: the disloy-

alty, revolt, disobedience, and alienation occur instead with the English declaration of war:

> Not in my single self alone I found,
> But in the minds of all ingenuous Youth,
> Change and subversion from this hour. No shock
> Given to my moral nature had I known
> Down to that very moment; neither lapse
> Nor turn of sentiment that might be named
> A revolution, save at this one time.
>
> (10.231–237)

Change, subversion, shock, lapse, fall: all the schismatic qualities that might have described the Revolution have been transferred to its super-scription, the English Counterrevolution. This is doubtless because for Wordsworth the Revolution was not a revolution at all: "All else was progress on the self same path / On which with a diversity of pace / I had been travelling" (10.238–240). Straight away, then, we may notice that Wordsworth has begun to circulate the terms. The Revolution progresses, it is a linear history; the hostile, conservative reaction to the Revolution is revolution, an expulsion from Paradise. This displacement is the result of the fact that the ideals and "spirit" of the Revolution are seen to be intimately involved with the same influences that Words-worth has been charting so patiently throughout the poem. Those influences, identified with his inner self, are now found to have assumed a more exterior, political expression.

> It could not be
> But that one tutored thus, who had been formed
> To thought and moral feeling in the way
> This story hath described, should look with awe
> Upon the faculties of Man, receive
> Gladly the highest promises, and hail
> As best the government of equal rights
> And individual worth.
>
> (9.242–249)

The ideals of the Revolution seem to be formed from the same substance as Wordsworth's own life; when he rejoices at the outbreak of the Revolution, it is because, as he puts it, "unto me the events/Seemed nothing out of nature's certain course,/A gift that rather was come late than soon" (9.252–254). Nature's power is now embodied in political power. Through his friendship with Beaupuy, Wordsworth achieves a complete identification of the Revolution with the benign inner processes of nature and his own spirit. Beaupuy himself seems to be about to "embody his deep sense/In action, give it outwardly a shape" (9.408–409). Nature's course, from its earliest apprehended murmurs of the Derwent, seems to be advancing, its vital spirit shaping itself into greater and greater forms "which could not be withstood." The Revolution, in short, is identified with nature itself, now "standing on the brink/Of some great trial" (9.405–406).

The Revolution is a natural progression, not a break. For that progression to take place, however, political power must revert to nature: it must also be a restoration, a revolution in the original sense of the word. For nature to pursue her course and cause, she must be freed from repressive social structures and "all institutes [be] for ever blotted out" (9.527). To break with society and its institutions is to break with the past, which is as much as to say with history. History must be abolished, as D'Alembert suggested, if man is to regain an original freedom. In this view, the breach of the Revolution is nothing less than a return to beginnings, its convulsions the birth-pangs of a second birth: "France standing on the top of golden hours,/And human nature seeming born again" (6.353–354).[24] The second birth is a reversion to the untrammeled childhood of man and nature; to resort to this Edenic memory, history must be erased. The Revolution is a return to the beginnings of history and must obliterate the history from which it recoils:

> To Nature then,
> Power had reverted: habit, custom, law,
> Had left an interregnum's open space
> For her to stir about in, uncontrolled.
> (10.609–612)

To blot out history is to achieve freedom through the repetition of a kind of primeval originary memory like that of the Infant Babe in Book 2. The Revolution, imaged as "an infant Godhead," shares the Babe's "infant sensibility,/Great birthright of our Being" (10.363, 2.285–286). The babe, like the child of the *Intimations Ode*, has no history aside from the Deity from which he derives. The child of the Revolution, however, already has a history in the text. The political product of nature's "second birth" is identified with the supreme image of Wordsworth's own inner life, the historyless image of his self to which he constantly repairs through the figuration of memory:

I behold
The lovely Boy as I beheld him then . . .
He hath since
Appeared to me ofttimes as if embalmed
By Nature; through some special privilege,
Stopped at the growth he had; destined to live,
To be, to have been, come and go, a Child
And nothing more.

(7.395–396, 399–404)

This "Alien scattered from the clouds," sealed up in his spot of time, does not grow up. But the Revolutionary child does; he acquires a history, stained with the blood of the guillotine:

Head after head, and never heads enough
For those that bade them fall. They found their joy,
They made it, ever thirsty as a Child,
If light desires of innocent little Ones
May with such heinous appetites be matched,
Having a toy, a windmill, though the air
Do of itself blow fresh, and make the vane
Spin in his eyesight, he is not content
But with the plaything at arm's length he sets
His front against the blast, and runs amain
To make it whirl the faster.

(10.335–345)

On the face of it the child with his whirligig is a devastatingly inappropriate image for the Terror, but the child has already been established in the text as the image of the Revolution. Wordsworth's mind, as he puts it in *The Excursion*, had seen in France "a seductive image of herself" (3.805). Now this self-image, "instinct/With Godhead," has been perverted and has acquired its own subversive history. This perversion is alarming not because it is the result of extrinsic circumstances, but because it is necessarily implicated in the structure of the second birth. Perversion and revolution have the same etymology ("to turn about") and are thus both enacted in the ever-increasing spinning of the child's whirligig. When nature is left "uncontrolled," its circular process will not stop. The reversion of the second birth cannot be separated from the convulsion of its birth-pangs. A return to the beginning must also involve a return to the destruction of the end, an endless spasm and repeated subversion. Revolution becomes a whirlwind from which one cannot free oneself, an irresistible process of necessity. This dark consequence has already been prefigured earlier in the book in the September Massacres nightmare, when Wordsworth realizes that to sow nature's breath is also to reap its whirlwind:

> 'The horse is taught his manage, and the wind
> Of heaven wheels round and treads in his own steps;
> Year follows year, the tide returns again,
> Day follows day, all things have second birth;
> The earthquake is not satisfied at once.'
>
> (10.70–74)

These extraordinary lines, in which the return becomes an endless circle, in which the millennium becomes an apocalyptic repetition compulsion, suggest the consequence and end of history as the second birth of nature. Birth becomes decomposition, a limitless ebb and flow of erasure and annihilation. Whirligig history, as we may call it, images history in the same terms that are often used in the poem for the senseless, unreadable, exterior world of cities. The "blank confusion" of London, for instance, is described as "the same perpetual flow/Of trivial objects, melted and reduced/To one identity by differences/That have no law, no meaning, and no end" (7.702–705). This exterior whirl is generally counterposed to the beat of an "inner pulse" (3.337), an intuition of nature's "inward meaning" (3.129), as in the Poet's Dedication in Book 4, or the Winander Boy episode in Book 5. But in the September Massacres nightmare a reassuring antithesis of inner to outer is not possible because it is nature itself that has been subjected to an apocalyptic unsealing, and revealed as uncontrolled and meaningless repetition.[25] The exterior but interior image of nature's whirling, its convulsions and erasures, becomes a kind of parodic doubling of the return and restoration of the spots of time. As De Quincey's description of the palimpsest might suggest ("In some potent convulsion of the system, all wheels back into its earliest elementary stage"), the convulsive wheeling cannot be entirely disassociated from the pulsing spot. The return of the spot's "inner pulse" finds a nightmarish mimicry in the repeated spasms of nature and history. The contamination of the whirl and the spot becomes more intricate when we recall that it is the experience of whirligig history that the spots come to repair, and that neither whirligig nor spot are given an assimilable meaning. The fact that the Massacres nightmare is both a "spot" (10.58) and a wheel, that it is dense with repetitions of words and phrases from other spots, also suggests the complicity of the effects that spot and wheel repeat.

The Prelude abandons France to the whirligig. In the last we hear of it, Napoleon appears as a "monster birth" like the Infant Prodigy, a "catastrophe" that is both another complete turn and another disastrous end. Wordsworth himself does not reach the whirligig until the experience of his own revolution, the English declaration of war. For him it is the Counterrevolution that is the "shock," the "lapse" and the "revolution," that "by violence at one decisive rent" tears him from his foundations (10.276). It severs him from his country, from his own society, and from his history, and thus reduplicates the severance of France from its history: "A veil had been/Uplifted . . . /a shock had then been given/To old opinions . . . / my mind was both let loose,/Let loose and goaded" (10.855–856, 860–864). "This threw me first out of the pale of love" (10.760): whereas at the beginning of the Revolution it had seemed that "Not favored spots alone, but the whole earth,/The beauty wore of promise" (10.701–702), Wordsworth is now expelled from the spot itself, to find himself in the whirligig:

> I, who with the breeze
> Had played, a green leaf on the blessed tree
> Of my beloved country; nor had wished
> For happier fortune than to wither there,
> Now from my pleasant station was cut off,
> And tossed about in whirlwinds.
>   (10.253–258)

This expulsion means that he is now formally aligned with the state of revolutionary France: they are both in whirlwinds, both "goaded," "let loose," and "uncontrolled," both subject to an apocalyptic convulsion that has followed the lifting of the veil. History has repeated itself, as effect but not as meaning.

For a moment we will leave Wordsworth and France revolving in their whirlwinds, to turn to a different form of history that the poem proposes at the same time that it puts forward those that have been described. Whirligig history both erases history and shows itself to be the process of history's decomposition. Simultaneously, however, Wordsworth proposes a view of the French Revolution that sees it as the very writing of history breaking forth. In this Girondist model, history is neither linear nor circular but altogether timeless. It is a "monumental writing" in the "book of Time" which is entered with the "name/Of note" and its heroic deed (10.1010–1011, MSS. A², C). These names and these deeds are inscribed in the book to form spots of history, out of space and time. Wordsworth tells how he and Beaupuy

> summoned up the honorable deeds
> Of ancient Story, thought of each bright spot
> That could be found in all recorded time
> Of truth preserved and error passed away,
> Of single Spirits that catch the flame from Heaven.
> (9.372–376)

The "punctual Presence" of the names of history provide their aspirations for the future. The French Revolution is expected to produce bright spots of mighty names and deeds that will join the "One great Society alone on earth:/The noble Living and the noble Dead" (10.968–969). In this scheme, Wordsworth's hopes for the Revolution amount to the desire that it will throw up a noble name worthy to be recorded and inscribed in history's timeless book. At one point he wonders whether he might not himself be the new name of history, the "one paramount mind" that would have taken the Revolution in the right direction, would "have cleared a passage for just government,/And left a solid birthright to the State" (10.185–186). But he recognizes that he would probably not have succeeded and would have perished nameless if he had tried. Beaupuy is only rescued from a similar fate by Wordsworth himself: "Beaupuis (let the Name/Stand near the worthiest of Antiquity)" (9.426–427). In Wordsworth's view the Revolution in fact throws up no name: Napoleon, significantly, is only alluded to. Insofar as the Revolution erases history, it also erases the possibility of a name:

> Carra, Gorsas, add
> A hundred other names, forgotten now,
> Nor to be heard of more, yet were they Powers,
> Like earthquakes, shocks repeated day by day.
> (9.179–182)

The name succumbs to the whirligig. Revolution once more becomes a process of deletion and superscription as name succeeds to name. The transience of the name here foreshadows the emptying of those great names already inscribed in history's book. As he lives through the events in France, Wordsworth exclaims:

> 'What a mockery this
> Of history, the past and that to come!
> Now do I feel how I have been deceived,
> Reading of Nations and their works, in faith,

Faith given to vanity and emptiness;
Oh! laughter for the Page that would reflect
To future times the face of what now is!'
                                    (9.171–177)

Mimicry becomes mockery, and Wordsworth's convulsive laughter at history's disfigured page looks forward to his own severance after the Counterrevolution.

With all forms of history inexorably drawn into the whirligig, Wordsworth actively tries to disjoin himself from the past, just as the heart in *Descriptive Sketches* had been "without one hope her written griefs to blot,/Save in the land where all things are forgot" (676–677). Godwinism promises that it will do what the doctors could never do for the spots of Lady Macbeth: it will "raze out the written troubles of the brain" (5.3.42) The futuristic intellectual promises of Godwinism reconstitute the mind as a *tabula rasa*: "And hence an emptiness/Fell on the Historian's Page" (11.90–91). History, its names, and its deeds are written off. The page of the book of history becomes a blank, an erasure, and a spacing:

Shall I avow that I had hope to see . . .
The Man to come parted as by a gulph,
From him who had been, that I could no more
Trust the elevation which had made me one
With the great Family that here and there
Is scattered through the abyss of ages past,
Sage, Patriot, Lover, Hero.
                                    (11.57, 59–64)

Godwinism erases not only the archetypes scattered in spots throughout time but also the history that has been the consequence of an earlier attempt to obliterate history, the now perverted French Revolution. A blank is followed by an "eclipse," but the whirligig cannot be escaped. Wordsworth is "confounded more and more,/Misguiding and misguided./ . . . now believing,/Now disbelieving, endlessly perplexed" (10.887–888, 892–893). The *tabula rasa* proves to be an abyss, without even the stability of the scattered spots. But the spots, like history, return. "All things have second birth."

IV

The figurations of history at play in *The Prelude* are all attempts to figure it out, to coerce it into meaning. In each case history, or its figuration, dissolves into meaninglessness, into the indifference of the whirligig's chance repetitions. But as the tortured and repetitive narrative structure of Books 9 and 10 indicates, even chance and repetition are subject to recuperative gestures. The accident that all histories repeat and become is itself the object of a slide in the argument of the poem — as Chase puts it, "in Book 5 . . . a defense of benign chance turns into a defense of chance disasters" (548). The preoccupation of Book 5 with the defense and enactment of accidents that Chase points to is, however, part of a much more pervasive reparatory movement in the poem. If this movement succeeds, it does so by repeating the doubled logic of historical inscription itself. At the same time it must fail insofar as such a logic resists any form of totalization, or ideological appropriation, by poet or reader.

Wordsworth had resorted to Godwinism because of a "heart which had been turned aside/From Nature by external accidents" (10.885–886). Like the educational sages in Book 5, "who in their prescience would controul/All accidents" (5.380–381), Godwinism had offered a "resolute mastery" that could shake off "The accidents of nature, time, and place,/That make up the weak being of the past" (10.822–823). "External accidents" of history prompt Wordsworth to try to shake off the very power of those external accidents. But what is an "external accident," or, elsewhere, "extrinsic transitory accidents" (8.780)? What could an intrinsic permanent accident be? A passage in Book 1 suggests that it is nothing less than a spot of time:

> the earth
> And common face of Nature spake to me
> Rememberable things; sometimes, 'tis true,
> By chance collisions and quaint accidents
> . . . yet not vain
> Nor profitless, if haply they impressed
> Collateral objects and appearances,
> Albeit lifeless then, and doomed to sleep
> Until maturer seasons called them forth
> To impregnate and to elevate the mind.
> (1.614–617, 619–624)

The spots, like the Revolution, come rather "late than soon," a deferred action that can only be interpreted retrospectively. They return to Wordsworth and demand that their "lifeless" writing now be read. The accidents that produced these traces are neither extrinsic nor transitory but quaint: wise, knowing, skilled, clever, ingenious, as well as strange and curious. A further passage, written for the Two-Part *Prelude* to link the episodes of the Drowned Man and the Gibbet-mast, develops the function of the quaint accident still further:

> I might advert
> To numerous accidents in flood or field,
> Quarry or moor, or 'mid the winter snows,
> Distresses and disasters, tragic facts
> Of rural history, that impressed my mind
> With images to which in following years
> Far other feelings were attached, with forms
> That yet exist with independent life,
> And, like their archetypes, know no decay.
>
> (1799, 1.279–287)

These accidents, which make up the spots of time, form a palimpsest, the inscriptions of the shocks and convulsions of history. The "archetypes" are "impressed" on the mind, and this Lockean terminology suggests that they are, literally, ἀρχι-τύπος, the first impress, stamp, or type. They are seals, cut into the mind, and accumulate and increase, remain and repeat, as shock reactivates shock. Each accident is superscribed upon the first, but it is only the superscription that makes the first first, and recalls it for reading.

In 1799 Wordsworth wrote confidently that the archetypes "know no decay." By 1805, he was not so sure. In Book 11 he is fearful that some accident might befall the inscription of the accident. Despite the frailty of books in the face of a cosmic accident, already agonized over in Book 5, he seeks to reinscribe the accidental inscriptions in *The Prelude* itself, in order to give them, "as far as words can give," "a substance and a life" (11.339–340). This desire to give the accident a substance suggests that a metaphysical scheme of history is here being broached. History can never, by definition, be present, so it can never be known directly. But it can be known indirectly. The "spirit of the past" has left a trail of accidents, and through the recollection of these accidents Wordsworth can deduce the presence of the substance. For Coleridge this view of the relation of the accident to the substance becomes "the law of the dependence of the particular on the universal, the first being the organ of the second." The accident, the extrinsic, becomes a writing that conducts its reader to the substance, the intrinsic, to produce the "translucence of the Eternal in and through the Temporal." Thus the external variety of nature "becomes the record and chronicle of her ministerial acts, and inchases the vast unfolded volume of the earth with the hieroglyphics of her history."²⁶ History, like nature, is a substance, a spirit, but it can only be apprehended retrospectively through its accidents, through the writing that it has left for a later reading. In this way the continuity and totality of history, and of the history of Wordsworth's life, could be seen not to be severed by the spots of time, but revealed in them. It is through the "particular" that he sees the "universal," through the accidental inscription that at a later time he reads the "written spirit" of his history.²⁷ But though the writing of nature may be translucent, in Wordsworth's case it is not at all certain that the writing that history leaves on the palimpsest of his mind is readable at all.

De Quincey, once again, gives a clear description of how, ideally, this form of history would work:

> The reader must not forget, in reading this and other passages, that though a child's feelings are spoken of, it is not the child who speaks. *I* decipher what the child only felt in cipher. . . . Whatsoever in a man's mind blossoms and expands to his own consciousness in mature life must have pre-existed in germ during his infancy. I, for instance, did not, as a child *consciously* read in my own deep feelings these ideas. No, not at all; nor was it possible for a child to do so. I, the child, had the feelings; I, the man, decipher them. In the child lay the handwriting mysterious to *him*, in me the interpretation and the comment. (*Suspiria*, 138–139)

For De Quincey history becomes a form of scripture. The present is underwritten by the past. But the spots of time, which stop the transitory accident and make a permanent inscription of it, are never read in the poem so as to become translucent. They are rather "involutes," "incapable of being disentangled" (*Suspiria*, 130). They never have been read, never been given a meaning and made translucent by Wordsworth or his readers. Inasmuch as they never have been read, they may be said to have no content; they are simply blanks, "spots," and have only effects. They wink at their reader and demand superscription, teasing him or her into interpretation. The spots are moments of time transformed into space, into writing. They persist through the figuration and disfiguration of history as a readable trope, as the return of nature or the book of names. They are the monumental letters that remain, repeat, and pursue. A present shock calls up the inner written shock. The spots erupt and revisit the poet as an "efficacious spirit" to repair the effects of disruption. Accident recalls accident, through what we may term the convulsion effect, but the archetypal accident only repeats the later incision that it is supposed to heal.

The accident of history, the French Revolution, is a fall, as the etymology of accident (*cadere*, to fall) suggests, and the fall is an accident. The whirling series of convulsions and erasures of the Revolution and Counterrevolution are repaired by the return of history's inscriptions, its compositions that bring back composure. The accidents of history are blotted out by accidents of rural history. History must be both a forgetting and a remembering, an erasure and a reinscription, a spot that blanks and a spot that remarks, a blot and a spot: "A thousand accidents may and will interpose a veil between our present consciousness and the secret inscriptions on the mind. Accidents of the same sort will also rend away this veil" (*Suspiria*, 91). Writing supervenes upon writing, both by superscription and by the reactivation of the traces that have already been inscribed and erased.

V

All these historical processes are entangled in a scene of writing that forms the first repairing spot: the convulsion effect of the spot itself, a repeated return, the name and the deed, and an inscription erased and superscribed. This is the episode of the Gibbet-mast, a "timely interference" in the text:

> We had not travelled long ere some mischance
> Disjoined me from my Comrade, and, through fear
> Dismounting, down the rough and stony Moor
> I led my Horse, and stumbling on, at length
> Came to a bottom where in former times
> A Murderer had been hung in iron chains.
> The Gibbet-mast was mouldered down, the bones
> And iron case were gone; but on the turf,
> Hard by, soon after that fell deed was wrought,
> Some unknown hand had carved the Murderer's name.
> The monumental writing was engraven
> In times long past, and still, from year to year,
> By superstition of the neighbourhood,
> The grass is cleared away; and to this hour
> The letters are all fresh and visible.
> Faltering, and ignorant where I was, at length

> I chanced to espy those characters inscribed
> On the green sod: forthwith I left the spot . . .
> (11.284–301)

This memory enacts the very work of the spots of time. Cynthia Chase has drawn attention to the way that in this spot an accident, "some mischance," leads the boy to "a scene of effacement, the erosion of the remnants of an execution, itself the effacement of a murder." In the Two-Part *Prelude*, the boy had seen "a long green ridge of turf . . . /Whose shape was like a grave" (1799, 1.312–313), but as Chase points out, when Wordsworth repeats "his reading of the 'spot' for the version of 1805, [he] rewrites these remains as literal *letters*. . . . The residue is writing. It persists through repeated defacements (of the moor's surface) and effacements (of the letters, as the grass grows back)" (553–554). The monument has demanded an epitaph, in this case the epitaph of the "naked name" (*Epitaphs*, 133). In the third of the "Essays upon Epitaphs" Wordsworth quotes approvingly Weever's assertion that "an Epitaph is a superscription (either in verse or prose) or an astrict pithie Diagram, writ, carved, or engraven, upon the tomb, grave, or sepulchre of the defunct" (158). The superscription on the grave is itself a superscription by the poet upon the residue of history in his own poem, and thus initiates a process that is repeated by successive critical interpretations. The epitaph "lovingly solicits regard" (131), and the boy chances "to espy those characters inscribed/On the green sod." But though he sees the name, he does not name it. The name appears as absent, a ghostly repetition of the absent name of the French Revolution, and of Wordsworth himself as the name of history. Like the "written paper" of the Blind London Beggar, the name is unread, and not to be found in the text. It is both there and not there, seen but not articulated.[28] The name becomes a cipher; its letters mark the spot. These characters do not yield to reading as nature's "Characters of the great Apocalypse" had done in Book 6. Instead, they mark and remark. The distinctive characteristic of this "monumental writing" is not only that it has been inscribed, but that it is continually reinscribed:

> and still, from year to year,
> By superstition of the neighbourhood,
> The grass is cleared away; and to this hour
> The letters are all fresh and visible.

The syntactical ambiguity here leaves us uncertain as to whether the grass is cleared away because the superstitious neighborhood wishes to preserve the lettering of the name, or whether it is a superstition of the neighborhood that the grass is cleared away by "some unknown hand," or whether it is a property of the letters that they mysteriously renew themselves, cutting back the encroaching grass. The letters thus enact the rhythm of the accidents of the spots and of language itself, which, in the "Essays upon Epitaphs," is said both to uphold and to dissolve, to feed and to vitiate (154). Here the letters both lay waste and renew, bare and repair. The spots of time "repair" in a double sense: they renovate, and, as "year follows year," they continually return.[29] In these lines we are also shown a *re-paring* in the "delineation . . . performed by the side of the grave" (129). The grass is cut away and the incision reinscribed, the accident exposed and recovered from its covering. The return of memory is also a re-paring: a rescraping or repeating of the accident so that its letters remain uncovered, "fresh and visible" like an open wound. The letters in the turf are, furthermore, sustained by a kind of memory. Superstition, which stands over them, is a form of history, a projection of the past on to the present. Like history, superstition can only be known through its effects, by accidents that repeat accidents, never allowing itself to be known directly: "The hiding-places of my power/Seem open, I approach, and then they close" (11.335–336).

The return of history becomes the process of superscription itself, a reinscription of the writing of the accident, a super-stition that repeats the deed with no name, the name with no author, and the nameless name. And the effect of history is that Wordsworth and his readers, like the Royalist officer "mastered by the times," keep returning to the spot:

> At the hour,
> The most important of each day, in which
> The public News was read, the fever came,
> A punctual visitant, to shake this Man,
> Disarmed his voice, and fanned his yellow check
> Into a thousand colours; while he read,
> Or mused, his sword was haunted by his touch
> Continually, like an uneasy place
> In his own body.
>
> (9 156–164)

The reading of history, as it returns day by day, produces a convulsion in the man. He repairs for reassurance to the same spot, to his sword. But the repeated return is made almost as if it is prompted by the pain of a wound that the news has reopened. As if the officer is diffused as a ghost within his sword, within his wound, whose punctual rhythm takes control of him. In the same way, history in *The Prelude* becomes a chapter of accidents, a spelling of convulsion effects that the spots themselves, and the superscription of criticism, repair in proliferating repetition.

NOTES

1. "To William Wordsworth," ll. 33–37, in *Coleridge: Poetical Works*, ed. E. H. Coleridge (Oxford: Clarendon Press 1967), p. 405.

2. René Wellek and Austin Warren, *Theory of Literature*, 3rd ed. (Harmondsworth: Penguin, 1963), p. 39.

3. See "The Limits of Pluralism" debate, *Critical Inquiry* 3, no. 3 (1977).

4. Terry Eagleton, *Walter Benjamin, or Towards a Revolutionary Criticism* (London: NLB, 1981), pp. 136, 138. See also Frank Lentricchia, *After the New Criticism* (London: Athlone, 1980).

5. "If the word 'history' did not carry with it the theme of a final repression of difference, we could say that differences alone could be 'historical' through and through and from the start." Jacques Derrida, *Speech and Phenomena, And Other Essays on Husserl's Theory of Signs*, trans. David B. Allison (Evanston: Northwestern University Press, 1973), p. 141.

6. René Wellek, *Concepts of Criticism* (New Haven: Yale University Press, 1963), p. 20.

7. Matthew Arnold, Preface to *Poems of Wordsworth* (London, 1879), p. xi.

8. Herbert Lindenberger, "The Reception of *The Prelude*," *Bulletin of the New York Public Library* 64 (1960):196–208. Lindenberger's account is limited by the fact that he discusses only eleven of the twenty reviews that appeared, but his estimate of the poem's reception in 1850 is frequently repeated.

9. *The Examiner*, no. 2217 (27 July 1850), pp. 478–479, and *The Prelude* (1850), 3: 607–609. Citations from the *Prelude* are taken from the Norton *Prelude*, ed. J. Wordsworth, M. H. Abrams, and S. Gill (New York, 1979), and refer to the 1805 version unless otherwise specified. I have retained capitalization and on occasion differed in punctuation. References are to book and line. Citations from the rest of Wordsworth's poetry are taken from *The Poetical Works of William Wordsworth*, ed. Ernest de Selincourt and Helen Darbishire, 5 vols. (Oxford: Clarendon Press, 1940–49).

10. *The Athenaeum*, no. 1188 (1850), p. 807.

11. Lindenberger, "The Reception of The Prelude," p. 198.

12. *The Examiner*, p. 478.

13. Coleridge, *Collected Letters*, ed. E. L. Griggs (Oxford: Clarendon Press, 1956–71), 2: 1104; De Quincey, *Recollections of the Lakes and Lake Poets*, ed. David Wright (Harmondsworth: Penguin, 1970), p. 169 (hereafter, *Recollections*); *The Spectator* 23 (1850): 738; *Graham's Magazine* 37 (1850):323; *The Westminster and Foreign Quarterly Review* 54 (1850):272; Macaulay, *Life and Letters*, ed. G. O. Trevelyan (London, 1876), 2: 279; Arnold, *Poems of Wordsworth*, p. xix.

14. A. H. Clough, *Poems and Prose Remains* (London, 1869), 1: 319.

15. R. H. Hutton, *Essays, Theological and Literary* (London, 1871), 2: 101.

16. Paul D. Sheats, *The Making of Wordsworth's Poetry, 1785–1798* (Cambridge, Mass.: Harvard University Press, 1973), pp. 205–206; Jonathan Arac, "Bounding Lines: *The Prelude* and Critical Revision," *Boundary 2* 7, no. 3 (1979): 41–42.

17. Cf. Genette on Proust: "Similarly no page of the *Recherche* can be regarded as truly definitive, none of its variants can be absolutely rejected. Starting from *Les Plaisirs et les Jours*, Proust's work exists and did not cease to move until November 18, 1922. This growth, this ceaseless metamorphosis, is not only a circumstance of its elaboration, which one might ignore, considering only its 'result,' it is integral to the work itself, it belongs to it as one of its dimensions.' ("Proust Palimpsest," in *Figures of Literary Discourse*, trans. Alan Sheridan [Oxford: Blackwell, 1982], p. 224). Genette's fascinating essay sees the palimpsest as a superimposition of discrete elements without the kind of contamination that I attempt to trace here.

18. Geoffrey H. Hartman, *Wordsworth's Poetry, 1787–1814* (New Haven: Yale University Press, 1971), pp. 243, 245. A more recent essay, "The Poetics of Prophecy," in *High Romantic Argument*, ed. Lawrence Lipking, (Ithaca: Cornell University Press, 1981), pursues the apocalyptic implications of Wordsworth's treatment of the French Revolution much further.

19. M. H. Abrams, *Natural Supernaturalism: Tradition and Revolution in Romantic Literature* (New York: Norton, 1971), pp. 338, 430–431. Abrams's assumptions about translation are questioned by J. Hillis Miller in his review of *Natural Supernaturalism*, *Diacritics* 2, no. 4 (1972): 6–13.

20. Cynthia Chase, "The Accidents of Disfiguration: Limits to Literal and Rhetorical Reading in Book V of *The Prelude*," *Studies in Romanticism* 18, no. 4 (1979): 547 (page references hereafter cited in text). See also Timothy Bahti, "Figures of Interpretation, the Interpretation of Figures" in the same issue, pp. 601–627, and J. Hillis Miller, "The Stone and the Shell. The Problem of Poetic Form in Wordsworth's Dream of the Arab," in *Untying the Text: A Post-Structuralist Reader*, ed. Robert Young (London: Routledge & Kegan Paul, 1981), pp. 244–265.

21. Terry Eagleton, *Criticism and Ideology* (London: NLB, 1976), pp. 187, 94.

22. Jacques Derrida, *Positions*, trans. Alan Bass (London: Athlone, 1981), pp. 57, 58. Cf. Barbara Johnson, "Nothing Fails Like Success," *SCE Reports* no. 8 (Fall 1980):7–16, and Andrew Parker, " 'Taking Sides' (On History): Derrida Re-Marx," *Diacritics* 11, no. 3 (1981): 57–73.

23. De Quincey, *Suspiria de Profundis*, in *Confessions of an English Opium Eater and Other Writings*, ed. Aileen Ward (New York: New American Library, 1966), p. 171 (hereafter, *Suspiria*). Cf. Stephen J. Spector, "Thomas de Quincey: Self effacing Autobiographer," *Studies in Romanticism* 18, no. 4 (1979): 501–520.

24. The return to beginnings and second birth are also part of the analysis of the Revolution in *Descriptive Sketches* (1793), ll. 520–521, 782–785.

25. Wordsworth has just visited the Place de Carousel, "few weeks back/Heaped up with dead and dying," and, like St John gazing on the book of the seven seals in Revelations, he looks on such sights "as doth a man/Upon a volume whose contents he knows/Are memorable, but from him locked up,/ Being written in a tongue he cannot read" (10. 49–52). In the "spot" that follows, the apocalyptic uncovering, or breaking of the seal, occurs.

26. Coleridge, *Lay Sermons*, ed. R. J. White (London: Routledge & Kegan Paul, 1972), pp. 72, 30, 73.

27. Cf. Wordsworth's comment in the second "Essay upon Epitaphs": "Doubtless, there are shocks of event and circumstance, public and private, by which for all minds the truths of Nature will be elicited," followed by the ambiguous "but sorrow for that Individual or people to whom these special interferences are necessary to bring them into communion with the inner spirit of things!" *Wordsworth's Literary Criticism*, ed. W. J. B. Owen (London: Routledge & Kegan Paul, 1974), p. 154 (hereafter, *Epitaphs*). On the

"Essays on Epitaphs," see Paul de Man, "Autobiography as De-facement," *Modern Language Notes* 94 (1979), 919–30.

28. It is intriguing that the letters Wordsworth claims to have seen really were illegible: TPM. In the section in the "Essays upon Epitaphs" that deals with puns on the name of the deceased, Wordsworth gives the following example: "Here lies, covered by the Earth, and paying his debt to sin, one whose Name is not set forth; may it be inscribed in the book of Life!" (*Epitaphs*, p. 139). Cf. Maud Ellmann's analysis of the letters in terms of scarification, "Disremembering Dedalus," in *Untying the Text*, p. 191.

29. The pun on "repair" as both a restoration and a return is pointed out by Geoffrey Hartman, "Poetics of Prophecy," p. 26.

6

THE MARBLE FAUN AND THE SPACE OF AMERICAN LETTERS

Henry Sussman

Nathaniel Hawthorne's romance, *The Marble Faun: Or, The Romance of Monte Beni*, can hardly be taken to task for the meanness of its aspirations.[1] This novel sets out to perform for all subsequent American letters no less than the function that graduate school fills for the preprofessional. It proposes to acclimatize, adapt, and socialize American letters within the institutional framework of European culture. Once this task is completed, there will be no tension or discrepancy between American writing, which issues from a geographical as well as conceptual margin, and a mainstream of European thought that emanates from far more venerable origins. There will be a coincidence between the sources of European and American culture: any fundamental difference or otherness will have been rooted out of the origins. The margins in the intertextual confrontation between Eastern and Western hemispheres will be resolved. American letters will have in effect studied in Europe on an exchange program so that it may someday join the faculty of a university of a universal Western culture. In this manner it will have attained literacy.

The splicing of American letters upon the trunk line of Western civilization is a major undertaking, and in order to bring it to fruition, Hawthorne mounts a multifaceted campaign. Hawthorne's urgency in cultivating American letters and bringing them to a state of moratorium[2] is so intense that it marshals a wide range of fictive resources and levels of conceptual complexity. Even the plot of the novel is an instrument fitted out for this construction job. Hawthorne literally sends his two American innocents, a painter named Hilda and a sculptor named Kenyon, to school in Rome. The novel begins in a Roman gallery as the Americans survey the artistic roots of their heritage like two criminals, drawn back to the scene of some indeterminate crime. So powerful is the setting of the European repository that Henry James will return to it at the outset of his first international-theme novel, *The Americans*, where Christopher Newman gawks at the treasures and copyists of the Louvre. As is befitting a novel in which so much material is devoted to an internal system of characters, qualities, and symbols, Hawthorne's Americans, Hilda and Kenyon, have already encountered a pair of counterparts, Miriam and Donatello, when the novel begins. In the first scene, Donatello is the conversation piece, for his companions have noted an uncanny resemblance between him and a Marble Faun by Praxiteles. The resemblance plays between Donatello and the statue, yet both sides of the resemblance themselves hover in figural suspension. Both Donatello and the Faun are grab bags of between-states. The Faun is an amalgam of opposites. It is "marvellously graceful, but has a fuller and more rounded outline, more flesh . . . than the old sculptors were wont to assign" (8–9). "The nose is almost straight, but very slightly curves inward" (9). Although stone, "it is impossible to gaze long at this stone image without conceiving a kindly sentiment toward it" (9). Just as Praxiteles' statue, a venerable and very substantial taking-off point for the Americans and American art in its culture-quest, fuses grace with fleshiness, geometry with organic form, and lapidary death with living affection, Donatello, the statue's human counterpart, is himself a synthetic manifold of opposites. "In some long-past age, he must really have existed. Nature needed, and still needs, this beautiful creature, standing betwixt man and animal, sympathizing with each, comprehending the speech of either race, and interpreting the whole existence of one to the other" (13). Native to two time-warps, the ancient and the modern, this beautiful Italian is also a hybrid or cross-breed linking the diverse families of the human and natural world, as articulated in terms of nineteenth-century anthropology and anthropocentrism. Yet while Donatello plays the role of synthesizer, of translator between the races, ages, and tongues, he himself is marked by "an indefinable characteristic . . . that set him outside of rules" (14). Donatello, the living Marble Faun, set in the age contemporary to the fictive time of the novel, sounds the keynote of the ambiguity and uncertainty that pervade all of the novel's characters (save Kenyon, the straight-man) and virtually all of its important actions. The Marble Faun is the occasion of and is occasioned by a resemblance. Both sides of the resemblance themselves turn out to be divided and uncertain. Even the resemblance that might seem to combine the incongruous parties is ambiguous, taken half in earnest and half jokingly by its perceivers. The ambiguity that the novel introduces in its title character and its ur-scene seems to make it a veritable program of contemporary theoretical interests and themes: its basis is a relation, a figure of speech. The novel seems to declare the priority of these linguistic facts over any more abstract reality. But this is a founding novel. The question is not *whether* such ambiguities as the above citations intimate are brought into play, but how they figure in the overall game plan. *The Marble Faun* is a novel that, while *acknowledging* certain concerns that are extremely *au courant*, entertains *higher* aspirations for its productions.

The other character to whom the Americans correspond in the novel's symmetrical coupling of transoceanic pen pals is Miriam, who in her own unique ways is as enigmatic as Donatello. Of uncertain ancestry and race, she is a sort of pan-European mongrel: she may be a German princess, "offspring of a southern American planter" (23), or even part Jewish. In one of her rare moments of serenity, Hawthorne couches her description in the Romantic conventions surrounding the image, a point that will figure in any historical assessment of the novel. Miriam hovers as much as her cohort. "She resembled one of those images of light, which conjurors evoke and cause to shine before us, in apparent tangibility, only an arm's length beyond our grasp, we make a step in advance, expecting to seize the illusion, but find it still precisely so far out of our reach" (21).

Yet for all her sprightly vivacity, which makes her an embodiment of the Romantic Appearance, or *Erscheinung*,[3] Miriam is plagued from the outset of the novel by dark memories and ominous threats. Miriam's torments, the dark side of her uncertain origins, soon appear on stage in the person of a swarthy and unkempt persecutor, who like Donatello is divided between ancient and modern emanations. This figure is known to the other characters as the Model, an appellation associating him with a certain evil, within a Manichean scheme, as indispensable to the work of art as its edifying qualities. When the Model, by pursuing and harassing Miriam, pushes the couple to the brink, Donatello responds in kind by throwing him over the precipice of the Capitoline Hill. This murder is the focal and climactic event of the novel.

Through this murder, the naive American artists are exposed to a timeless, congenital, and ineffaccable corruption or stain that haunts the European bedrock of American culture. It is for this reason that Hawthorne repeatedly describes Rome as a heap of concentrated and somewhat excremental junk, anticipating a fundamental concern with garbage on the part of such twentieth-century writers as T. S. Eliot, Ezra Pound, and Wallace Stevens.[4] "Rome, as it now exists, has grown up under the Popes, and seems like nothing but a heap of broken rubbish, thrown into the great chasm between our own days and the Empire, merely to fill it up. . . . If we consider the present city as at all connected with the famous one of old, it is only because we find it built over its grave. A depth of thirty feet of soil has covered up the Rome of ancient days; so that it lies like the dead corpse of a giant, decaying for centuries, with no survivor mighty enough even to bury it" (110). Having removed his American innocents to a culture-Mecca set upon a quagmire of putrescence and morbidity, a scenario not unlike the quaking that Faust discovers in the Grecian foundation of civilization in *Faust II*,[5] Hawthorne makes Hilda and Kenyon accessories to the murder by forcing them into the position of voyeurs of witnesses to Miriam and Donatello's activities. A scene in Chapter 12, in which the Americans, unnoticed, observe Miriam as she is pursued by her tormentor, rehearses the Americans' role as implicit accomplices in the crime. This collusion in the crime of two Europeans who are as enigmatic as their ancestries are timeless goes to the heart of the novel's program. Hawthorne exposes his exemplary Americans to the congenital disease within the European past so that *we* may live. By Texan standards, Rome is only a few steps or train stops away from the Venice of Thomas Mann and venereal disease.[6] Hilda and Kenyon contract the venereal disease inherent within European history so that the American public — contemporary to its writing and future — will be shielded, vaccinated, against the infection. If the Americans Hilda and Kenyon get a bit soiled in the course of their odyssey, their fall is nonetheless fortunate, for it ensures the moral and physical health of future generations. Hawthorne fuses the time-worn motif of the fortunate fall with the advances of nineteenth-century immunology in synthesizing a recuperative historical framework for American letters. Just as Hilda and Kenyon will return home sadder but wiser, American letters will recuperate, make the most of, the degeneracy to which it is exposed when grafted upon the tree trunk of European cultural history.

In the wake of the murder, the quartet of paired characters splits up. Donatello retires to his ancestral Tuscan home, Monte Beni, where he later receives Kenyon for an extended visit. Monte Beni is the setting of the deepest penetration made by an American into European culture and its past. Here Kenyon imbibes the Sunshine wine that is a quintessence of presence and locality, and he also hears the legend identify Donatello as a living bridge to the most primordial stratum of myth.[7] The two friends go on a walking tour of Italy devoted to the philosophical as well as perceptual activity of observation. Their trip is described as a sequence of absorptions into self-sustaining scenes which are invested with iconic sacredness. The tour terminates when, by prior arrangement with Kenyon, Miriam appears on the scene. The Euro-

pean lovers reunite both to consummate their knowing love and to prepare for their inevitable punishment. During this time Hilda has with-
drawn in order to expiate her rather tenuous guilt. In the wake of her
failure to restore her sense of moral uprightness through a solitary
appreciation of artworks, she turns to a priest at St. Peter's. While she
resists her urge to convert to Catholicism, her confession to the priest
reconciles her both with the fallen ways of the world and with the historical tradition consummated by the Church, whose otherness she previously experienced as rejection and loss. Hilda's confession is her
equivalent to Kenyon's sojourn at Monte Beni. If Kenyon effects the
aesthetic and historical facets of the American-European graft, she
accomplishes the same on the theological front.

The ending of the novel is a sequence of reminiscences in preparation for a predetermined close. Kenyon discovers Miriam and Donatello
in the Roman campagna, where they set him on the track of the absent
Hilda. He finds her amid the anarchy of the Roman Carnival, having
caught one final glimpse there of his European cohorts. Particularly
telling with regard to Hawthorne's cultural program is the fact that in
the aftermath of their European experience and discoveries, Hilda and
Kenyon renounce their art or drastically revise their artistic activities.
Hilda rejects the amorality of art (338–339), whereas Kenyon disso-
ciates himself from the burden and contagion of the European past
(409, 412). The *culmination* of Hawthorne's historical-cultural program thus includes a *retreat* from its aesthetic concerns and activities.
In his masterplan for American culture, Hawthorne is ultimately content with an illiterate audience, one incapable of reading the moral
indeterminacies that he playfully sets before it.

I have provided a thumbnail sketch of the manner in which the plot
serves as a vehicle for the novel's cultural and institutional program.
One basic paradox that certain of the details that I have cited suggest
is that in concretizing a recuperative and synthetic program, Hawthorne has frequent, almost obsessive recourse to *negative* qualities and
operations. The narrative freely admits the limits of its knowledge
about the characters and its inability to establish clarity and coherence.
In a description that could only please the palate of contemporary taste,
the novel describes itself as an embroidered text "into which are woven
some airy and unsubstantial threads, intermixed with others, twisted
out of the commonest stuff of human existence" (6). Such a scenario is
tantalizing, as are the novel's repeated allusions to hovering, ambiguity,
and mystery, and its fascination with figures and relations such as the
status of the *resemblance* between Praxiteles' statue and Donatello.
Such concerns might suggest that Hawthorne cast the future of Amer-

ican letters on a foundation of "poststructuralist" apprehension, that the American Renaissance was simultaneous with "the end of the book and the beginning of writing."[8]

Homer Obed Brown has often surmised that all American literature may be regarded as a construct of European Romanticism.[9] Another way of interpreting the negative capabilities that Hawthorne incorporates into the novel, one perhaps more fruitful than a simple appropriation of nineteenth-century American literature in line with current concerns, would be to regard the uncertainties proclaimed by *The Marble Faun* as part of a positive system: the speculations about understanding, reflection, and intuition formulated by such Romantic writers as Schlegel and Hegel. The ambiguities in the novel, the mysteries that Hawthorne introduces when the facts will not tally, the farce in which the novel ends do not comprise the violation of a systematic thought so much as a specific system in its own right. Recent critics such as Jean-Luc Nancy, Philippe Lacoue-Labarthe,[10] and Rodolphe Gasché[11] have performed the inestimable service of formulating the limits conditioning constructs that would otherwise seem to hypostatize infinity and unrecuperable negativity. Hawthorne may allow a certain amount of ambiguity to play in his novel, but when necessary, when historical and institutional destiny call, he rewinds the slack in his narrative line in the interest of the cross-cultural graft outlined above. *The Marble Faun* may thus serve as a case of repressive fictive tolerance in nineteenth-century American literature.

To this point we have examined the wider outlines of Hawthorne's project primarily in relation to the story line. Yet in addition to the story, Hawthorne fitted out two other primary dimensions of the novel as implements of the grafting process. In its literary allusions and historical references, the novel constructs a *historical framework* whose operation is analogous to the problems involved in its cultural aspirations. If a historical system may be discerned in the work, in which mythological, theological, art-historical, and Romantic sources are appropriated as sequential yet overlapping contexts for the novel's inscription, a system of characterization is also at work in which figures and events become legible in terms of a comprehensive, semiological code. By endowing all the major characters with the same attributes, including an artistic medium and a color, Hawthorne constructs a lexicon for the novel in terms of which its actions and assertions are to be decoded. Hawthorne's cultural and institutional program, both for the novel and American letters, receives its positive assertion in the form of these systems of history and characterization. On a thematic level, the novel's ambiguities and mysteries, such as the question whether Donatello's ears really resemble those on Praxiteles' Faun, or the vanishing of Hilda before Kenyon reclaims her at the carnival, collide with these systems. The narrative *professes* a whimsy, playfulness, and impenetrability that seem to belie its attempt to construct a historical platform for American letters and a characterological system for itself. But the work of Nancy, Lacoue-Labarthe, and Gasché enables us to discern the collaboration of the novel's subsystems with the imponderables that seem to undermine them. The novel's professed and dramatized hovering, its narrative gaps, and its closing farce are in collusion with its restricted systems and belong to the nineteenth-century traditions of reflection, imagination, and irony. At stake in the conflicts of *The Marble Faun* are not merely the novel and the American literature adjacent to it but the aesthetic and philosophical traditions to which it annexes itself.

Before even venturing to determine whether the novel's ambiguities overthrow its systematic arrangements or are in collusion with them, some more basic observations may be useful, specifically regarding the text's historical and characterological systems.

I. THE THEORETICAL FRAMEWORK

Like a hyperanxious parent, Hawthorne pursues his ambitions for his novel by trying to secure for it the best possible *connections*. When in Chapter 27, "Myths," he traces Donatello's ancestry back to a point when mortals freely disported with nymphs and other supernatural creatures, Hawthrone "connects" American literature to the Pelasgian creation myth, as far back, in Western terms, as one can go. The novel's historical program proceeds by establishing connections. *The Marble Faun* is Hawthorne's D-Day for American letters, securing four successive yet simultaneous bridgeheads on the European coast. By means of allusion, Hawthorne summons ancient myth, early Church history, the Renaissance, and British Romanticism to different contexts and in relation to different characters. We have already observed the mythological dimension of Donatello. The malevolent Model derives from the early Church by virtue of his association with the legend of Memmius. This particular moment captivates Hawthorne because it precedes the Protestant-Catholic schism. In light of Hawthorne's ambition to couple American culture to a *unified* mainstream of the Western tradition, the Protestant-Catholic break is an inconsistency that must be circumscribed. Hawthorne repairs this tear by appealing to the legends of the early Church and in staging Hilda's confession to the priest, even though neither the narrator nor Kenyon can resist ventilating their anti-Catholic prejudices.[12] Miriam is a character surrounded in the high drama of the Renaissance, and that is why she is repeatedly linked to the Medicis and Cencis, whereas Hilda is a sisterly figure from the pages of Wordsworth, a woman endowed with a certain ambiguity but deprived of action.

It is important to emphasize that the novel's four primary allusive areas serve Hawthorne both in sequence and in a randomly scrambled arrangement. Just as Donatello and the Model are divided between eternal and contemporary emanations, the novel's temporal framework encompasses both diachronic and synchronic configurations. In this fashion Hawthorne achieves an effect similar to that of the *mise en scène* of D. W. Griffiths's film epic, *Intolerance*, in which alternating scenes of Egyptian barbarism, Christ's crucifixion, and the French Revolution form a backdrop to the birth of the American republic. Making *his* four historical contexts for the novel simultaneous or synchronous enables Hawthorne to ground any character or event in a European connection. Donatello's forbears were protohumans who conversed with the demigods; Miriam steps, as it were, off the canvas of Guido's "Beatrice Cenci," and so on. Hawthorne can and does flit back and forth between mythology and Romanticism as the occasion demands or suggests. But a sequential sense of the epochs also has a place within the novel's strategy. Both Hawthorne's novel and Griffiths's film operate as historical syllogisms. In order, the historical frames function as the premises of an argument whose conclusion consists of the artwork and the world of its setting. The historical precedents of these artworks retrospectively endow them with the force of inference or necessity. The latest historical moment of these works, whether the American Revolution and march of the Ku Klux Klan in Griffiths's film or the nineteenth-century emigré art world in the novel, becomes the inevitable conclusion to the preceding historical events.

In his historical design for the novel, Hawthorne wants things both ways. He coordinates his buttressing of the events in the historical past at every point with a more encompassing sequential movement of historical and logical dimensions. This split or doubled historical configuration and imperative explains why so many characters and artifacts in the novel, notably fountains, marble basins, cemeteries, and Rome itself, require both a continuous existence and a sequential one.

The intricate coordination that grafts the living present of nineteenth-century America and the fictive world of the novel upon the predetermined and hopelessly corrupt past informs virtually every significant character, object, and event in the novel. So pervasive is the influence of this temporal juggling act that one could argue that the novel's motifs of hovering and indeterminacy are a function of its synthetic temporal framework. The gesture of superimposing the contemporary time of the novel on the continuum of history becomes the novel's exemplary act in founding American culture and in fulfilling its genealogical and cultural imperatives. This act is repeated throughout the novel's settings and with regard to its privileged symbols with a ritualistic urgency. Donatello is described at several points as an evolutionary primitive, who somehow preserves the animalistic, autochthonous, and Dionysian qualities of his forbears. Yet if the instinctive Donatello hovers at the border of statuary representation in the form of Praxiteles' statue, Roman marble, which Hawthorne describes in terms of female genitals, moves in just the opposite direction, toward the organic and the slightly seedy. In the fountain in Miriam's courtyard thrive "the patches of moss, the tufts of grass, the trailing maidenhair, and all sorts of verdant weed that thrive in the cracks and crevices of moist marble, tell us that Nature takes the fountain back into her great heart" (38).

The paradox of the hard but sexually soft and fecund fountain extends throughout the novel's system of indeterminacies, itself a paradoxical formulation. Ephemeral persons and experiences, typified by the "Sunshine wine" from Donatello's estate, which is so rooted in its local point of origin that it spoils if moved, can evoke the remote past. Under the influence of Donatello's primitive and Dionysian revelry, the likes of which Keats projected onto his urn, to which the narrative makes sure to allude (88) — "Here, as it seemed, the Golden Age came back again, within the precincts of the sunny glade; thawing mankind out of their cold formalities; releasing them from irksome restraint; mingling them together in . . . gaiety" (88). Conversely, statues and artifacts of marble, while receptive to gradations of movements and emotion, sublimate the eternal out of the ferment of the ephemeral. The repose that Kenyon, who as a sculptor or shaper is God and Hawthorne's strongest lobbyist in the novel, extracts from Cleopatra is an example of the novel's temporal oxymoron from eternity's eye-view. "A marvellous repose . . . was diffused throughout the figure. The spectator felt that Cleopatra had sunk down out of the fever and turmoil of her life, and, for one instant — as it were between two pulse-throbs — had relinquished all activity" (126). "Soon apotheosized in an indestructible material, she would be one of the images that men keep forever, finding a heat in them that does not go down, throughout the centuries" (127).

Nor is Hawthorne content merely to *intimate* the idealism of the aesthetics that prevails in the novel and that serves as a prolegomena to any future American art. When Kenyon, on the eve of Miriam and Donatello's final judgment, discovers an ancient statue in the Roman campagna, its description is couched in terms of the Hegelian classicism in which the artwork and the ideal merge:[13] "The beautiful Idea at once asserted its immortality, and converted that heap of forlorn fragments into a whole, as perfect to the mind, if not to the eye, as when the new marble gleamed with snowy lustre; nor was the impression marred by the earth that still hung upon the exquisitely graceful limbs, and even filled the lovely crevice of the lips" (423–424). So sublime and ethereal is this artwork, an inspiration for American as well as European art, that the narrator exhorts us to ignore the dirty space between its labia. Organic as well as classical, this artifact is an exemplary inspiration to a Romantic aesthetics.[14]

The countertemporalities of the ephemeral-eternal and the eternal-ephemeral bonded by the artworks in the novel imply a sexual division of labor as well, one to which we will return. The feminine is, so to speak, the workhorse behind these historical and cultural programs, acknowledged as an energy-source but kept well under harness. For the moment, in line with the novel's temporal order, it is worth noting that the masculine art of sculpture with its aspirations to permanence is to be sharply contrasted to the painting practiced by Miriam and Hilda, which is evidently a feminine medium. Miriam describes her own art as "too nervous, too passionate, too full of agitation," that is, too hysterical and rooted in the present, for the repose of sculpture (116). The cause of Miriam's suffering is apparently the fact that instead of assuming Hilda's submissive role as a copyist, she has pretentions of being a productive artist in her own right. From the evidence supplied by the text, Miriam's sin is not some mysterious deed shared by herself and the Model but her artistic hubris, compounded by the fact that her studio is littered with her portraits of other haughty and castrating women: Jael, Judith, and Salome.

II. THE SYSTEMS OF CHARACTERIZATION AND SYMBOLISM

The novel's systems of characterization and symbolism are every bit as determined and coordinated as its temporal scheme. This conclusion becomes particularly unavoidable in light of the observation that each of its five major characters is identified at least by means of a double, an artistic medium, a color, a natural element, a metaphysical realm, and a judgment. Not only do the main characters comprise arch- or prototypes, but certain of their qualities or activities are associated with objects that acquire symbolic consistency or equivalence. The functioning of a closed symbolic system within the novel is reinforced by the fact that certain of its symbols, notably sunshine, snowflakes, stains, the color red, and shadows are repeated in similar contexts in other of Hawthorne's novels and tales.[15] In addition to his historical project, then, Hawthorne undertook a lexicographical one: that is, he attempted to found an American lexicon of symbols and moods. As has been superbly documented in John Irwin's recent book on the American hieroglyph, Champollion's decoding of the Rosetta stone and its American impact could well comprise the historical context for such an enterprise.[16] Hawthorne's lexicon, of course, begins with the letter A, specifically, the sinfully ornate scarlet letter that survives within an American cultural repository, the Salem custom house: "a certain affair of fine red cloth, much worn and faded. There were traces about it of gold embroidery, which, however, was greatly frayed and defaced. It had been wrought, as was easy to perceive, with wonderful skill of needlework; and the stitch (as I am assured by ladies conversant with such mysteries) gives evidence of a now forgotten act."[17] The narrator's disclaimer regarding his intimacy with such effeminate activities as embroidery notwithstanding, the impetus for *The Scarlet Letter's* narration consists of a partially eradicated but nonetheless radical trace of writing, whose marginality is linked to a "certain affair" in the novel. The origin of Hawthorne's moral melodrama in a love affair and a piece of tracery parallels *The Marble Faun's* setting off from the *omphalos* of a riddle, concerning Donatello's ears. Yet as uncontainable as the original mark may be, Hawthorne devotes enormous resources to civilizing it. He even goes so far as to build a native American dictionary around the A. This dictionary, with its built-in *grammar* of customs and usages, extends as far as his last novel, *The Marble Faun*, where it confines the characters to rather tightly fitting costumes.

The term that Hawthorne applies to his program of containing his characters in an iterable symbolic system is allegory. And he announces his allegorical design on at least two occasions: in describing the frescoes of the saloon at Monte Beni in Chapter 15, and, more important, in describing the bracelet that Kenyon gives Hilda as a wedding present, which is the last act of the novel. Because the bracelet had once belonged to Miriam, it symbolizes the passing of the mantle of the European past into American hands. Its own rigorous order intimates those of the novel's characterological and symbolic systems: It "became the connecting bond of a series of seven wondrous tales, all of which, as they were dug out of seven sepulchres, were characterized by a sevenfold sepulchral gloom" (462). As the proof and contract of Hilda's forthcoming marriage to Kenyon, the bracelet weds the system of the novel's characterization to the equally closed and teleologically oriented metaphysics of marriage.

The typecasting of *The Marble Faun*, then, is not merely accidental or even lazily obsessive; it is a strategic weapon within an arsenal devoted to the grounding of American culture from the bottom up, from the letter A. Within this system Donatello serves as an ancient-modern, animal-human shifter who opens the space for the novel's coordinative movements. His medium is dance; his natural element is sunshine, hence his own vintage of Sunshine wine; his colors are green and gold; and his origin is the earth, the rustic Tuscan countryside from which he stems. He has two doubles, an inanimate one in the form of Praxiteles' statue and a mythological one in Pan (90). His consort Miriam, on the other hand, has as her double a witch who would be as at home in Salem as in Rome or Munich; among her artistic productions is the painting of a "woman with long dark hair who threw up her arms with a wild gesture of tragic despair, and appeared to beckon him into the darkness along with her" (41). Miriam's medium is original painting; her natural element is shadow; her origins are indeterminate both in nationality and in time, making her a figure for European historicity; she communicates with the supernatural. She bears the burden of an original sin introduced into the narrative as a literal metaphor. "Men have said that this white hand once held a crimson stain," her tormentor reminds her the only time they converse in the novel (97). In the novel's color code, Miriam is associated with red, a color that for Hawthorne combines the allure of sensuality and the perdition of Hell.

As an American Lucy Gray or paragon of the Romantic Woman, Hilda will only truck with pure white. She is often the occasion for the novel's ample supply of allusions to the English Romantics. The narrator asserts that "all of us, after a long abode in cities," have a need of "rural air" (75); "there was no motion in them, now" (173), referring to the hands of the dead Model or monk, and at one point the figure of Shelley's Beppo makes a walk-on appearance in the narrative (111). Whereas Miriam is "subject to fits of passionate ill-temper" (35), Hilda is "even like a flower" (55), although the narrator does not add "half-hidden from the eye." In a metaphoric sense, Hilda even dwells "beside the Dove," for her double consists precisely of the doves whose caretaking comes with her apartment.[18] If Miriam communicates with the underworld, Hilda's residence above the city and its mortality affords her an immediate access to Heaven. It is by virtue of her innocence and almost excessive spirituality that "since her arrival in the pictorial land, Hilda seemed to have entirely lost the impulse of original design" (56). A total woman, her relentless and formless empathy qualifies her to be a copyist. "She was endowed with a deep and sensitive faculty of appreciation. . . . She saw, no, not saw, but felt — through and through a picture; she bestowed upon it all the warmth and richness of a woman's sympathy; not by any intellectual effort, but by this strength of heart, and this guiding light of sympathy, she went straight to the central point" (56–57). Although going directly to the central point may get her in more trouble than she has in mind, Hilda does not waste any intellectual energy in the effort. In fact, she does not have any intellect to waste, having been relieved of hers by the narrator's system of stereotypes. If Donatello is a living image, Hilda is the ideal antenna or receiver of images (58–59).

One of the few variations allowed by this rigid machinery of pairs and common denominators consists of the possibilities opened up by a fifth party. If Donatello and Miriam are lovemates united in Manichean opposition, Miriam's true soulmate, with whom she shares elective affinities, is the Model. Like Miriam, the Model belongs to a realm of shadows and communicates with the underworld. His artform is precisely modeling, that is, serving as a representational source rather than being a producer of painted images. As a source of images, the Model usurps the place of God in art: he interposes himself between the artist and the sanctioned nothingness known as divine inspiration or absolute knowledge. His color is black; his mode of existence is persistence; as a usurper, his double is Satan, and he is the only one of the characters condemned to anything more substantial than moral death.

In sharp contradistinction to the Model, Kenyon is an original artproducer in the full sense of the term. His "grand, calm head of Milton" was not copied from any one bust or picture, and yet is "more authentic than any of them," because of his omniscience regarding "all-known representations of the poet" (117–118). If not an exact double of God within the novel in the sense that no character could be one, Kenyon is at least a high priest: Marble, according to the narrator, "ensures immortality to whatever is wrought in it. . . . Under this aspect, marble assumes a sacred character; and no *man* should dare to teach it unless he feels within himself a certain consecration and a priesthood, the only evidence of which, for the public eye, will be the high treatment of heroic subjects, or the delicate evolution of spiritual, though material beauty" (117–118). As a sculptor, Kenyon is thus the pope or at least the American archbishop in an idealistic religion of art. His feet are so much on the ground from which emanates stone, his personnality is so marble that he even elicits the narrator's occasional irony, the only character to do so. He is also the single one whose origins, however murky, are not specifiied, a truly self-made American Man.

Such a heavily coded system of characterization comprises a grid for the decoding of actions and symbols. The dramatic characters in the story become symbolical ciphers in a language proper to the novel. Because the novel's facts are organized on a grid, the dramatic characters are able to fill in missing information about themselves and each other. Thus the natural antipathy felt by a character as healthy as Donatello for the Model telegraphs how loathesome the latter is before we know exactly why. Given Hilda's fully documented profile as a paragon of spirituality and chastity, we are to infer that during her absences nothing in her propriety goes amiss, even though she eventually turns up at carnival time suspiciously dressed as a white domino.

Such a coded deployment of dramatic characters drastically reduces the distance between characters in the sense of human surrogates and characters as ideograms or talismans. The novel's great images are as dramatic as its characters; conversely these symbols are every bit as much typecast and encoded. Our foregoing discussion of the novel's historical framework suggests what the coordinates of the internal symbolistic index might be. Virtually all of the novel's memorable images are described in terms of their temporal conditions, the state of hovering, or both. There are many passages in the novel of striking poetic power and complexity: yet even the most forceful descriptions, whether of Rome or the Capuccine burial ground, demand decipherment in terms of these codes. If sunshine and snowflakes exist at an extreme of immanence and temporal immediacy in the novel, the permanent sublimation effected by statuary and marble is its diametrical opposite. Virtually all of the novel's other recurrent images are to be situated between these extremes. Gardens, whether the Borghese or Medici, and the fountains they contain, regard the temporal synthesis between process and permanence from the perspective of change. Rome, as a decaying labyrinth and historical palimpsest, and sarcophagi and graves, while tolerating a measure of activity, are closer to the repose achieved by marble. The artifacts at both ends of the continuum belong to the infinite cycle of nature and art, in which nature ultimately recuperates the artifice extracted from it. The infinity that Hawthorne ascribes to these stately cycles is a stock-in-trade of Hegelian dialectics, where the diametrical opposites, when they can no longer stimulate linear growth from each other, begin to revolve around each other in infinite cycles.[19] "The shifting, indestructible, ever new, yet unchanging, up-gush and downfall of water" (143) in a Roman fountain is thus merely the *liquid* version of a temporal paradox assuming both solider and more ethereal forms. And of all the examples of change that we might select, whether of the "frail, yet enduring and fadeless pictures" cast by stained-glass windows (304), or of the Roman cathedral to which Hilda, in the wake of the murder, retires, where worshipers "in the hottest fever-fit of life . . . can always find, ready for their need, a cool, quiet, beautiful place of worship" (355) — of all the novel's many temporal oxymorons, none is as shining as the Capuccine burial ground: "But, as the cemetery is small, and it is a precious privilege to sleep in holy ground, the brotherhood are immemorially accustomed . . . to take the longest-buried skeleton out of the oldest grave, and lay the new slumberer there instead. Thus, each of the good friars, in his turn, enjoys the luxury of a consecrated bed, attended with the slight drawback of being forced to get up long before day-break, as it were, and make room for another lodger" (192–193). Despite the passage's image of mortuary substitution and a funereal residue or palimpsest, it belongs to a controlled economy in which the temporalities of randomness and evolution are coordinated.

III. RIDDLES, MYSTERIES, SECRETS, THE FARCE

Our appreciation of the overdetermination and coordination in the novel's historical framework and its systems of characterization and symbolism now places us in a position to return to our initial, possibly central question: For all its rehtorics of indeterminacy and epistemological limit, is the novel a post-structuralist classic, whose historical home base in the nineteenth century is merely a fictive illusion, an indiscretion to be glossed over? Or is it possible that the novel's overtly espoused cloudy spots, rather than being *at odds* with the highly manipulated temporal and semiological systems we have explored, *belong* to these almost clumsily managed economies? If this is the case, to *unhinge* the novel we would have to do so *elsewhere* than in its publicly announced blind spots. In other words, the novel's blind alleys, appearing on the literal level in the labyrinthine Rome that anticipates Jorge Luis Borges's landscapes,[20] are a *screen*[21] diverting our reading from touchier points. To deconstruct the novel we would have to *resist* following the leads that it provides, and find an entrance less to its liking.

The Marble Faun is thus an instance of a text that attempts to mislead its readers by opening the *wrong* facade to critical penetration. While undertaking a historical program that could only be regarded as irreproachable by its audience, the novel nonetheless resists the honorable task that it proclaims and so laboriously fulfills. The playful gestures by which Hawthorne *retracts* the arrangements that he organizes place the contemporary reader in a double-bind that may well be the ultimate extension of the question concerning Donatello's ears. We can, on the one hand, point to evidence that the novel's assertions of indeterminacy belong to Romantic conventions of irony, reflection, and infinity–and argue that the novel is what it is, a Romantic text that, because of transoceanic time-lag, was composed in 1860 instead of 1810. Our contemporary ability to reconstruct an epoch in terms of its epistemological and metphysical limits would thus open the door to a revised notion of literary history, one in which even violent textual manifestations can be placed, if not dated.

Yet in addition to this historical response, the novel's double signals afford us at least one other out. If the novel's *stated* indeterminacies do not finally unhinge it, there may be other indiscretions that do, of the sort that beg to be glossed over. The novel's misogyny, the structurally superfluous but persistent allure of a feminine sexuality *everywhere* in Rome and the narrative, would be one instance of a given that it takes for granted, but upon which it founders. In addition to the traces of a persistent femininity that the novel cannot assimilate, and greets only in a confusion of embarrassment and revulsion, it makes mistakes in terms of its own characterological systems, it breaks its own codes. Of many such instances, a striking one is that Miriam, in shadowing Kenyon and Donatello in their travels, steps into the shoes of her tormentor. Also in this vein, certain key symbols entertain variant meanings. Joyous sunshine appears once as deception (152), and at the end of the novel the previously pristine marble becomes a medium of death (377, 390–391). Yet even its exceptions marshal an appeal to the system that initiated the symbolical division of labor. If there is something to the novel's riddles, to the sleight of hand that the narrative underscores as it disclaims any knowledge of Donatello's ears or Hilda's whereabouts, this something consists in the schizophrenic bind in which the text still places the reader. *The Marble Faun* is a novel that is Romantic for all the reasons it would presume to be modern; yet it lends itself to our contemporary critical practices precisely where it is Romantic. It is this anomaly that makes the novel compelling today, for all the positivity of its program and the tedium of its execution.

What remains in this survey of the novel, then, is to suggest some of the novel's fake transgressions and their sources, and to suggest what some of the camouflaged entries into its systems might be. It could well be argued that the novel's most aggressive profession of its radicality consists in the secrets to which it is privy but that it withholds from the readership. From the novel's ur-scene in the museum to its retrospectively annexed conclusion, the narrative transpires between riddles. The novel opens and closes in tantalizing us with the ambiguity concerning Donatello's ears. This riddle, which conceals in the act of indication and innuendo, is the model for the novel's other acts of striptease. Why does Hilda have to deliver a package for Miriam to one Luca Barboni at the Palazzo Cenci? Where does Hilda disappear? The novel's secrets impose a double loyalty on the characters. Sometimes they are in the know, they collaborate with the narrator, as when in the conclusion Hilda dangles before the reader an answer as to her whereabouts. But Donatello's ears connote an area of knowledge the narrator withholds from all, except for Donatello, of course. In the novel's professed and dramatized secrecy, it enters the split epistemological field of Romantic irony, extending from Hegel's multiple perspectives of *in itself*, *for itself*, and *for us* to Kierkegaard's fictive surrogates.[22]

But secrets assert far more than ambiguity and imponderability. As Neil Hertz observed in his illuminating analysis of Freud's *Case of Hysteria* (1907),[23] secrets, on both sides of their striptease, their provocation and their masking, act out a hysterical assertion of authority on the part of the bearer of knowledge. And indeed, it is precisely in some of the novel's most congenial passages, those bestowing their fullest blessing on current critical conventions, that narrative control most blankly asserts its authority.

> In weaving these mystic utterances into a continuous scene, we undertake a task resembling, in its perplexity, that of gathering up and piecing together the fragments of a letter, which has been torn and scattered to the winds. Many words of deep significance — many entire sentences, and those possibly the most important ones — have flown too far, on the winged breeze, to be recovered. If we insert our own conjectural amendments, we perhaps give a purport utterly at variance with the true one. Yet, unless we attempt something in this way, there must remain an unsightly gap, and a lack of continuousness and dependence in our narrative. (92–93)

This is merely one of several introjections by the narrator that present the highest level of diacritical awareness encompassed by the text. The concerns with textuality, fragmentariness, and absence introduced thematically in this passage make it and the novel irreproachable. The passage returns to the frayed letter, which is the architrace of yet another founding novel; it describes the narrative as woven; it acknowledges losses in its continuity that imply the impossibility of any totalization in representation. Yet this passage, which is so straightforward, almost noble, in its acknowledgment of representational limits, also betrays the dependence that it fosters. And this betrayal takes the form of a disclaimer: in *eschewing* gaps, lacks, and narrative dependence, the text intimates the pattern of manipulation that it establishes. Ostensibly undermining the forms of narrative authority that it disavows, it asserts the reader's dependence on it, as well as its own authority — its power to disseminate, withhold, and doctor evidence. Rather than denying the structure of authority, this passage disqualifies competitive and ostensibly other varieties of authority in reserving its own. Between the lines of this ironic, winking voice, then, are the assertions of its own indispensability, inviting the reader into complicity with its authority. For the reader to laugh with this narrative voice at its jokes of impenetrability is for him or her to participate in a masochistic punishment. It is for this reason that the novel labors so tediously and unsuccessfully in the direction of good jokes.

Closely related to such disclaimers of coherence and totality, which emanate from the voice of the narrator, are the novel's settings of farce, frivolity, and abandon. For Søren Kierkegaard, the farce, whose ancient ancestor was Aristophanes' *Clouds*, was the privileged vehicle for irony.[24] The farce unveiled in Kierkegaard's brief tract, *Repetition*, demolishes the orders into which it collides. It robs the proscenium arch of its effectiveness as a theatrical and epistemological divider; it briefly revolutionizes the social order by telescoping the classes together; it incorporates both stupidity and randomness into theatrical design, disqualifying the generic profiles of aesthetics.[25] So too did Hawthorne hope, in composing Romances, confections neither too frivolous nor nihilistic, to synthesize an aesthetic hybrid, if you will, a generic New World. But whereas the farce at the center of *Repetition* detonates tensions within a pradoxical, double inquiry into the structures of displacement, desire, and objectivity, the farce of the *Marble Faun* acts out a violence that the novel's temporal and symbolical systems never entertained. Whereas Kierkegaard's farce is the aesthetic correlative to an aphoristic utterance that resonates in discontinuity, that abandons any argumentative line or ulterior design in building a cloud chamber of incongruous assertions, the pandemonium of *The Marble Faun* is ultimately held in check for illustrative purposes. The "riotous interchange" of the carnival where Kenyon goes to find Hilda is described in terms that associate the scene with the apocalyptic paintings of Brueghel and Bosch. "A biped, with an ass's snout, brayed close to his ear, ending his discordant uproar with a peal of human laughter. Five strapping damsels (so, at least, their petticoats bespoke them, in spite of an awful freedom in the flourish of their legs) joined hands, and danced around him, inviting him, by their gestures, to perform a hornpipe in the midst. Released from thse gay persecutors, a clown in motley rapped him on the back with a blown bladder" (445). It is this world of anomie, transvestitism, and excess, replete with Flemish hybrids and bladders, that the exemplary American must negotiate before he can claim his mistress, a scene reminiscent of the horrifying *rite de passage* depicted in the film *Zulu*. Yet just as Brueghel and Bosch's apocalyptic panels depend on the evolutionary and teleological schemes that they with such a flourish violate, the revelry in this novel does not go to waste; it serves a higher purpose. Even during the novel's pandemonium, its violence is allegorical in a naive sense, belonging to well-established patterns of representation. The Titaness who makes an untoward display of sexual aggression to Kenyon in this scene, shooting a popgun at him in revenge for his indifference, is like Miriam a foil to Hilda's acceptable submission (445–446). The mock coroner's inquest that Kenyon observes after this assault does not stray too far from Kenyon's own situation: an anxious, even morbid uncertainty just at the moment when his private portion of the eternal-feminine[26] is to be revealed and his separation ended. The historical utility of the novel's slapstick and farce is only confirmed by the ease with which Kenyon can repress such disturbing manifestations: "Fortunately, the humours of the Carnival pass from one absurdity to another. . . . In a few moments, they vanished from him, as dreams and spectres do, leaving him at liberty to pursue his quest" (446–447). This speculative quest for a woman who is a revelation, a fate, and a destiny is undertaken on behalf of the American public as much as to satisfy Kenyon's drives. The allegorical uses of the carnival violence rout this historical, metaphysical, and sexual *Wanderlust* in a closed representational system.

If the novel's secrets and farce ultimately succumb to its genealogical imperatives, so too does its elaborately dramatized fascination with the image. We have already observed how both Hilda and Miriam share the imagistic qualities attributed to women by Romantic writers as diverse as Hegel, Goethe, and Wordsworth. Yet the narrative's imagistic concern extends to an entire rhetoric of observation, indication, and setting. Hawthorne invests both the frames around aesthetic objects and the sites of scenes with considerable reverence. Whether paintings, statues, or scenes, the images in Hawthorne's text increase in sacredness when they are arranged in sequence, in the halls of a museum or by a roadside. The primary rite in Hawthorne's art-religion for an emerging American *cultus* consists in pilgrimages, several of which take place in the novel, through stages or stations of the image. In his program for American letters, Hawthorne would convert the European museum into a secular cathedral. It is in accordance with this quasi-theological imagistic reverence that Hawthorne begins the novel in a museum, that he applies the formulation "Scenes by the Way" as a rubric for Kenyon and Donatello's peregrinations, and that concurrent with these wanderings Hilda experiences "The Emptiness of Picture Galleries." It is under the influence of the aesthetics of the image that moments such as Donatello's dance and the ramble of the aesthetic emigrés are set in such tightly constructed and closed scenes. In his reverence for images, Hawthorne accords them enormous power. The eloquence to which the narrative would rise in its key descriptions, such as of Roman ruins or the Cappucine cemetery, constitutes Hawthorne's effort to harness this divine, yet somewhat uncanny power. The hope that the narrative founds in scenes and images is no less than messianic. The title of Chapter 33, "Pictured Windows," describes not only the glasswork of a gothic cathedral but also Hawthorne's fictive program, in which the image is the source of energy and illumination. Not only does the statue that Kenyon unearths in the campagna mediate and represent the ideal; it is a talisman for the magic hopes that the novel invests in the Romantic tradition of the image: "How happened it to be lying there, beside its grave of twenty centuries? Why were not tidings of its discovery already noised abroad? The world was richer than yesterday, by something far more precious than gold. Forgotten beauty had come back, as beautiful as ever; a goddess had risen from her long slumber, and was a goddess still" (424).

The only apotheosis that Miriam and Donatello are permitted as they prepare to pay society back for their crimes is that they are transformed into an image. "He still held Miriam's hand; and there they stood, the beautiful man, the beautiful woman, united forever, as they felt, in the presence of these and eye-witnesses, who gazed so curiously at the unintelligible scene" (323). Images thus not only inhabit the privileged space of a mandala, but constitute the possibility of redemption and salvation.

But for all the sacredness in which the novel's images are sheathed, it remains an open question whether they ever gather the energy to break the centripetal force exerted by the novel's representational system. The images of this narrative share the fate of its pandemonium. Their potential autonomy and self-referentiality is proferred and then retracted by an allegorical system that simply will not relax in its assimilative compulsion. Hawthorne's images are toilet-trained spots of time, engendered by the same speculative system but abortive in the pursuit of their own fragmentation. Thus it is that the mock autopsy at the carnival must immediately be applied to Kenyon's interpretative quandary and that the "figure in a white robe" is not allowed to walk alone. "Such odd, questionable shapes are often seen gliding through the streets of Italian cities" (392). Yet no sooner is this one mentioned than its glide comes to a halt, for while the narrator concludes that the figure is a mystery, he fills in its possible significations, all related to the expiation of guilt.

In its appeals to secret knowledge, the image, farce, and narrative unreliability, the novel lifts the curtain on a theoretical New World: yet like Dr. Strangelove, it cannot restrain its gestures of a far more questionable loyalty, to its native land of Romantic conventions. The novel *claims* a certain indigenous American radicality, yet what the novel *betrays* is its subservience to and replication of fixed systems of sexual identification, historical determinism, and symbolical equivalence, all varieties of the metaphysics of representation. This work thus opens the space for, initiates, a tradition continuing until today, one under which we still all labor. On the one hand, there is a freedom of expression in American culture that encourages the shock-values of yesterday and today, from gothic horror to the very literal representations of violence and sexual activity in television and film. Coinciding with, perhaps underlying this literal freedom is a suspicion toward language corresponding to the closed economies, the enforcers of restraint, in the novel. The marginal placement of the university and the cartoon vision of intellectuals throughout the history of the American cinema and electronic media are manifestations of this suspicion. One of the latest American fads, a series of films in which a violence of unprecedented literality is acted out against liberated or sexually aggressive women, is illustrative of *The Marble Faun*'s double-bind. These films achieve new heights of shock and explicitness, yet underlying them are very old, even classical fears and inhibitions. Miriam is an ancestor of the horny housewife in *Dressed to Kill* and the teacher in *Looking for Mr. Goodbar*. Even more fundamental than the fear of the aggressive woman is the suspicion of the linguistic capabilities that she contains. When Kenyon and Hilda trivialize and revise their aesthetic commitments, they consummate a program in which Hawthorne's fiction will permanently wean the American public of its interest in aesthetic and linguistic ambiguity.

In writing of the closure and obsolescence of a Romantic text, I myself have violated certain conventions. The basic values of entertainment and critical showmanship compel me to write alluringly of an ambiguous text to the triple credit of the text, the theoretical attitudes I bring to bear on it, and myself. Yet my own previous attempts vacillated in the interatioo between the text's counterimperatives: to regard it either as uncannily contemporary or as deceptively radical. The "radical" casting of this work convinced me that I was merely paraphrasing or updating Romantic conventions in textual terms, that I was creating, in effect, a "new, improved" *Marble Faun*. So unsatisfactory was this alternative that I acquiesced to another that was not without its own limits. In writing of a Romantic work from the perspective of its closed subsystems, I was opening the door for a literary-historical division of labor, in terms of ages, sequences, and developments. I hope that it will be possible to distinguish placing the work in its conceptual and metaphysical age from merely *dating* it in any simplistic sense. For these reasons I wrote about *The Marble Faun* as a Romantic text in the light of its Romantic conventions. The experience has certainly been romantic.

NOTES

1. All citations of *The Marble Faun* refer to the Centenary Edition: Nathaniel Hawthorne, *The Marble Faun* (Columbus, Ohio: Ohio State University Press, 1968).

2. I use the term "moratorium" in the sense applied to individual development by Erik Erikson in *Young Man Luther* (New York: Norton, 1962), pp. 43, 100–104.

3. In Hegel's *Phenomenology of Spirit*, for example, Appearance is the illusion first of an interior, then of a transcendental domain, that makes possible abstraction and all advanced works of logic, theology, and art. See the chapter on "Force and the Understanding" in G. W. F. Hegel, *The Phenomenology of Spirit*, trans. A. V. Miller (Oxford: Oxford University Press, 1977), pp. 86–103.

4. I have in mind such works as Eliot's *Preludes* and *The Waste Land* and Stevens's *The Man on the Dump*. The creative recycling of the archaeological remains of a wide variety of cultures is not only a vital theme of Pound's *Cantos*; it comprises the performative dimension of the work's production and textuality.

5. See Johann Wolfgang von Goethe, *Faust*, trans. Walter Arndt (New York: Norton, 1976), pp. 178–194 (ll. 7080–7097, 7495–7549).

6. I refer, of course, to Mann's novella, "Death in Venice," in *Death in Venice and Seven Other Stories by Thomas Mann*, trans. H. T. Lowe-Porter (New York: Random House, 1960), pp. 3–75.

7. Cf. Chapter 27, "Myths," in *The Marble Faun*, pp. 242–248.

8. This is a chapter heading, claim, and program in Jacques Derrida's *Of Grammatology*, trans. Gayatri C. Spivak (Baltimore: Johns Hopkins University Press, 1976), pp. 6–26.

9. This during numerous personal conversations and academic functions at SUNY/Buffalo, 1978–79.

10. Lacoue-Labarthe and Nancy, in *L'Absolu littéraire* (Paris: Seuil, 1978), assemble and elaborate a set of discursive conventions, including the fragment and the image, that dominate early Romanticism. In so doing, they demonstrate how the sublime and enigmatic moods of Romanticism participate within, rather than oppose, the traditions of metaphysical speculation.

11. In recent and forthcoming work, Rodolphe Gasché attempts to distinguish deconstruction from the negativity accommodated by standard speculative procedures. See his "Deconstruction as Criticism," *Glyph 6* (Baltimore: Johns Hopkins University Press, 1979), pp. 177–215.

12. See, for example, *The Marble Faun*, pp. 53, 266, 366, 368.

13. I refer to Hegel's discussion of classical Greek art in his *Vorlesungen über die*

Ästhetik. See G. W. F. Hegel, *Werke in zwanzig Bänden*, Theorie Werkausgabe (Frankfurt: Suhrkamp, 1970), 14: 13–30.

14. "Romanticism" and "Romantic" are obviously pivotal formulations in this argument. By no means do I mean to imply that the particular artifacts produced during the era conventionally known as "Romanticism" are devoid of or inherently alien to textuality and linguistic apprehensions, as the works of Goethe, Wordsworth, Shelley, Melville, and a hoard of others amply attest. For the purposes of the present discussion, however, I employ Romanticism in a more general, historical sense, as a rubric for the configuration assumed by speculative conventions at one extended moment in the tradition of metaphysics. Here, I believe, I follow a lead implicit in Lacoue-Labarthe and Nancy's *L'Absolu littéraire*.

15. For example, *The Marble Faun* receives its color symbolism virtually intact from *The Scarlet Letter*. The painted image (of old Colonel Pyncheon, Chapter 2) plays a decisive role in *The House of the Seven Gables*, where marble also figures (Chapter 15). An entire tale, "The Snow-Image," elaborates a figure (snow) that appears merely as the briefest shorthand in *The Marble Faun*. I am suggesting that Hawthorne's work is at least in part organized as a lexicon to itself; that certain texts assume the task of decoding and translating images presented elsewhere as rebuses, out of context and with a minimum of explanatory material. The iterability of Hawthorne's symbols allows him to play the duplicitous role of both the *placer* and the *solver* of enigmas.

16. See John T. Irwin, *American Hieroglyphs: The Symbol of the Egyptian Hieroglyphics in the American Renaissance* (New Haven: Yale University Press, 1980).

17. Nathaniel Hawthorne, *The Scarlet Letter*, Norton Critical Edition (New York: Norton, 1962), pp. 27 28.

18. All these descriptions of Miriam and Hilda derive from Wordsworth's *Lyrical Ballads*. Miriam's moods allude to the first line of "Strange Fits of Passion Have I Known." Hilda, in her modesty, seclusion, and her association with birds and flowers, becomes a creature of one of the so-called Lucy poems, "She Dwelt among the Untrodden Ways."

19. See, for example, the cycles of infinity and life in Hegel's *Phenomenology of Spirit*, pp. 99–100, 106 107.

20. See, for example, the tortuous Paris streets superimposed upon the map of Buenos Aires in "Death and the Compass," or the Chinese labyrinth of time that expands toward completion in "The Garden of Forking Paths." Jorge Luis Borges, *Ficciones* (New York· Grove Press, 1962), pp. 96–98, 133–134.

21. The smokescreen by which the novel camouflages its most suspect variables is closely akin to both the false entrance protecting Kafka's "Burrow" and the Freudian notion of the screen memory. The screen memory is a benign memory substituted for a traumatic one. See "The Psycho-Pathology of Everyday Life" in the *Standard Edition* (London: Hogarth, 1960), 6: 43–52.

22. I am referring here to the complex surrogation by which the counteraesthetic texts comprising *Either/Or* are at least two steps removed from Kierkegaard. The texts, themselves introduced by the fictive narrator, Victor Eremita, are ascribed to one "Aesthete A" and one Judge William. I am also suggesting that this fictive distancing device in a philosophical text is already implicit in the Hegelian perspectival division of labor that articulates *in itself*, *for itself*, and *for us*. See Søren Kierkegaard, *Either/Or*, trans. David F. Swenson and Lillian Marvin Swenson (Princeton: Princeton University Press, 1971), 1: 3–15.

23. See Neil Hertz, "Dora's Secrets, Freud's Techniques," *Diacritics* 13 (1983): 64–76.

24. For Kierkegaard's reading of *The Clouds*, see Søren Kierkegaard, *The Concept of Irony* (Bloomington: Indiana University Press, 1968), pp. 158–181.

25. See Søren Kierkegaard, *Repetition: An Essay in Experimental Psychology* (New York: Harper & Row, 1964), pp. 61–65.

26. The figure of the eternal-feminine derives from the end of Goethe's *Faust*, p. 308 (ll. 12104–12111).

7

THE ACADEMIC DEVELOPMENT OF
THE WASTE LAND

Peter Middleton

Discuss the view that *The Waste Land* "uses the images of the past to reveal, but also to transform, the horror of the present."

Although lacking the interrogative, this sentence insists on its imperative from the first word, even before presenting the reader with its carefully displayed "view." Like the poem itself often does, an absent, unnamed speaker is implied by quotation marks, but not allowed to sign this appearance. For the words of the quotation are being used without the endorsement of their putative original speaker, but that anonymous speaker is reproduced here as a sign not of that name but that authority of which the whole question is a structural part. Yet this authority is not one of fact or truth or theory, for it is represented as a view, "the view," and views depend on standpoints. So the question both notes the authority of this unnamed speaker and insists on a pluralism of views. There is a view and it becomes an object of our attention and analysis, to be discussed, for words to cartograph accurately. As it stands, the question (and the absence of the interrogative makes the idea of an "answer" deliberately ambiguous) does not involve *The Waste Land*, except as some external measure for the operation of "discussion" and "view," as the relative triangulations of this particular diagrammatized view are measured against the testing ground, this piece of waste ground, *The Waste Land*.

This demand cannot be answered. The conditions that prevent a solution to this apparently transparent request will be the concern of this essay. I cannot directly answer this question and do not intend to try, but instead to investigate the terms of this request. It will appear that it tells us more about the poem than any critic could do.

I cannot answer the question partly because the conditions under which it could be answered as it demands no longer exist. This innocent request was question 8 on an examination I took on Thursday, 14 June 1973, at 9:30 A.M., entitled "7(f). Yeats and Eliot," as part of the "Honour School of English Language and Literature" at Oxford University. I did not answer the question then but opted for an alternative — "What part is played in the *Four Quartets* by *either* music *or* time?" — and "discussed" the "musical" organization of the poems, a nondiscursive analogue, as a way of discussing structure purely in terms of its repetitions, and elaborating the conventional idea that music is the purest art because it has no content. I can only write from memory about that answer because I have never seen it since. Once it had been assigned a mark, its useful role was finished, and it was either filed and kept in secret, or destroyed, and certainly not allowed to enter the society of those other writings from which the quotation had come. The context of the question demanded not only an answer but a marker, and that special reading of my text was its final resolution. There was to be no future intertextuality for it. Even if I had answered the question on *The Waste Land*, it would function only as a largely erased text, in memory alone, with no textual existence to qualify as an answer now.

Therefore even if I could now write to a timed examination mode, mimicked for authenticity, an answer to that request for a "discussion" about *The Waste Land*, it would not be complete until it had been "marked," and the "mark" would be a mark of its banishment from the discourse in which literary criticism is viewed as discussion, in the way that this paper will, I hope, be received. However much I discussed the quotation, it could never be *the* discussion that had been demanded because that would require this closed circuit of secrecy — the examination hour and room, the examinee and examiner.

Yet this request and the quotation are worth discussion, and once it is understood that *this* discussion is not an answer to that closed artifact with which we began, it is possible to proceed with a further exploration of this innocently unanswerable invitation. An innocent invitation that will soon appear less than innocent and yet innocent of its methods for transforming horror, and the present, into examination questions.

Its appearance in a paper that formed part of an examination on the carefully and nationalistically labeled "English" language and literature deserves comment to begin with. Neither Yeats nor Eliot were "English" insofar as one was Irish, admittedly Anglo-Irish, and the other American and only a British citizen as the result of a legal process that occurred nearly a decade after the poem was published. This is not to assert some chauvinistic point but to indicate that the inclusion of these writers as English (which in its specific use describes that part of the United Kingdom which excludes Wales, Scotland, and Northern Ireland, although they are all governed from London) is an act of cultural appropriation. Its full significance lies outside the scope of this paper, but Eliot's case can be considered a little more. Eliot's anglicization represented a significant countermovement to the growing American cultural hegemony that was felt by intellectuals in Britain during the thirties, forties, and fifties. Films, popular music, and popular fiction seemed to dominate cultural production. Therefore Eliot's repudiation of America by taking up English citizenship could be understood as a triumph, and the inclusion of his work on the syllabuses of English literature courses was then a strategic demonstration of the force of English culture, whose hegemony has been challenged throughout the twentieth century not only by the United States but also and almost as powerfully by Scotland and Ireland.

Eliot was included not because he wrote in the English language — so did Ezra Pound and Hilda Doolittle, who both lived in London for crucial years in the development of modern English literature. They did not appear (unless on a paper on American literature offered alongside medieval German, Icelandic, and Latin literature papers among others that seemed to indicate foreign sources for English literature) on the English examination papers because of their failure to qualify by nationality. Only Eliot among the American expatriates was allowed. His anglicization was fortuitous because his poetry and criticism has become essential to the academic institutional and especially pedagogic enterprise.

It is an observation still too little made that in the words of the French critic Pierre Macherey, "it is essential to study the material history of texts."[1] A text like *The Waste Land* enjoys its significance, its meaning (if that word can be allowed to stand for unanalyzed complexities for a moment), because of the way it is re-presented, republished, and taught. Macherey's work has been unfortunately associated with a rigid Althusserianism based on a clear distinction between science and ideology, and the problematic that creates significant absences, but in brief essays and interviews since *A Theory of Literary Production*[2] he has made succinct observations about the way literary meaning is constructed that merit attention. In an interview he repeated his idea that literary texts conceal their operations until interpretation can free them: "The type of analysis which I propose is precisely to read the ideological contradictions within the devices produced to conceal them, to reconstitute the contradictions from their system of concealment."[3] The difficulty with this formulation, despite its suggestiveness, is that it presupposes a critical method, which, in terms of our opening question is not a "view." It should be an objective "scientific" mapping of the contradictions. However, Macherey makes this point in a limited context, and that narrower frame of reference gives the method a more precise function. The range is that of the educational system. "I think literature exists — in the most physical, immediate, and obvious sense — not for those who consume it but for those who use it, namely schoolchildren. . . . These schoolstudents and their teachers have a direct relationship to literature."[4] It is easy to hear the self-criticism of the intellectual who feels removed from the tangible workings of the world outside the analytic field of the academy, but the contextualization of the earlier remark by this reference to literature as what is studied, the practice of literary studies, in schools and universities, is of great help for the present discussion. Can we use, or use in an altered form, these comments in an attempt to account for that opening question and its invocation of *The Waste Land*?

That question can only be answered by an extended consideration of both the poem as the educational apparatus in Britain and the United States has exploited it, and the role of that apparatus from which that questioning synecdoche began this inquiry.

Waste land. Words to describe land that is not productive, not being cultivated, cultured by human beings, but which the term implies either ought to be or cannot be because of some inherent failure of the land, its users, its position, or its constituents. Waste land is not usually wilderness, national park, or jungle. The value of exploitation and use is implied by these terms, which we shall see are precise indicators of the uses that the textual operations of the poem propose. This land has been *wasted*. It awaits redevelopment, the culture of useful products or the erection of inhabitable structures, and both have been obligingly provided for the project of that title by the literary institutions. And yes the valorized puns are not random releases of inhibition as easy laughter. All production begins with raw material, but the academic literary production of *The Waste Land* has been marked by concealment and contradiction, to use Macherey's words.

Success is always a matter of consensus. The chorus of academic critics singing the praises of Eliot's poem is remarkably harmonious, and that alone would be enough to pronounce it a success. A typical example of the importance of Eliot for the academy occurs in an essay by Robert M. Adams published in a collection of essays in 1973 to mark the fiftieth anniversary of *The Waste Land*. He writes, "my own education . . . seems to have been soaked in an awareness of Eliot" and adds a little ambivalently, "Eliot imposed himself on the literary con-science of my generation."[5] It was only an imposition in the sense that Eliot's work had to be assimilated thoroughly and not without difficulty by the academy. Adams is explicit about the educational processes sur-rounding Eliot. "Writing a paper on T. S. Eliot in 1972 is easier, on at least one preliminary level, than it ever used to be. There are all sorts of books and articles on the topic: they are all on the shelves. There is a way of saying this that makes the remark sound malignant and trium-phant; I mean no such tone to be heard. It is an occasion for surprise only because, for almost forty years, I have been accustomed to find a snarl of students buzzing over and about books by and about T. S. Eliot." The latent theriomorphism and the curious disclaimer remind us of how imbedded in the hierarchic social relations of the university Eliot's work has become, and the remark about the ease of writing about Eliot suggests that specific interpretative responses have been very clearly marked out. A similar note can be found in the writing of a British critic, Frank Kermode, who remarks in an essay examining The Waste Land that "our most lively sense of what it means to be alive in poetry continues to stem from the 'modern' of forty years ago."[6] Both writers testify not only to Eliot's significance but also to the academy as the site of that importance. Kermode's collective pronoun *our* and the explicit reference to students by Adams should make that clear. To be alive *in* poetry and know what that means comes from Eliot and his contemporaries. The preposition stresses the full occupation of the poetic work by the critic.

This use to which Eliot's work has been put by education institu-tions is in apparent contradiction to Eliot's own early pronouncements about art. In an editorial in *The Criterion* for July 1923 Eliot attacked the new journal, the *Adelphi*, edited by John Middleton Murry, for its credo that made "life" the absolute measure of art. "It is the function of a literary review to maintain the autonomy and disinterestedness of literature, and at the same time to exhibit the relations of literature — not to 'life,' as something contrasted to literature, but to all the other activities, which, together with literature, are the components of life."[7] In the first issues of *The Criterion* Eliot published *The Waste Land*, the Malatesta Cantos of Ezra Pound, a long essay on Freud, and various other literary and nonliterary works. What is striking about Kermode's no doubt accidentally contradictory remark is the way it points to the opposite term in Eliot's editorial — autonomy. Autonomy is further glossed as a "preoccupation with literature and art for their own sake." It is this that really animates Eliot's modernism and which is the hidden binary term implied by that vitality that Kermode invokes. We shall see that it is one of the central ways Eliot's work, and especially *The Waste Land*, has been so useful to the literary academy.

Even the few dissenters to the chorus of praise for the poem have not questioned its pedagogic importance. David Craig voiced criticisms typical of the dissent in a 1960 essay. He objected to the way the poem as it was taught "encourages a superior cynicism in young students," because although the poem was the record of a "defeatist personal depression," it was projected "in the guise of a full impersonal picture of society."[8] Craig tries to challenge the pedagogic dominance of the poem by denying its historical validity and significance, but his denial only reinforces our sense of the educational role it has played. Craig writes, "*The Waste Land* is not the representative work of the present age, *and to make it so* implies that pessimistic view of the present age which I have already challenged" (my italics). Craig tries to discuss the "view" of a hypothetical "quotation" from the academy and in doing so is unable to step outside the circle. His comments only confirm the importance of the poem for teachers of literature.

My own favourite testimony to the supremacy of Eliot in the literature department (at least until recently) occurs in an essay with a deliberately outrageous title, which jarringly confronts high and low, dominant and ethnic cultures. In "Tom Eliot Meets the Hulk at Little Big Horn," two poets, Marge Piercy and Dick Lourie, argue that a certain kind of poetry survives only as a teaching text, as an academic discipline.[9] It tends to "support a large critical apparatus (thus keeping in a minor way, the wheels of the economy turning)." Not only is there some truth in this polemic despite its overstatement, but what is of particular interest here is that they take Eliot as the central representative figure in their presentation of poetry as the terrain for academic discipline, research, the land on which the critical industry operates. The main purpose of their essay, to make available poetry as a popular artistic practice, is not immediately relevant here, but one remark in this context is. In Eliot's name we are told, "Poetry which upholds the status quo is considered apolitical." This provides a very useful starting point for considering in greater detail the reasons for the centrality of *The Waste Land* to educational practice.

There are two main overt reasons for this importance. The first is the critical challenge the poem appeared to offer. Until recently, almost all critical methods aimed to demonstrate the unity of a work according to criteria of different kinds, and a poem like *The Waste Land* provided an opportunity to test these to destruction. Or so it was allowed to appear. Actually the strength of the critical doctrine was usually demonstrated, and the poem's unities strained into place.

Most discussion of Eliot's *Waste Land* follows two lines. It attempts to show that the poem does have a unified structure of some kind despite the surface irregularities and apparent disorganization, and it also, usually simultaneously, draws forth this unity in terms of reference points that are allegedly alluded to by the pervasive quotations and literary echoes. The poem is traced back to its sources and is brought forward into an extrapolated wholeness.

Since Cleanth Brooks said that the poem was a "unified whole"[10] and F. R. Leavis said that "the unity the poem aims at is that of an inclusive consciousness" and a "musical" organization,[11] the majority of critics have echoed these formulations. Leavis was careful to stress that the poem was not a "metaphysical whole" but "an effort to focus an inclusive human consciousness" and then to use as a measure of its unity terms of mental activity rather than material subjects. Recent critics seem to have echoed this argument with even greater emphasis, probably because it shifts the burden of unity away from the need to prove it with the surfaces of the poem, onto the assumed unity of the human ego. In a very recent study of Eliot, A. D. Moody argues that the poem is "struggling to unify a vastly more inclusive and complex sensibility" than we ordinarily recognize.[12] "Its complexities proceed from the complexities of his consciousness; and its ultimate coherence is a matter of the unifying of his sensibility."[13] This extraordinary shift from poem to author and the odd idea that the ultimate measure of the poem is the unification of the author's "sensibility" should not distract us from the basic strategy that runs through this account, like the others. The poem, it is said, reveals a unity because it shows *consciousness* extended to its limits yet brought to a focus. All these critics agree that it is consciousness of "the state of a civilization," or "the horror of the present" as our opening question put it, that is apparent in the poem.

A further element in the standard critical accounts is the tendency to stress the value of the poems's allusiveness. Most salient for my purposes, Leavis (echoed by many others, George Williamson in *A Reader's Guide to T. S. Eliot*, for example[14]) finds a "*wealth* of literary borrowings" and a "*rich* disorganisation" in the poem[15] (my italics). These submerged metaphors for material wealth assimilate the literary works of the past to the market discourse for art treasures. They are a way of reminding the reader that *The Waste Land* can be read as a glossary of literary works, a guidebook to the tradition, or in terms of the metaphor, as a bank statement of the literary investments currently made. This is the measure of what Hugh Kenner called "the contemporary cultivated consciousness" of the poem.[16]

Some recent attempts to write about the poem have been quite self-conscious about these assumptions. Robert Langbaum writes that "one sign of a great poem is that it continues to grow in meaning,"[17] thereby justifying continued attention to the poem, continued exegesis, and by implication the critical industry, in a circular fashion, and using a curiously dated organicist metaphor to do it. His version of the "consciousness" of the poem is "new concepts of identity,"[18] but he is still able to refer to a "central consciousness" that he finds in the Stetson passage and the opening of Part 3.

Strangely, the best and almost the only sustained attempt to counter these views was written more than forty years ago (but not so strangely given the enormous critical investment we are now auditing) by an unreasonably neglected critic, Alick West. In 1937, in *Crisis and Criticism*,[19] he devoted the opening chapters of the book to a consideration of T. S. Eliot and especially *The Waste Land*. His study is still valuable, despite the naiveté of its vocabulary and pscyhology, because it questions the way the poem appears to demand a certain kind of interpretation and the way critics have responded. He argues, "As a statement with so many meanings in it cannot be conceived as being made by an individual mind, it seems to be the expression of a mystery. The poem as a whole makes the reader feel some greater unity, of which all these elements, though unrelated according to the way 'we' see life when drinking coffee in the Hofgarten, are parts in the greater whole."[20] This comment inverts what most critics say. They represent the achievement of interpretative unity as a struggle in the face of great opposition, whereas Alick West suggests that it is the deliberate strategy of the poem to satisfy such a need for struggle and unity. "The poem thus corresponds to modern criticism." Unfortunately these remarkable insights are followed almost immediately by a lapse back into some of the terms of the critics he was opposing. He says, "what unites the parts of the poem is that they are *seen* in relation to one another, and seen by a type of mind of which Tiresias is an expressive symbol."[21] Once again the idea of a unifying consciousness is filtering back into the account through this attempt to centralize Tiresias. West's difficulty lies in finding a discourse for subjectivity. He writes of the opening of the poem with a good understanding of the subject positions offered, and hence the politics and metaphysics of the pronominal shifts, but cannot substantiate his observations. The opening passage of the poem, he writes, "depends to a considerable extent on the alternations in the meaning of 'us,' which Mr. Eliot conveys with such skill. . . . When I do not know any longer who are the 'we' to whom I belong, I do not know any longer who 'I' am either. 'I' can no longer be projected into a poem as the source of the creative energy felt in it."[22] The potential brilliance of that final sentence is marred only by the vagueness of the gesture toward a conjunction of science and art in one—"creative energy." Much of the opening of the opening of the book is an attack on the centrality of the subject for contemporary literary criticism and so seems once again of great interest.

It is to the great psychologist of the subject that we need to turn for further insight into the critical procedures that have been sketched here. Despite the emphases on ambiguity, allusiveness, and even the "rich disorganisation," critics of the poem always attempt to restore the surface of the poem, to step over the cracks rather than to include them in the topology of the poem. Freud's attention to dreams is of some interest here precisely because of his conviction that the gaps and elisions in a dream were the points at which important material had been repressed and were therefore part of the meaning of the dream.

The Waste Land is a pattern of transitions, gaps, blurrings of event and perspective, and it might seem that interpretations should heed Freud's vast demonstration of the way gaps and fragments of a dream are the result of repression working as displacement and condensation through what he called at the time of *The Interpretation of Dreams* the "censoring agency": "There can be no doubt that the censoring agency, whose influence we have so far only recognised in limitations and omissions in the dream-content, is also responsible for interpolations and additions in it."[23] He then explains that sometimes the dream work revises this faulted structure so that it appears seamless and whole: "This function behaves in the manner which the poet maliciously ascribes to philosophers: it fills up the gaps in the dream-structure with shreds and patches."[24] This patching up of a whole is a false kind of interpretation. "Dreams which are of such a kind . . . appear to have a meaning, but that meaning is as far removed as possible from their true significance." That "true significance" will involve the rediscovery of the flaws in the dream, the discontinuities that are present and conceal the intensities of affect. Analysis is very powerful. "It is often possible by means of analysis to restore all that has been lost by the forgetting of the dream's content."[25] In the context of Freud's theories about the process of condensation, "the very great number of associations produced in analysis to each individual element of the content of a dream,"[26] a process which is the basis of the formation of dreams, the analytic approach begins to bear curious resemblances to that applied to *The Waste Land*.

Freud argued that the gaps in a dream are the sites where repression is often most active, where important material has been omitted. The literary-critical desire for unity has entailed a concealment of the gaps in the poem. These gaps, elisions, transitions, and fractures are precisely those points where the activity of forbidden desire has disrupted the flow of meaning across the surface. Unity enables the critic to ignore this disturbance by explaining away the dislocation.

It is crucial to recognize that these gaps are occurrences at different levels of the production of meaning that constitute a reading. There are simple shifts of speaker, and breaks in syntax, but there are, at another level, gaps in readings that have been offered as the propaedeutic for students "studying" Eliot. Moreover the analogy with Freud's attention to dreams is more than that, for it is part of a general hermeneutic for the period of the poems's writing and critical reception. Although Freud everywhere acknowledges lacunae in the surface of the dream, he also invariably finds sources, origins, explanations beyond, beneath, and before the topography to be explicated. The gaps are illusory. Critics of *The Waste Land* have conflated the process into a search for sources, and it is this denial of the surface that finds not only the Freudian analysis but also the poem's presentation deeply complicit. The history of the poem would find a parallel in the history of the reification of analytic processes as alienated objects of scientific scrutiny outside language, in the history of psychoanalysis, especially in relation to the theorization of the subject and the ego, and the general amnesia about linguistic productivity.

Before examining this complicity of poem and interpretation that has encouraged academic exegetes who would restore it to its unbroken origins among the sources, it is necessary to say a little about the *general* importance of Eliot to the academic teaching of literature. Eliot's critical doctrines were of enormous significance for the growth of academic literary studies from the thirties to the sixties. To begin with, Eliot repeatedly stressed the autonomy of literature, as the quotation from *The Criterion* shows very clearly. This was an important defense for the growth of autonomous literature departments during those years, departments that did not want to be a subsection of sociology, history, linguistics, or whatever. This stress on autonomy was linked to another pervasive theme in Eliot's criticism, its expressionism.

This aspect of Eliot's work has been documented in my own research on the period and in a helpful study of literary expressionism from a Wittgensteinian standpoint by John Casey in *The Language of Criticism*.[27] Eliot presents the process of literary composition as essentially the expression of a "sensibility" (most famously in the idea of an "objective correlative"), which implies that a mental content exists *prior* to any linguistic manifestation. As a consequence of this separation of mind and language, Eliot is forced to produce various arguments about "impersonality" and the need to put conscious mental activity into abeyance (finding further confirmation in the Freudianism current at that time). A failure to restrain the conscious mind would result in the distortion that Freud finds everywhere in dreams, and moreover a contamination by merely personal beliefs, prejudices, and concerns. Only the unconscious could guarantee universality and poetic conviction. In his essay on Ben Jonson he critcizes the poet for a lack of depth owing to the fact that "unconscious does not respond to unconscious"[28] in his poetry. Eliot therefore campaigns for a poetry that is expressive of the unconscious and eschews personal commitment of any kind. The active involvement with history or ideas, so often called political, is therefore exiled from the republic of poetry, and a natural development is possible for the New Criticism's neglect of history and social context. Engagement with ideas in literature as other than expressions of an artist's mind is excluded. Ideas cannot be argued with in the way philosophers and scientists challenge and modify the concepts published by other thinkers. Literary studies could be kept pure.

Eliot's criticism also made acceptable a renewed interest in the seventeenth century, supposedly an era of "undissociated sensibility," a pure and uncontaminated source for the expression of sensibility in poetry and literature in general. Although it was always argued that social conditions made this cognitive homogeneity possible, the history could be treated in selective, discrete samplings. Today the attraction of the seventeenth century seems obvious, as a period before civil war forever upset the monarchic system of patronage and the regal Christian order. The mediated relation with the authority of God still lingered before the final wave of the puritan revolution established the personal search for definition and identity in self-questioning relations with God, as a political order. Literary academics were largely able to enjoy a political position without the problems of making it explicit.

The final aspect of Eliot's importance, his anglicization, was obviously more important in England, but it supported and justified a European bias in the teaching of literature in America, against which so many writers struggled in the fifties. That lies outside the scope of this paper. What is common to all these aspects of Eliot's criticism as it has been received is the way that his critical writings could be and often have been used to endorse and perpetuate the teaching practices of the academy. Even Eliot's insistence on "tradition," which he used to replace the concept of history, could be used to support the notion of a canon or syllabus of great authors and their texts, existing in a transcendent realm as passive subjects for study.

Eliot was not the instigator of English studies, nor were his writings aimed at the institutionalization of literature. He often said that only practitioners should be taken seriously as critics of literature. Reviewing and literary journalism were his critical activities. Yet his ideas have been essential to the theorization and fascia of academic literary practice, and his poetry the justification, the validation, or credentials for their deployment, and no poem more so than *The Waste Land*. It was presented as the proof of the claims of the critic behind the impersonal mask of the great modern poet. It proved that these doctrines produced great modern art, endorsed the synoptic, synchronic literary history that had been established — and by devaluing the present, including itself, devalued the practice of writing as a part of literary study, because this writing would partake of the "horror of the present." And finally it offered certain gratifications to the reader and teacher if read in ways that did not challenge the formulations of the poem, in the academic nexus.

Britain and the United States diverge over the issue of the location of that "horror," that "waste land," and that is reproduced by their respective approaches to the teaching of literature as the practice of writing. In Britain almost no literature departments teach writing because literature is generated as part of a process of literary historicism and evaluative judgment. Contemporary literary practice, new writing, finds no place in this closed ceremony of analysis. In the United States a sense that the "waste land" was elsewhere, in the past as frontier, abroad as the exhausted culture of Europe, engendered a confidence in the possibility of academic control of the validation of potential writers. In both countries there is an underlying common factor. The writing must be controlled within the system of marks and legitimation, or excluded. We can see once again how prophetic William Carlos Williams was when he said that with *The Waste Land* Eliot handed poetry back to the academics.[29]

The Waste Land was important as a demonstration of the validity of certain critical doctrines, but it also offered other satisfactions. Those I wish to examine here are images of the present, transformed into unspoken pleasure for certain readers. These are its presentations of war and sexuality, and in particular the disquiet over female emancipation and the enormous loss of life during the First World War. Although war and sex are everywhere discussed in critical exegeses of the poem, the politics of both treatments is almost never examined because the relations presumed present in the poem are always tacitly endorsed. There has been at work a critical unconscious, allowing the reader and the academy to perpetuate certain ideas by failing to engage with them except as passive reference to the words of the poem by quotation.

Literary works provide formal or imaginary solutions, in many

cases, to unresolved social contradictions, within the circumstances of
their reproduction in institutions. These are effective while unread, unexamined, and seen as part of the unquestioned solidity of background
from which the semantic drama emerges. I think once we examine *The
Waste Land* closely we can see that certain readings are possible which
are rarely openly discussed in the academic literature on the poem, but
which offer gratifications to certain sexual and political complacencies,
and have been allowed to do so because unexamined. It is this which
can be called a critical unconscious. No moral judgment is intended
here, but rather an attempt to understand the operations whereby the
poem came to stand in that peculiar discourse that opened the paper but
can never be answered. Lacan's formulation offers a useful analogy.
"The unconscious is that chapter of my history that is masked by a blank
or occupied by a falsehood: it is the censored chapter."[30] I want to look
at the censored chapters of *The Waste Land*.

Many aspects of sexuality are depicted in the poem, but I want to
explore just two. One is the poem's offer of homosexual gratifications to
the male reader, and the other is its presentation of a strong antifeminism, what used to be called misogyny. The latter can only be fully
understood in the context of debates about birth control and female sexuality during the first world war, debates that then continued in muted
form until the sixties, but were always alive enough to make the poem's
pleasures worth having.

Women are the most salient figures in the poem, and they exhibit
a whole range of depravity: corruption, indulgence, moral confusion,
shallowness, and superstition. Their dissolution is symptomatic of the
modern waste land. Male depravity is hardly mentioned. This hostility
toward women is ameliorated slightly in the final version, and the
underlying violence of feeling can only be seen openly in the drafts.
There it is vivid. Women are depicted as types—Magdalene, Jenny,
martyr, bitch, puss cat, favorite, slattern, doorstop dunged—and apart
from possibly the martyr, all are defined by their sexual relations to
men, and in ways that stress their corruption and animality. Women
suffer from both emotion and intellect. "Women grown intellectual
grow dull," but on the other hand most women exhibit "unreal emo-
tions and real appetite."[31] They are damned both ways. Most unpleas-
ant of all is the earlier version of "A Game of Chess," in which the rich
idle woman is "aroused from dreams of love and pleasant rapes /
aroused from dreams of love in curious shapes." These examples were
excised for publication, but the traces remain in the seductions, the
neurasthenia, the fortune-telling. Take the case of Philomel. Keats's
nightingale represented presence, continuity, art, permanence. Eliot's

nightingale is likewise "inviolable" but only because she has been raped, violated.[32] She is a woman become attractive by ceasing to be a woman, having become pure music, pure art. She has lost her power of speech. Only "dirty ears" hear her music as words that signify, that is, give her an active role in discourse. The word *jug* is flung out as a deliberately Freudian symbol. She, Philomel, is in the desert, the wasted land, pursued by the world, from which, by the syntax, the reader is separated. So the woman here is excluded from language and any form of representation by the sexual violence of a man, and now the world, but thereby allowed access to a pure art that is powerless and desolate. It is a pattern that can be read both as offering a justification to the unconscious reader for a sexual fantasy of violent transmutation, and, when so read explicitly, as a way of isolating and analyzing such metaphorphoses of male desire in art.

The antifeminism is a response to the other threat that this patriarchal power was encountering particularly strongly during and after the First World War, but which has resurfaced ever more meaningfully for the masculine order in the twentieth century. In Britain the First World War had meant a chance for large numbers of women to work in the factories while the men were away fighting, and it was as a direct result of this sudden economic independence that some of the demands that the suffragette movement had been making for several decades were finally conceded. In 1918 women over the age of thirty were given the vote and the Maternity and Child Welfare Act was passed giving women greater security in child care. Women were allowed to sit on juries for all except sex crimes. In 1919 the Sex Disqualification (Removal) Act opened many jobs to women from which they had been barred, especially in the legal profession. These developments had similar parallels in the United States, where the drive for adequate birth control was also under way in the hands of Margaret Sanger and others, and soon had a marked influence in Britain.

Margaret Sanger became convinced of the need for birth-control facilities after seeing women in New York die of self-induced abortions and the demands of endless childbearing in very poor conditions. "In this atmosphere abortion and birth become the main theme of conversation,"[33] she later wrote, and this is clearly the background to the pub sequence in *The Waste Land*. Margaret Sanger's autobiographical writings located her involvement with one woman in particular, Sadie Sachs, who was unable to take the doctor's advice not to let her husband sleep with her, and who subsequently died in appalling conditions, as her turning point. She wrote stirringly about women, birth control, and sexuality, in a discourse that shows traces of Christian evangelism. A woman "goes through the vale of death alone, each time a babe is born,"[34] Sanger wrote. The biblical terms are used to dignify the process but are themselves subverted and transformed. The attempt to enlist women's fight for a successful birth into the discourse of Christian heroism would change the structure of metaphor surrounding the body, sexuality, and death. It is no accident that *The Waste Land* also uses those terms of struggle and death, the valley of death, because it is operating in the same linguistic territory where a battle is being fought over the definitions of sexuality, courage, and death.

Sanger also wrote in *Woman and the New Race*:

> Woman must not accept; she must challenge. She must not be awed by that which has been built up around her: she must reverence that within her which struggles for expression. Her eyes must be less upon what is and more clearly upon what should be. She must listen only with a frankly questioning attitude to the dogmatized opinion of man-made society. When she chooses her new, free course of action, it must be in the light of her own opinion - of her own intuition. Only so can she give play to the feminine spirit. Only thus can she free her mate from the bondage which he wrought for himself when he wrought hers. Only thus can she restore to him that of which he robbed himself in restricting her. Only thus can she remake the world.[35]

This is the language of puritanism linked with the politics of revolution, and it is that which is most threatening in this movement for emancipation. The present is rejected in favor of the future, and there is a very strong repudiation of the past. The world must be remade. The implied obligation "must" is very emphatic. Her own attempts to remake the world were appropriately fervent but also pragmatically specific. In her birth-control leaflet (1917) she insisted that women were not passive sexual characters like those presented in *The Waste Land*. "A mutual and satisfied sexual act is of good benefit to the average woman, the magnetism of it is health giving. When it is not desired on the part of the woman and she has no response, it should not take place."[36] The passage implies that such unwanted acts should be defined as a form of rape. For such suggestions the leaflet was banned for obscenity when published by Marie Stopes in 1922. Prosecution counsel argued that "birth control was a danger to the race and against nature's law."[37] It was only a year since Marie Stopes had opened the first family-planning clinic in Islington, the same year that *The Waste Land* was begun.

In Part 2 of the poem an unidentified narrator outlines the dilemma that women found themselves in. Of the woman identified as Lil, we are told, "She's had five already, and nearly died of young George," and that she has taken pills to induce an abortion. The details seem true to the circumstances at that time, and so is her sense that she has no choice. It is the narrator who traps Lil in this difficult double bind, however. "He wants a good time,/And if you don't give it him, there's others will, I said." So she accepts Albert's demands and is willing to compete for Albert's attention. But in response to Lil's complaints about her health, the narrator is seemingly saying the opposite—"Well, if Albert won't leave you alone, there it is, I said." Again there is a euphemism for sexual intercourse, again an implied judgment, this time of Albert's desire, followed by a resigned acceptance of the present state of affairs, "there it is." Lil's dilemma appears to be an unsolvable paradox. She loses Albert if she does not "give it him" and loses anyway if she does, through her own probable death. What is not mentioned here is the possibility of contraception. The reader is placed in a complex relation to this material, which is reported speech, in the first person, that denies access to Lil and therefore prevents direct concern for her problem, and teases the reader into a critical relation to the speaker. Her competitiveness and lack of sympathy suggest that this state of affairs is women's fault. The narrator both confirms Lil's pain and prevents her from resolving it, making it possible for the reader to perceive the same dilemma as Margaret Sanger but to respond with an attitude of blame and resignation.

The problem seems to begin with the war's end and Albert's return. After the First World War there were two years of great social instability in Britain. "Bitter heroes in arms and women who had tasted a fleeting independence and begun to shed the illusions of sexual subordination."[38] Troops like Albert had been promised a new world and better homes—promises that were largely not kept. There was an atmosphere of near insurrection, strikes, riots, and even the police on strike. Yet this period soon ended with the restoration of an earlier economic hierarchy, and women were gradually excluded from the work force again. There was an ideological reaction to their independence, a backlash which blamed social ills on women's mistaken desire for independence. Sheila Rowbotham describes how one novel of the period, *This freedom* by A. S. M. Hutchinson, showed a young woman whose rebellion leads to her death after a back-street abortion: "She lay . . . upon the altar of her gods of self, of what is vain, of liberty undisciplined, of restless itch for pleasure."[39] *The Waste Land* covered similar political territory.

It was not only in Britain that such arguments were rife. Some participants in the Russian Revolution (where the towers of the old order had also been falling), most notably the feminist Alexandra Kollontai, believed that it heralded a sexual revolution as well. "The waves of the sexual crisis are sweeping over the thresholds of workers' homes and creating conflicts every bit as acute as the sufferings of the 'refined bourgeois world.' "[40] She and other Russian feminists were soon to be disappointed. It is interesting that the link between political and sexual change is so explicit and made in an image characteristic of the discourse of sexuality in *The Waste Land*, but the government response to these ideas was even more striking. Lenin and other leaders denounced these ideas fairly quickly. In the following passage the idea of drinking water as a natural human function is used for powerful rhetorical effect to support female sexual passivity — men are drinkers, women are water. Lenin refers to the "famous theory that in communist society the satisfaction of sexual desires, of love, will be as simple and unimportant as drinking a glass of water."[41] He then derides it. "This glass of water theory has made our young people mad, quite mad. . . . Of course thirst must be satisfied. But will the normal man in normal circumstances lie down in the gutter and drink out of a puddle, or out of a glass with a rim greasy from many lips?" The possessiveness and fear of female sexuality are obvious. This discourse about sexuality also occurs in *The Waste Land* with similar images of madness, thirst, and the dangers of water.

The success of *The Waste Land* was partly due to the retrenchment and comparative quiescence of feminism from the twenties to the sixties, which showed itself in a commitment to gradual reforms and no longer made sexual and egalitarian political demands. In this period sexuality was not often a political issue, and the association of sexual independence and social or moral corruption that *The Waste Land* proffers as one of its textual productions was likely to find a receptive readership. Both men and women would be *subject* to the sexual ideology, but men would find a position of interrogation looking for an explanation outside itself, a position of mastery, confirmed, at the expense of a gendered blame, while women readers would find their experience also partially confirmed. A reader who does not acquiesce would have a struggle to outline a response that did not dissolve into hostility or incomprehension. My own subjective impression is that surprisingly few female critics have written about the poem, and those that have tend to subordinate it to discussions of the later, more religious work.

In the passage quoted from Part 2 of the poem, the anonymous speaker says, "he wants a good time,/And if you don't give it him, there's others will." This statement is completed with the simple formula, "I said." A reader is therefore placed in the subject position and party to the attempt to lure Albert away from his wife for the sake of desire. Just one of many instances in the poem when the reader is placed in the position of a woman about to be the sexual object of male attack, this hints at a pattern in the poem that offers a male reader a kind of resolution of sexual ambiguity that is both taboo and desired. A very obvious case occurs in the drafts of the poem.

> Then he wished he had been a young girl
> Caught in the woods by a drunken old man
> To have known at the last moment, the full
> taste of her own whiteness
> The horror of her own smoothness.[42]

The desire to be a woman and be seduced is there made explicit, whereas in the final version it is simply implicit. As Claire Pajacowska puts it in an article on the way female desire is conceptualized in film theory, "The positions of masculinity and feminity are never unequivocally resolved or completely achieved, gender identity must always be laboured towards in order for its crises to be transcended."[43] I believe that *The Waste Land* is only a particularly salient example of a modern text that allows a male reader to negotiate homosexual desires that relate to uncertainty about sexual identity in ways that offer wish fulfillments and the satisfaction of their denial. It is, after all, the female figures that enact the drama. The poem offers this possible position to the reader while concealing it, and thus paralleling the general silence about the "processes of homosexuality in the psychic structures of signifying practice."[44] This remains a largely taboo area of discussion, but we need to consider it if we are to understand the cultural role of a work like *The Waste Land* in our educational processes.

Tiresias, following Eliot's footnote, has often been called the central consciousness of the poem. He offers a point from which the male reader can enjoy sexual relations with another man. "Old man with wrinkled dugs," he is ambisexual, androgynous. He has foresuffered all, in other words, always already been seduced. His condition is like that of Philomel, but as a man, or part man, he has been released into discourse, made able to enter the subjectivity of others. "I too awaited the expected guest," he says. We are in the woman's position, but in a sense replacing her, at this unacknowledged site of desire that is displaced from the women in the poem. "And I Tiresias have foresuffered all/Enacted on this same divan or bed." Here the verbs displace the event into some timeless place. The effect of this is both to conceal the pleasure of participation in the sexual act and to generalize the displaced condition of desire. Lacan's comment seems apt here on the mechanism at work despite its implied value system. "One might add here that male homosexuality in accordance with the phallic mark that constitutes desire, is constituted on the side of desire . . . these remarks should really be examined in greater detail, from the point of view of a return to the function of the mask in so far as it dominates the identifications in which refusals of demand are resolved."[45]

If the poem allows mysogyny and homoerotic desire a place, it also deals with the fears that arose from an event that created a traumatic realignment in the male psyche as great as the suffragette movement. The Great War. The poem offers a response to the war which operates as part of a general denial of history in favor of the transcendent world of the imaginary, but in the case of the war, in terms of a psychic transformation that is similar to the treatment of sexuality, and which appears in a form discussed by Freud.

Death in the war occurred on such a scale that people were initially unable to cope, and we owe the growth of modern psychiatry in part to the development of ways of treating the victims of shock. References to war abound in the poem, but the implied resolution of the horror and fear evoked have been allowed to operate unchecked and unexamined. *The Waste Land* offers a way of denying death through a series of devices, most strikingly through the images of the uncanny, and pervasively through the synoptic, transcendent allusiveness.

In "Tradition and the Individual Talent" (1919), Eliot wrote, "In English writing we seldom speak of tradition, though we occasionally apply its name in deploring its absence."[46] Tradition is absent, what is not present, although Eliot means to imply that it could or should be. What then can be done about it? A good poet can write so that, "not only the best, but the most individual parts of his work may be those in which the dead poets, his ancestors, assert their immortality most vigorously " So tradition is the dead, death, that otherness which Eliot wants to allow full possession of the subject, and of the subject's discourse. Quotation and parody are thereby acts of resurrection, an overcoming of death. This idea reaches its conclusion in the emphatic assertion that "no poet, no artist of any art, has his complete meaning alone. His significance, his appreciation is the appreciation of his relation to the dead poets and artists." Being able to signify, able to enter the symbolic realm, entails a relation with death, represented by the dead poets. The strategy here, then, is to assert that tradition, and death, are essential to the signifying process, but that the linguistic is then able to transcend death at the moment that the self, the I, of the present day poet disappears. "And the poet cannot reach this impersonality without surrendering himself wholly to the work to be done. And he is not likely to know what is to be done unless he lives in what is not merely the present, but the present moment of the past, unless he is conscious, not of what is dead, but of what is already living." The need is to resume the dead, to give them a place, a meaning, a significance. The war presented a human event that seemed to devour significance so that discourses were only slowly able to reform themselves. It was the time of Dada in art. Moreover the passages from Eliot's essay mark a fear of the present and the future which should be contrasted with the revolutionary optimism of the feminist discourse.

The Waste Land offers an extensive attempt to deny death, absence, by quotation, parody, incorporation, allusion, and the imbrication of old and new (O O O O that Shakespeherian Rag). It also offers a very precise use of the uncanny as Freud defined it. Section 5, lines 359–365 presents a questioning voice asking about a double. The doubled figure that appears alongside a companion, the addressee of the passage. According to Freud in "The Uncanny" (1919), the image of the double in supernatural fictions is an "energetic denial of the power of death,"[47] a form of narcissism, and a general reminder of the repetition compulsion. Freud argues that the uncanny is a way of understanding death in a very primitive way and is related to fears about the return of the dead, and at the same time the desire for just that to happen. Eliot's "tradition" would describe this process as well. Freud has difficulty in defining the manifestations of the uncanny without enumerating artistic devices used to produce the effect, but manages to offer a general definition that is closely descriptive of the effects of the poem. "An uncanny effect . . . is often and easily produced by effacing the distinctions between imagination and reality."[48] Most obvious are Eliot's references to the "unreal city" where the dead walk familiar London streets, or the "bats with baby faces." There in 1921 Eliot was using just these effects in order to resolve fears and doubts about the war, and the attendant deaths, perhaps even using the essay as a guide, quite consciously. Much else in the poem does suggest a conscious manipulation of contemporary theory. Whatever the genesis, the poem has continued to be read in an era in which mass death is familiar, and so the poem's pleasures have continued to be effective.

Rather than speculate on the pedagogic implications of these fantasies about death, which would require some extensive historicizing, I intend to examine in a more general way the strategies that the poem offers for dealing with history, the pressure of events in a national and personal narrative, of which the fantasy denial of the war is only a part. Those pedagogic implications are perhaps best adumbrated here by our opening question, which takes this point and links it with a seemingly innocent reference, backed by the authority of the quotation, to the "horror of the present," that present with which the English studies must therefore not directly engage. Instead it is the past that must be entered and simultaneously denied as a history that produces literature, as our writing is a product of our history, inescapably so.

One obvious effect of the Pound revisions and excisions on the poem manuscripts was an abrupt termination of almost all references to specific social circumstances. "The inhabitants of Hampstead have silk hats" but no longer stroll through the poem, although the Bradford millionaires do make a ghostly appearance. As these contemporary figures were apotheosized in symbolic utterances, so one figure became preeminent, that of the waste land itself, and the story of Parsifal and the Fisher king. And in the background the absent paradigm of the Holy Grail that formed the rationale of the whole Arthurian cycle.

It is worth remembering that although *The Waste Land* is always viewed as a *terminus ab quo*, it actually looks back directly to Victorian medievalism, that desire for an age distinguished by a noble unity of purpose within the overarching gothic heaven of a universal faith. It was dominated by a desire for a code of chivalry that could give a beautiful gloss to the patriarchal relations of men and women.

The Grail legend is well-known and especially that aspect of it referring to Parsifal (or Perceval depending on the version) and his ill-fated journey to the Grail king or Fisher king, as Chretien de Troyes distinguishes him.[49] A few aspects relevant to our purposes need to be recalled, however. The king is Parsifal's uncle and is, in terms of the narrative, a male replacement for the mother who apparently dies of grief. He pursued sexual, earthly love without permission and is punished with a wound in his own sex. All the Grail community remain of the same age. Parsifal's failure to ask the question is usually given by critics as the most relevant feature of this story for *The Waste Land*, but in the light of this inquiry it should be clear that the kinship status as a male repetition of the female origin is also important, as is the sexual wound, which transforms the king into a genitalized Tireseias. The story presents castration anxiety and the need to transform that fear into adult sexuality. Such an analysis is far too neat, however, if only because it omits the apparently happy sexual relation between Parsifal and Conwiramurs. That relation is marginalized to the point of extinction by the poem's emphasis on the episode at the Grail castle which leaves everything unchanged.

The poem has no simple relation to this material, which has been transmogrified into the fragmentary dramas of absence and death in the poem. The material is allegedly secondary anyway, having come from the Jesse Weston book *From Ritual to Romance*[50] according to the footnotes, but as F. R. Leavis observed, "repeated recourse to *From Ritual to Romance* will not invest it with the virtue it would assume."[51] This becomes an astute comment when it is realized that it is precisely an ethical maneuver that is occurring here. That anthropological study is presented as if it were the source, the validation, and true meaning of some thematic aspect of the poem. If that is so, it will not be because of some simple program tracing the poem's surface to its true origin and meaning, however.

Jesse Weston's study was a late offshoot of the school of Cambridge anthropology, euhemerist, evolutionary, and above all dedicated to the return of mythic narrative to ritual origin. In Jane Harrison's capable hands, for example, it becomes a subtle method for tracing the formation of belief, but for Jesse Weston the oppositions of truth and fantasy are simple, binary, and morally imperative.

"The poets and dreamers wove their magic webs, and a world apart from the world of actual experience came to life. But it was not all myth, nor all fantasy; there was a basis of truth and reality at the foundation of the mystic growth, and a true criticism will not rest content with wandering in these enchanted lands, and holding all it meets with for the outcome of human imagination."[52] The building, the topology, the landscape of narrative is then a surface that is fantasy or myth, and only the foundation offers "truth and reality," hidden beneath that surface. Like the knight on a quest, the interpreter has to question what is seen, to distinguish the merely human from the original. Evolutionary thought has been used to amplify the Romantic theme of an original knowledge become corrupted into story and poetry.

Jesse Weston spends most of the book tracing the origins of the Grail legend to the "basis of truth and reality" in order to demonstrate that

> in the process of transmutation from ritual to romance, the kernel, the Grail legend proper, may be said to have formed for itself a shell composed of accretions of widely differing material. It is the legitimate task of criticism to analyse such accretions, and to resolve them into their original elements, but they are accretions, and should be treated as such, not confounded with the original and essential material.[53]

She wants to dismantle the Romance, interpret the surface, so that nothing remains except that reversal toward the foundations of the semantic and syntactic space. A characteristic hermeneutic maneuver but one that does a particularly good job of effacing the operations of the text in favor of a movement back to the ideal origins and transhistoric realm of the mystery that is revealed, in a process that confirms the methodology at work. In *The Waste Land*, as in *From Ritual to Romance*, the Grail legend disappears, and in the poem the reader/critic becomes the wandering knight who is invited to see through this illusory linguistic surface to the true sources beyond. The poem appears to make sure that this time the quester will ask the question. The poetry is a dream, a fantasy that needs to be analyzed in a certain way, traced to its "real" origins. To help the reader, footnotes are included in the later editions of the poem, so that sources and authorities can be made explicit. Effacing the poem, checking it against the measure of its origins apparently becomes easier. These footnotes are a structural projection of the anthropological method, and by analogy, they are the voice of the quester who never appears in the poem. Parsifal speaks out in the footnotes, having absented himself from the broken surfaces of the poem, and therefore inserts into the poem an alien discourse. Footnotes are a functional interrelation whereby a discourse is made coherent and purposive, given a past. Not all discourses use footnotes because some, like poetry, depend too much on linguistic density, rather than isolable, defined terms, for the genealogical system to work. Moreover, footnotes are an institutional extension of the filing system for useful retrieval and recording of the institution's decisions. Parsifal has apparently become an academic, and the academy has recruited him the moment he walked out of the poem, leaving it in pieces to be deciphered, archaeologized, and restored to a likeness of the implied original unity.

The trouble is, as Jack Spicer noted in his sequence of poems *The Holy Grail*, that the academic expropriation had found the Grail in the way Galahad did—"Found it in such a way that the dead stayed dead, the waste land stayed a waste land."[54] It was against this need to penetrate the surface of the language to find out what was "hidden," original, ideal, that Wittgenstein wrote the *Philosophical Investigations* (which does not escape all the problems either). Wittgenstein's comment on philosophy is that "since everything lies open to view there is nothing to explain. For what is hidden, for example, is of no interest to us."[55] And he says earlier, "The problems arising through a misinterpretation of our forms of language have the character of *depth*."[56] Academic interpretation of *The Waste Land* has gone straight along the paths laid out by those footnotes signposting the way to the deep foundations of the poem that is believed to be only an illusorily visible linguistic surface.

According to Spicer, Perceval also suffers in the search for the Grail, asking the wrong question and left hanging at the end of the line of the stanza. There is an implicit commentary here on the Arthurian legend as well as on poetry and its pedagogic transformations. Like Guinevere, as we look back over this history of a poem like *The Waste Land*, we might say, "I am sick of the invisible world and all its efforts to be visible." Preeminent in these efforts is the Grail. It is the Other, the other pole in the endlessly deferred circuits of desire within the field of the signifier. It figures an ideal that in our context would be the unified interpretation, the perfect explanation, the transmission of a complete view of the poem from teacher to students. Spicer also has a comment to make on this comparison.

> The Grail is the opposite of poetry
> Fills us up instead of using us as a cup the dead drink from
> The Grail the cup Christ bled into and the cup of plenty in Irish
> Mythology
> The poem. Opposite. Us. Unfulfilled.[57]

Compared to poetry, the grail seems accessible, plenitude, promise. This might be a poetic gloss on the rhetorical images of a monstrous swallowing and destruction by tradition that F. R. Leavis reveals in a comment on *The Waste Land*. "The traditions and cultures have mingled, and the historical imagination makes the past contemporary; *no one tradition can digest so great a variety of materials*, and the result is a breakdown of forms and the irrevocable loss of that sense of absoluteness which seems necessary to a robust culture"[58] (my italics).

Spicer has the last word on these matters in "Lancelot." "The horse he rides on (Dada) will never go anywhere."[59] It cannot move because it is not a real horse. According to one account of the origins of the meaningless name Dada given to the artistic activities of those in Zurich during the First World War, it was chosen from a French dictionary that assigned the child's name for a wooden horse as its meaning. Lancelot will never get anywhere because he rides on a wooden unreal horse, literally the art of Dada. And Dada will never *go* anywhere.

The Waste Land is a ready-made academic poem with interpretations already included, and the recent publication of the facsimile has only extended its operation as a dadaist text. It is "about" the consumption of poetry, or rather it is compiled of many layers of material that offer themselves openly to a hermeneutic impulse. There is no space here to elaborate on the practices of Dada in the way they require to show why the critical quester is astride a wooden horse, but we can look at a few features of the movement, and its great publicist Tristan Tzara, to suggest the outline of an explanation for the horse's woodenness, and the opening question's unanswerability.

Dada "ne signifie rien," in Tristan Tzara's words. Or as the poem puts it, in the words of another, "I can connect nothing with nothing." The subject returns with a precise paradoxical description of its place in the signifying activity, where signifiers are nothings, that is, have no reference, and where the subject of the enunciation, the "I" that speaks, has no power over the signifiers that speak it, and is possessed by the voice from Shakespeare. According to Richard Huelsenbeck writing in 1920, Tzara was "the prophet of a word, which only later was to be filled with a concept."[60] It was a "filling" that was resisted as thoroughly as possible by Tzara. "Everybody knows that Dada is nothing."[61] It can be seen that the artists were putting in question the way certain signifying practices were immediately co-opted into preexisting discourse. Their strategies involved the production of a recognizable object of art discourse and then the masterful denial of its credentials for admission to the realm of the meaningful, respectable art form. As Tzara put it, Dada "est contre et pour l'unité."[62] It is a strategy familiar to *The Waste Land*. Taking away significance by simultaneously reading poems aloud, turning objects into performance, writing poems that did not arrive at a semantic grail castle, were all part of their work. Above all, the conventional high valuation of art was constantly in question. Tzara's own poems are peculiarly interesting examples of this, and also point toward Eliot's practice. In "Droguerie Conscience" appear the lines "si tu pense si tu es content lecteur tu deviens pour un instant transparent/ton cerveau éponge transparente/et dans cette transparence il y aura une autre transparence plus lointaine/lointaine quand un animal nouveau bleuira dans cette transparence,"[63] and it is clear that transparency, the riding through language into its deeper meanings, is blocked. A regression of the point of true meaning perceived through the linguistic interface is imaged here.

Tzara even wrote a poem that reads like a predecessor to *The Waste Land*, called "Printemps." One parts reads, "le roi en exil par la clarté du puits se momifie lentement/dans le jardin de légumes."[64] It does not matter whether Eliot's poem has another source here in any interpretative sense, but it is further help in orienting that critical reader on the wooden horse in quest for the *answer*. The poem need not be read as the support for the authoritarian pedagogic practice of interpreting literature in a series of fading views, which will eventually compile into a final holographic picture or geodetic survey of the unified meaning of the text (a meaning that validates the ceremonies of student examinations). It can be opened up to many of the issues that are discussed when we are not discussing literature. The voice of the thunder, of the law of the father that speaks the supposedly root syllable of IndoEuropean, "Da," may be heard again as stuttering out the word that is looking for a concept, the wooden horse that goes nowhere, but suddenly wakes us to the reality of the place we are actually in. Let another poet say it.

> No
> poetic gabble will survive which fails
> to collide head-on with the unwitty circus:
> no history running
> with the french horn into
> the alley-way, no
> manifest emergence
> of valued instinct, no growth
> of meaning & stated order:
> we are too kissed & fondled
> 1.0 longer instrumental
> to culture in "this" sense or
> any free-range system of time.[65]

The Waste Land will go on questioning us for a long time to come, despite our wrong questions, fear of the "unwitty circus" of history, sexuality, and surfaces that are not institutionalized. Those of us who teach literature must go on listening to what the poets are saying, and think hard about whether the questions we are asking ourselves and our students have answers or, like that opening question, remain in perpetual motion that occurs in the closed system of interpretation, astride a wooden horse.

NOTES

1. Pierre Macherey, "Interview," in *Red Letters* no 5 (Summer 1977): 7.
2. Pierre Macherey, *A Theory of Literary Production*, trans. Geoffrey Wall (London: Routledge & Kegan Paul, 1978).
3. Macherey, "Interview," p. 5.
4. Ibid., p. 4.
5. Robert M. Adams, "Precipitating Eliot," in *Eliot in His Time*, ed. A. Walton Litz (Princeton: Princeton University Press, 1973), pp. 129–130.
6. Frank Kermode, "A Babylonish Dialect," in *T. S. Eliot: A Casebook*, ed. C. B. Cox and Arnold P. Hinchliffe (London: Macmillan, 1968), p. 234.
7. T. S. Eliot, "The Function of a Literary Review," *The Criterion* (July 1923): 421.

8. David Craig, "The Defeatism of The Waste Land," *T. S. Eliot: A Casebook*, p. 200.

9. Marge Piercy and Dick Lourie, "Tom Eliot Meets the Hulk at Little Big Horn: The Political Economy of Poetry," *TriQuarterly* 23/24 (winter/spring 1972): 60.

10. Cleanth Brooks, "The Waste Land: Critique of the Myth," in *Modern Poetry and the Tradition* (North Carolina: University of North Carolina Press, 1939), repr. in *T. S. Eliot: A Casebook*, p. 128.

11. F. R. Leavis, *New Bearings in English Poetry* (London: Chatto and Windus, 1932), p. 103, 95.

12. A. D. Moody, *Thomas Stearns Eliot: Poet* (Cambridge: Cambridge University Press, 1979), p. 79.

13. Ibid. p. 81.

14. George Williamson, *A Reader's Guide to T. S. Eliot* (London: Thames and Hudson, 1967).

15. Leavis, *New Bearings in English Poetry*, pp. 90–91.

16. Hugh Kenner, *The Invisible Poet* (New York: Mcdowell Obolensky, 1959), p. 160.

17. Robert Langbaum, "New Modes of Consciousness in *The Waste Land*," *Eliot in His Time*, p. 95.

18. Ibid. p. 97.

19. Alick West, *Crisis and Criticism* (London: Lawrence and Wishart, 1937).

20. Ibid., p. 30.

21. Ibid., p. 31.

22. Ibid., p. 4.

23. Sigmund Freud, *The Interpretation of Dreams*, trans. James Strachey, in *The Standard Edition of the Complete Psychological Works* (London: Hogarth Press, 1953), 5: 489.

24. Ibid., p. 490.

25. Ibid., p. 517.

26. Freud, *Works*, 4. 280.

27. John Casey, *The Language of Criticism* (London: Methuen, 1967).

28. T. S. Eliot, "Ben Jonson," in *Selected Essays* (London: Faber and Faber, 1951), p. 148.

29. William Carlos Williams, *The Autobiography of William Carlos Williams* (New York: Random House, 1951), p. 174. Williams also specifically refers to the classroom as the destination of the poem, and possibly for all new poetry.

30. Jacques Lacan, *Ecrits: A Selection*, trans. Alan Sheridan (London: Tavistock, 1977), p. 50.

31. T. S. Eliot, *The Waste Land: A Facsimile and Transcript of the Original Drafts*, ed. V. Eliot (London: Faber and Faber, 1972), p. 27.

32. T. S. Eliot, *The Waste Land*, in *Collected Poems: 1909–1962* (London: Faber and Faber, 1963).

33. Margaret Sanger, *My Fight for Birth Control* (New York: Farrar Rinehart, 1931), in *The Feminist Papers: From Adams to De Beauvoir*, ed. Alice S. Rossi (New York: Columbia University Press, 1973), pp. 522–523.

34. Ibid., p. 525.

35. Margaret Sanger, *Woman and the New Race* (New York: Brentano, 1920), in Rossi, *The Feminist Papers*, p. 535.

36. Margaret Sanger, *Family Limitation* (pamphlet) (New York, 1917), in Rossi, *The Feminist Papers*, p. 520.

37. Sheila Rowbotham, *Hidden from History* (London: Pluto Press, 1975), p. 150.

38. Ibid., p. 120.

39. Ibid., p. 124.

40. Alexandra Kollontai, "Sexual Relations and the Class Struggle" (1911/1920), quoted in Cathy Porter, *Alexandra Kollontai: A Biography* (London: Virago, 1980), p. 318.

41. V. I. Lenin, quoted in Gail Warshofsky Lapidus, *Women in Soviet Russia* (Berkeley: University of California Press, 1978), p. 88.

42. *The Waste Land facsimile*, p. 93.

43. Claire Pajacowska, "The Heterosexual Presumption," *Screen* 21, no. 3 (1981): 89.

44. Ibid., p. 90.

45. Jacques Lacan, *Ecrits*, p. 285.

46. T. S. Eliot, "Tradition and the Individual Talent," *Selected Essays*, p. 13.

47. Freud, "The Uncanny," *Works*, 17: 234.

48. Ibid., p. 244.

49. Although for the purposes of this paper I have not distinguished between versions of the story by Chretien de Troyes, Wolfram von Eschenbach, and others, the distinctions are of course very important. "Perceval" by Charles Mela, in *Yale French Studies* 55/56 (1977), gives a useful psychoanalytic reading of Chretien's story, which sharpens distinctions only outlined here.

50. Jesse Weston, *From Ritual to Romance* (Garden City, N.Y.: Doubleday, 1957), p. 186.

51. Leavis, *New Bearings in English Poetry*, p. 106.

52. Weston, *From Ritual to Romance*, p. 186

53. Ibid., p. 163.

54. Jack Spicer, "The Book of Galahad: part 4," *The Holy Grail*, in *The Collected Books of Jack Spicer*, ed. Robin Blaser (Los Angeles: Black Sparrow Press, 1975), p. 207.

55. Ludwig Wittgenstein, *Philosophical Investigations*, trans. G. E. M. Anscombe (Oxford: Basil Blackwell, 1976), p. 50, no. 126.

56. Ibid., p. 47, no. 111.

57. Jack Spicer, "The Book of Gawain: 3," *Collected Books*, p. 188.

58. Leavis, *New Bearings in English Poetry*, p. 91.

59. Jack Spicer, "The Book of Lancelot: 7," *Collected Books*, p. 197.

60. Richard Huelsenbeck, from *En Avant Dada: A History of Dadaism* (1920), in *Theories of Modern Art*, ed. Herschel B. Chipp (Berkeley: University of California Press, 1968), p. 379.

61. Tristan Tzara, "Lecture on Dada" (1924), in *Theories of Modern Art*, p. 385.

62. Tristan Tzara, "Manifeste de Monsieur Anti-Pyrine," *Oeuvres complètes* (Paris: Flammarion, 1975), 1: 357. The quotation "ne signifie rien" comes from "Manifeste Dada 1918," p. 360 in *Oeuvres*.

63. Tzara, "Droguerie Conscience," *Oeuvres*, p. 96.

64. Tzara, "Printemps," *Oeuvres*, p. 106.

65. Jeremy Prynne, "L'Extase de M. Poher," in *Poems* (Edinburgh-London: Agneau 2, distributed by SPD Inc., 1784 Shattuck Ave., Berkeley, Cal. 94709; 1982), p. 161.

8

CAUGHT IN THE ACT OF READING

Samuel Weber

W hether or not the work of Wolfgang Iser is indeed, as he claims, phenomenological may be debated; what is beyond doubt, however, is that it is definitely a phenomenon. Since the generation of Auerbach and Curtius, no German-language literary critic has enjoyed anything like the success accorded the author of *The Implicit Reader* and *The Act of Reading*, if success can be measured in terms of sales or of ongoing discussion in journals such as *Diacritics*.[1] It is true, of course, that Iser writes on English texts and is therefore accessible to a larger audience in the Anglo-American sphere than would be the case of a critic working entirely within the bounds of German literature. But this hardly suffices to account for the wide interest accorded Iser's work here (and elsewhere). For the fact is that, especially in his theoretical writings, Iser is not easy. His critical position derives in large part from a tradition (Husserl, Ingarden, the group "Poetics and Hermeneutics") that has remained outside the mainstream of North American critical theory, where his work has found its greatest resonance. Furthermore, his style of writing, no less than his style of theorizing, would hardly seem conducive to the wide response his work has evoked. Indeed, one would rather have expected a reaction such as that voiced by Stanley Fish, for whom Iser's theory "is finally nothing more than a loosely constructed network of pasted-together contradictions; push it hard at any point, and it immediately falls apart."[2] And yet even a reader as hard-headed as Fish has difficulty in escaping the seductive charms of what he himself acknowledges, however ironically, to be a "marvelous machine."[3] For however categorically Fish condemns *The Act of Reading*, he finally resorts to Iser's own categories in order to dismiss him. Iser's theory, Fish contends, is like the very literature it describes, "full of gaps (that) the reader is invited to fill . . . in his own way." And this, Fish concludes, is why "no one will ever be afraid of Wolfgang Iser."[4] For Iser, Fish asserts, "pulls the sting from pain," and indeed, who would be better qualified to judge than the author of *Is There a Text in this Class*? But what, then of that *wound* that Iser, no less than Fish, claim to treat? In a culture as given to painkillers as is our own, the question is of more than local interest. The following remarks attempt to indicate a possible response.

I

The question is no more alien to Iser than to Fish. From the very first, *The Act of Reading* presents itself both as a diagnosis of a discipline in crisis and as a remedy. Traditional literary criticism, Iser announces in his opening pages, "has clearly had its day" (10) — and none too soon. For the day of this tradition is well on its way to becoming a long day's journey into night. "The referential reduction of fictional texts to a single 'hidden' meaning" — Iser's description of traditional literary interpretation — has not merely outlived its usefulness: its continuation poses a threat to the very survival of literary criticism as a discipline. This is so for two reasons. First, traditional hermeneutics, increasingly incapable of reducing the complexities of modern art to its norms of unity, order, and harmony, has begun to "interpret itself instead of interpreting the art" (13). By thus usurping the (traditional) prerogative of its object, Iser contends, to which it was "originally subservient," such interpretation runs the risk of becoming solipsistic and thereby losing its raison d'être. Second, the traditional conception of the work of art as a repository of univocal meaning has historically contradicted itself by failing to produce critical consensus. And yet this very ideal, Iser argues, would, if ever realized, mean the end of criticism as a vital enterprise: "For what can be the function of interpretation if its sole achievement is to extract the meaning and leave behind an empty shell?" (5).

Traditional criticism is thus damned if it does and damned if it doesn't: success would be suicide and failure is fatal. If such criticism nonetheless survives, Iser remarks, it is because it lives — parasitically — off the very insecurity it perpetuates. Placed on the defensive both by modern art itself and by the contradictions inherent in its own enterprise, the traditional critic clings all the more stubbornly to the very norms that have helped produce the dilemma, but which also appear to offer "a high degree of assurance" (17). However, the cure is not merely worse than the disease: it *is* the disease, since it reproduces and augments the insecurities it claims to remove.

If this is the problem, as Iser diagnoses it, the solution he proposes is for the critic to stop looking for hidden meaning in texts and to concentrate instead upon the process by which meanings are produced. The critic, Iser argues, should replace the traditional "referential model . . . by an operational one" (14).

What Iser recommends, then, is that the patient become a clinician: instead of working "to explain a work," the critic should "reveal the conditions that bring about its various possible effects." In this way the critic need no longer "fall into the fatal trap of trying to impose one meaning on his reader," and instead—in the words of T. S. Eliot—"simply elucidate: the reader will form the correct judgment for himself" (8). But is it really so simple to "simply elucidate"? And will the reader "form the correct judgment for himself"? The struggle to resolve these questions in the affirmative constitutes the major effort of *The Act of Reading*. However the reader may judge its success, what is clear from the start is that the stakes are high. For beneath Iser's measured and reassuring tone, there is no mistaking the sense of urgency: literary criticism will either follow the direction laid down or continue along its suicidal path until it is no more.

But if contemporary criticism is thus in critical condition, the cure, Iser assures us, is fortunately close at hand. It begins with the simple recognition that "it is in the reader that the text comes to life" (19). *The Act of Reading* is nothing less than Iser's attempt to describe this birth. Before taking it up in detail, it may be useful to invoke an image, or rather scenario, in order to depict the conception of reading that emerges in the course of the book, mindful, of course, of the simplifications that any such imaginary analogy must inevitably entail. But since reading, according to Iser, is inseparable from the production of images, I offer the following as an image of *The Act of Reading*:

> Imagine a room containing a box that is suspended from the ceiling; not far from the box, an individual is seated on the floor. At a given moment the box opens slightly, and, one by one, in orderly sequence, pieces of a picture-puzzle begin to fall upon the ground. The individual picks up one piece after the other, studies them, and then tries to fit them together. S/he thus forms figures, gestalten, which s/he in turn seeks to combine into larger units. Some pieces fit, others do not. As the pieces accumulate, the player must at times disassemble certain of the already assembled units in order to integrate the new pieces into more comprehensive combinations. In fitting the pieces together, s/he is guided by a variety of factors. First,

there are the objects depicted upon the individual pieces; certain pieces are easily recognizable, for they represent familiar objects; others are more obscure and must be put aside until a place for them can be found. Second, the player is guided by the contours of the individual pieces, which indicate possibilities of their being matched with other pieces. Finally, and perhaps most important, there is the conviction that every puzzler shares, and which reflects what may be described as the basic, unwritten rule of picture-puzzles: the belief that they are *complete*, that they form a whole. (If not, the puzzler would be entitled to a refund — or to another puzzle.) As with any good puzzle, the fun is measured by the difficulties encountered — and surmounted. So, too, with reading, for it is precisely by dint of the obstacles overcome in the assemblage of the text (the puzzle) that the player becomes aware of previous expectations and is able to transcend them.

This image of the act of reading as a picture-puzzle game is, of course, itself neither complete nor entirely adequate. But despite its obvious limitations, it does direct our attention toward some of the more prevalent features of reading as Iser describes it. The first of these is the importance of visualization: notwithstanding his use of the term "text," Iser conceives reading as essentially a process of visualization (or image-construction). The text is first and foremost something to be *seen* (and something that in turn *sees*). It is constituted by "perspectives," which offer the reader "a channelled view of an object" (113). These "perspectives" or "segments" are "given" to the reader even before s/he begins to read, or rather, as the first step of that process. These "perspectives" give reading its start, as it were, but as such, they must be conceived as already constituted *before* reading itself begins to operate. As perspectives, they offer the reader a double view: "a particular view of the intended object . . . and also a view on the other perspectives" (96).[5] Like the pieces of the picture-puzzle, the perspectival segments that constitute the elements of the text are already constituted and directed by *another intention*, directed at an "object," before they meet the reader's eye. Indeed, the reader only can set eyes on the text, in this sense, because the latter is *already* the expression of that other intention, and as such, predetermined or "given." We shall return to this later.

In any case, the process of reading, as Iser construes it, begins with visualization, and it also ends in visualization: in establishing the connections between the various perspectives, in revising and reassembling their relationships, the reader constructs an "aesthetic object," which represents a totalization of the aspects of the text. Such a totalization includes, as it were, the difficulties encountered by the reader, who "sees" not merely the imaginary object s/he produced, but also himself in the process of production. S/he recognizes the limits of previous experience and expectations, and transcends them in following out the directives of the text, which moves, ineluctably, toward its own "actualization": "The observer is . . . involved and he watches himself being involved" (134).

The process of reading thus entails a progressive growth of *insight*: of the reader into the text as something *other* than himself, and into himself as one who is transformed by this encounter with the text. But this transformation and self-transcendence is only possible, Iser stresses, because of the power that the text has *to control* the responses of the reader: "Only the controlled observation of that which is instigated by the text makes it possible for the reader to formulate a reference for what he is restructuring" (134). But such "controlled observation" in turn is only possible because it is the text that is the *instigator*, and not the reader.

Thus, Iser's injunction to his readers to recognize the vital role of the reader — that is, of themselves — in bringing the text to life is in fact more complex than it seems. For if the reader can be said to vivify the text, it is only the power of the text which can guarantee that what the reader brings to life is, in truth, the text — and not *something else*.

There is, in short, a priority of the text over the reader, although both are obviously indispensable parts of the act of reading. The priority consists in the presumption that the text is already present, as potentiality, when the reader appears upon the scene. Indeed, the reader can only be said to *actualize* the text inasmuch as the latter is understood to be *potentially present*, in the "perspectives" and "segments" that are *already there*, waiting to be read. This potential presence of the text, prior to its contact with the reader, brings us to the second basic point Iser's account of the reading process shares with the picture-puzzle. This relates to what I have called the unwritten but basic rule of picture-puzzles, which holds equally for the text as Iser conceives it: both, picture-puzzle and text, are construed as potential wholes, as *totalities*: possessing the principle of their coherence within themselves. As opposed to the picture-puzzle, of course, the text, Iser argues, can be assembled in various ways; however, those different possibilities will all be framed, as it were, by the contours established by the originally existing segments of the text "itself." In this sense, Iser can repeatedly insist both that the textual segments "are aspects of a totality that the reader must assemble," but also that "in assembling it he will occupy the position set out for him" (141). Indeed, it is only in occupying the "position set out for him" *by the text* as totality in *potentia* that the reader can even be said to be reading at all, and not simply fantasizing, hallucinating, or dreaming.

However active, therefore, the role of the reader may be, the range of his activities is carefully controlled, in advance and throughout, for "the written text contains a sequence of aspects which imply a totality," and it is this — *and nothing else!* — which "must be assembled in the course of reading" (151).

The relation of reader and text is thus by no means reciprocal or symmetrical. For there can be no doubt that, for Iser, it is the text that controls and defines the possibility of its totalization by readers. The only question, then, is: *who — or what — controls the text?*

II

The Act of Reading claims to offer, as its subtitle indicates, "A Theory of Aesthetic Response." This theoretical undertaking, Iser asserts, is to be understood as a "construction," one which at the same time is a "description of the operations by which aesthetic response is set in motion through the reading-process" (x). Since this description is designed to "provide a framework" that will "enable us to assess individual realizations and interpretations of a text in relation to the conditions that have governed them" (x), the theoretical construction itself must be independent of what it seeks to describe and to frame. Reading, construed as the process by which the potentialities of a text are actualized, must comprise the *object* of the theory, not its method.

Iser is therefore understandably reluctant to get involved in interpretive squabbles concerning the reading of individual texts, for it is just such squabbling that *The Act of Reading* seeks to transcend and to bring under control, by presenting its theory as an arbiter designed "to facilitate intersubjective discussion of individual interpretations" (x). Since Iser hopes "to focus upon the assumptions that underlie" individual readings *in general*, and thus "to promote reflection on presuppositions operative both in reading and interpreting" (x), it is evident that his own theoretical effort must at all costs avoid getting bogged down in what it seeks to describe: "individual interpretation."

And yet, despite all of its efforts to remain within the sphere of theoretical construction and description, *The Act of Reading* cannot entirely avoid . . . reading. This is a cause of some concern. For if what purports to be a *general* theory of reading must also partake or participate in what are inevitably *individual* readings, the very project of "describing" reading as such can no longer be taken for granted. The *general* validity of the *theory* will depend upon the *particular readings* from which it is *generated*. This is a question that Iser seeks to side-step in the Preface to his book, by asserting that the individual readings invoked "are not meant as interpretations of a text, but simply serve the purpose of clarification" (x). But the problem is not so simple. For if these readings are to be regarded not as "interpretations" of the texts they claim to read, but only as "clarification," the question is: *what* can they be said thus to clarify? Once reading in general has been determined as the "actualization" of a text, can a reading that is not an interpretation by considered to be a *reading at all?* Once their status as interpretation is bracketed, all that such "readings" *clarify* is the *intentions* that inform *The Act of Reading*: what its author *meant to say*. But since what the author *does* say, again and again, is that reading is the actualization of the *text*, how can he hope to clarify this by the use of readings that may not actualize (i.e., interpret) the texts they purport to "read"?

Such questions compel us to take a closer look at the way in which individual readings operate within the overall economy of Iser's theoretical discourse. These readings are of two kinds: first, there are those that address literary texts, and it is these that are said to be not interpretations, but merely illustrations. Second, there is another kind of reading to be found in *The Act of Reading*, one which addresses theoretical texts. Of his readings of such texts, Iser has nothing explicit to say; perhaps he does not even consider them to be readings at all. At any rate, it would be difficult to regard them as mere "clarification" or "illustration" of the theory, since they contribute directly to its elaboration. Let us therefore examine first an instance of Iser reading one such theoretical text, and then turn to his reading of a literary work, in order to discover what happens when *The Act of Reading* reads.

To begin with, it should be noted that Iser's use of theoretical texts hardly appears to be a "reading" at all. Rather, it takes the form of what might be called "authoritative citation." A theoretical text is cited, reinscribed, often only as a phrase, in order to articulate, substantiate, or indicate a position then assumed by *The Act of Reading*. Such abbreviated citation presents the reader with the end-result of a process that has been pursued elsewhere. This procedure is, of course, by no means peculiar to Iser; it is characteristic of the manner in which literary critics or theorists generally read nonliterary texts. What is remarkable about Iser's "use" of his theoretical authorities is the strange way in which it exemplifies the theory under construction. Such *exemplification*, however, as we shall see, is by no means the same as *confirmation*.

The instance I want to address occurs in the course of Iser's discussion of "consistency-building," a term he borrows to designate the spontaneous, preconscious effort of the reader to make sense of the text. Consistency-building, for Iser, is both that which "involves" the reader in the text and also "the habit which underlies all comprehension" (129). In his attempt to understand the text, the reader assembles its diverse elements into figures and configurations, into gestalten. Such gestalt-formation entails both the *selection* of certain elements and the *exclusion* of others. A tension thus results between the "formulated gestalten," which serve to establish consistency, and their excluded "shadows," which continue to "bombard" them and "thus bring about a reorientation of our acts of apprehension" (126). The problem that thereby emerges concerns the status of such "reorientation." On the one hand, it too must depend upon new selections and exclusions, something that Iser, in an earlier chapter, has already acknowledged: "In order to orient ourselves we constantly and automatically leave things out" (84). On the other hand, however, if consistency-building is a process that leads to "comprehension"—which it must be, since reading, for Iser, is conceived as the progressive "actualization" or "totalization" of the text—then such reorientation must also entail, necessarily and in principle, an increase in insight, commensurate with the unfolding of the text in and through the reader's response.

It is in this context that Iser "reads"—that is, cites—a remark of Gombrich, approvingly it would seem: "Gombrich is right when he says: Whenever 'consistent reading suggests itself . . . illusion takes over' " (124). Iser then makes the following comments about the citation:

> Consistency-building itself is not an illusion-making process, but consistency comes about through gestalt groupings, and these contain traces of illusion [*ein illusionäres Moment*] in so far as their closure—since it is based on selection—is not characteristic of the text itself, but only represents a configurative meaning. (124)

While thus apparently citing Gombrich as an authoritative source, Iser rejects the unsettling implications of his assertion that consistency-building necessarily and structurally entails illusion and projection. For were this to hold, consistency-building could no longer be considered "the indispensable basis for all acts of comprehension," since all such acts would only be accomplished at the cost of new sets of exclusions. This in turn would call into question the power of the "text" to control the ideational acts of its readers, since the latter's involvement *in* the text would be indistinguishable from the reader's projection *of* the text. And thus, the very notion of "the text itself" — the notion of a text possessing a "self," *in potentia* — would be radically undermined. Iser's reading of Gombrich thereby *exemplifies* the very process under discussion: it *selects* the description of consistency-building as a process of selection and exclusion and at the same time seeks to *exclude* Gombrich's conclusion that "illusion takes over." But his exclusion of illusion returns to "bombard" the "gestalt" that excludes it; Iser's effort to include exclusion by declaring it to be a "*Moment*" — that is, a part of a more comprehensive process of totalization — supposes a standpoint situated *outside* the process he is seeking to describe. In order for illusion and exclusion to be mere "moments" of a process that transcends them, they must be recognized as such by the reader. To support this contention, Iser is drawn to cite Gombrich once again. But as before, his citation exemplifies the problem rather than providing a solution:

> Though we may be intellectually aware of the fact that any given experience *must* be an illusion, we cannot, strictly speaking, watch ourselves having an illusion. (127)

Whereas Gombrich here states that we can never entirely *distance* ourselves fully from the "illusions" in which the desire to be *consistent* inevitably involves us, Iser 'reads' the passage in order to assert the very opposite conclusion:

> Here illusion means our own projections, which are our share in gestalten which we produce and in which we are entangled. This entanglement, however, is never total, because the gestalten remain at least potentially under attack from those possibilities which they have excluded but dragged along in their wake. (127)

Thus, while Gombrich stresses precisely the illusionary aspect of consistency-building, Iser seeks to include the projective, illusionary aspect of consistency-building stressed by Gombrich within a process that transcends it. He thereby arrives at a conclusion that is in direct contradiction with Gombrich's assertion that "we cannot, strictly speaking, watch ourselves having an illusion." On the contrary, for Iser the reader can and must be able to "see himself being guided from without," since

> only the controlled observation of that which is instigated by the text makes it possible for the reader to formulate a reference for what he is restructuring. (134)

Indeed, were the "observations" of the reader *not controlled* from *without*, there would be no basis for the assertion that consistency-building is the "basis" of comprehension. The movement of reading, proceeding from one selective inclusion to another, would inevitably entail a concomitant set of exclusions, and progress in insight would be structurally inseparable from progress in blindness. This in turn would exclude the conception of the text as a potential totality, and of reading as its progressive totalization and actualization.

The question that imposes itself here is: does Iser "read" the texts of Gombrich, and if so, in what sense? If reading consists in a process of selection and exclusion, the answer must be in the affirmative. Yet if such selections and exclusions are considered to be moments in a process of totalization, through which "the text" "controls" "the reader," indeed Iser may not be reading Gombrich at all.

But the question is even more complex: for the "actualization" of a text—at least, of a "literary," "fictional" text— is, as Iser repeatedly insists, not simply the repetition of its marks, or the sum of its explicit statements. As "potentiality," the fictional text is precisely the result of its implicit relationships. Does Iser's practice in citing and commenting Gombrich imply that the same holds true for theoretical texts as well? And that, therefore, in *contradicting* Gombrich's explicit assertions he in fact is *actualizing* their potential *implications*? If this is so, what then of the assertions contained in Iser's own text? Can we take them any more literally than he has taken those of Gombrich? When he first states that, yes, Gombrich is right, illusion is inevitable—and then goes on to argue that no, he is wrong, for illusion is only a moment and ultimately recognizable as such, can we take him at his word? But if we cannot take him at his word, how can we be certain that we are taking "him" —that is, his "text"—at all? How can we know that we are not, in turn, being "taken," or more precisely, *taken over* by our own desire to make sense of the text, to read it *consistently*? How, in short, can we determine just where projection, exclusion, and illusion stop and truth begins?

The Act of Reading is by no means unaware of such questions, and indeed it is the need to respond to them that directs its course. Iser's theory stands or falls with its ability to establish the power of the text to control the reader's response, for only then can reading be regarded as a process by which the potentiality of the text is actualized. In this ongoing struggle for control, two notions emerge as of particular importance: the "blank" and "negativity." The former is described as follows:

Between segments and cuts there is an empty space, giving rise
to a whole network of possible connections which will endow
each segment or picture with its determinate meaning. Whatever regulates this meaning cannot itself be determinate, for
. . . it is the relationship that gives significance to the segments. (196)

If the blank "itself" cannot be determinate, it is nonetheless situated in
a determinate place: "between segments and cuts," which therefore
must be considered as already constituted, precut as it were, predetermined. Neither these predetermined segments and cuts, nor the blank
as their "unformulated framework" (198), can therefore be products of
the reading-process. Rather, they comprise its condition of possibility:

The blank, as the unformulated framework of [the text's] interacting segments . . . enables the reader to produce a determinate relationship between them. . . . The blank exercises
significant control over all the operations that occur within the
referential field of the wandering viewpoint. (198)

It is the blank, then, which emerges as the negative embodiment of the
potentiality of the text, and hence, which sees to it that the "wandering
viewpoint" does not go too far astray and get lost. It is the blank that
prevents the "segments and cuts" of the text from cutting up uncontrol-
lably, by enclosing them within a "framework." The blank, in short, by
delimiting the "whole network of possible connections" defines the potential identity of the text and its power to control the illusionary element of the reader's consistency-building.

But this account of the blank encounters the same problem that we
have already seen at work in the discussion of consistency-building. For
the blank can only be actualized inasmuch as the reader selects certain
relationships while excluding others. In order for the blank to be considered a property of the text, however, it must be possible to distinguish between those relationships which are *possible* — that is, which
are already potentially inherent in the "text" — and those which are
impossible, in the sense of being mere projections of the reader, having
nothing to do with the text itself. That it is difficult to establish any
purely formal category capable of sustaining such a distinction is indicated by the insistence with which Iser returns — is compelled to return — to this problem. At the very end of the book, he appeals to something he calls "negativity" to do the job. Negativity is described as "the
basic force in literary communication" (226) and as "the nonformula-

tion of the not-yet-comprehended" (229). To it falls the task of legitimating exclusion; working through what Iser calls "the aleatory rule," negativity "does not lay down the course to be followed, but only indicates those courses which are *not* to be followed" (230). Negativity, then, is Iser's final theoretical attempt to name the "force" capable of *controlling* the illusionary process of selection and exclusion, and thus of assuring that its movement "leads not to diffusion but to a new meaning" (230).

But if Negativity is thus required in order for the reading-process to be determined as insight rather than as blindness, as meaning rather than as diffusion, it itself, Iser asserts, is "to be experienced rather than to be explained" (226). For if he is eloquent in describing all that Negativity must accomplish in order for reading to be kept within bounds, Iser is at a loss to explain just *how* this *force* is able to exercise its control over the otherwise so refractory and refractive selections and exclusions practiced by "the reader."

All the more reason, then, for us to be thankful for the illustrations and clarifications presented in *The Act of Reading*, which demonstrate Iser's categories at work. One such instance is of particular, indeed exemplary importance, since it deals not merely with a literary text but with one whose thematic content seems closely related to the very process of reading Iser seeks to describe. The texts concerned are the novels of Ivy Compton-Burnett, of which Iser gives the following generic characterization:

> The characters all stem from the same background, and so their communication is governed by the same code. Furthermore . . . they ask one another questions in order to ensure that they have grasped what has been said. It would scarcely seem possible for the conditions of successful speech acts to be more completely implemented. And yet the result is continual failure and, indeed, disaster. The various speech acts do not serve to promote understanding as regards facts and intentions, but instead they uncover more and more implications arising from every utterance. The pragmatically oriented speech act of every day dialogue is thus replaced by the imponderability out of which speech arises. As every utterance is embedded in complex preconditions, the dialogue here brings to the fore the unending range of implications. The words of each speaker leave something open; the partner tries to fill the empty space with his own utterance, and this in turn leaves further blanks which again must be filled by the partner, and so on. The ramifications of the dialogue are endless. (193)

Iser is well aware that the characters he so describes are "engaged in a process which would otherwise be carried out by the reader as he assembles the meaning of a text" (193). But the figures in the novels of Compton-Burnett are less lucky than the reader of *The Act of Reading*. Unlike the latter, they do not move from error to insight but from error to error: each attempt to fill in the blanks of the partner's discourse only "gives rise to new blanks," since the "answer will also contain hidden motives. . . . And so the utterances themselves become more and more unpredictable, and the characters' images of each other become more and more monstrous" (193). What, then, distinguishes Iser's reader, as he seeks to describe him in *The Act of Reading*, from this monstrous double in Compton-Burnett?

Iser's response repeats and condenses the theory it is meant to illustrate; what enables the reader to read Ivy Compton-Burnett with more understanding than the characters in her novels is the *blank*: "The Ivy Compton-Burnett novel leaves behind a many-sided blank in respect to what people really are [*eine reich facettierte Leerstelle hinsichtlich dessen, was die Menschen nun wirklich sind*"] (194). If the reader can avoid the monstrous fate reserved for his fictional doubles, it is only because, after all is said and done (and even if in the novel all is never said nor done), there is a distinct and determinate residue which defines the coherence and contours of Compton-Burnett's novels. The phrase "what people really are" is the decisive "operator" in Iser's account of the *blank*: situated ambiguously between an assertion and a question, the phrase attributes a "salient structure" to the text and thereby affirms its capacity to "control the otherwise uncontrollable concepts prevalent in ideational activity" (194). Once this controlling instance has been established, the reader is able to distinguish himself from his fictional mirror-images, "stepping back from [his] own conceptions" in order to "take a critical look at them." But the *source* of that "critical look" can only be a reader who does more than merely read. For the reader who is able to identify that "many-sided blank" has gone beyond reading: s/he has recognized its enabling condition. The phrase "*was die Menschen nun wirklich sind*" defines and delimits the blank as "the unformulated *framework* of [the text's] interacting segments" (my italics); it determines which responses can be considered "actualizations" of the text, and which not. It *prescribes*, in short, *the permissible range of readings* beyond which *reading cannot be said to have taken place at all*. As such, this axiomatic master-phrase cannot itself be a subject of discussion or debate, since it is required in order to define just what, in this particular case, reading *is*.

If the reader of Compton-Burnett does not become entirely lost, if he can aspire to a "critical look" at the text and at himself, it is only because of *the possibility of some such prescriptive utterance, which will speak directly for the text itself*, for its "unformulated framework." In such an utterance, the "negativity" of the text comes into its own: in it, the "non-formulation of the *not-yet*-comprehended" is at once formulated and comprehended; in it, the "not-yet" *is* no longer, the text-potential is actualized in all its potency through the discourse of a reader who is no ordinary reader, but rather a critic, or more precisely, a critical theorist. The critical theorist can establish the decisive framework of the text, separating the space of reading from its other, only if he can *contemplate* the whole, in the potential relation of its parts. Only then can he offer his decisive utterance as both unquestioned description and authoritative prescription, since it identifies both what is (*in potentia*), and what should be (*in actualitas*).

All the more remarkable, therefore, is the fact that Iser's *prescriptive* formulation of the blank that Compton-Burnett's novels "leave behind" — but just where is this *behind?* — in no way follows from, or accords with, his own *description* of those novels. For while the assertion/question "*Was die Menschen nun wirklich sind*" supposes, as its basic reference, something like a generalized essence of human beings, what Iser describes is not *human nature as such* but members of a *particular* social class in an equally *particular* culture, all sharing a code and thus highly determined both socially and historically. If Compton-Burnett's characters, as Iser describes them, are unable to communicate with one another, if their every utterance is caught up in "the unending range of implications," this would seem to indicate not some general "imponderability out of which speech arises," which in turn might be related to a universal quality of human nature, but rather *the incapacity of a specific code to impose closure upon the process of selection and exclusion* that comprises the operations of language. If this situation therefore raises questions, they would seem to involve the relation of *consciousness*, *language*, and (social) *code* in determinate contexts, rather than the nature of "people" in general.

This in turn should direct our attention toward an aspect of the reading-process that has hitherto been neglected. So far we have followed Iser in his efforts to describe that process in terms of the dyadic interaction of "reader" and "text." His description of Compton-Burnett, however, introduces a new element into the configuration. By demonstrating that the interaction between subjects in language presupposes the operation of a common code, the question is raised — implicitly, at least — as to the *conditions* under which such a code can effectively *impose closure* upon the "otherwise uncontrollable" selections and exclusions characteristic of language, and of reading in particular. Iser's attempt to attribute such closure to the implicit, unformulated aspect of the text, which then requires an explicit formulation by the reader-critic, simply presupposes what it seeks to demonstrate: the intrinsic, if potential self-identity of "the text."

There is another place in *The Act of Reading*, however, where such identity is not simply presupposed, but examined and discussed. This is where Iser endeavors to establish the *systematic* character of "the literary text." And here again we encounter one of those remarkable reinscriptions that might, or might not, be described as a "reading," but which in any case exemplify the problematic character of the theory they are designed to illustrate.

Iser begins his discussion of the systematic aspect of literature by citing a passage by the German sociologist Niklas Luhmann describing the general characteristics of *systems*:

> "All systems are linked to the world around them by means of selective references, for they are less complex than that world and so can never incorporate it in its totality. . . . The world around the system can, to a certain extent, be . . immobilised through the *institutionalization* of *particular forms* of *experience-processing* (habits of perception, interpretations of reality, values). A variety of . . . possible modes of conduct is reduced and the complementarity of expectations is secured." (71, author's italics)

Although Iser cites Luhmann here in order to establish and authorize his subsequent discussion of the literary system, he steadfastly ignores what the sociologist places in italics for special emphasis: the notion that the system is formed by a *nontotalizable* process of selection and exclusion, which therefore must be construed as the *institutionalization* of *particularity* ("particular forms of experience-processing"). This is why the conception of "institutionalization" remains *isolated*[6] in Iser's text, which invokes the notion of system in order to argue precisely what Luhmann denies: "The literary text must comprise the complete historical situation to which it is reacting" (80). For Iser, literature is systematic precisely insofar as it constitutes a process of totalization, and it does this by incorporating what the extraliterary system, to which it responds and refers, leaves out. If the literary system is to be capable of performing this feat of totalizing incorporation, as Iser would have it, it cannot be "institutional" in Luhmann's sense, which implies its *irreducible particularity*. Hence, in place of Luhmann's insistence upon the partial, partisan, nontotalizable structure of the system qua institutionalization, Iser derives the systematic character of literature from a governing *intention*:

> Although in structure basically identical to the overall system, the literary text differs from it *in its intention*. Instead of reproducing the system to which it refers, it almost invariably tends to take as its dominant "meaning" those possibilities that have been neutralized or negated by that system. (72, my emphasis)

Through what he calls "depragmatization," the "existing norms" of the extraliterary system are transported, "in a state of suspended validity," into the system of the literary text. The latter, by recognizing just where the blind spots of these systems are situated, is able to integrate and appropriate what those systems necessarily exclude, "balancing out" the latter's "deficits" in an economy of equivalence and of totalization.

Instead of Luhmann's notion of institutionalization, as that which imposes a relative stability through the establishment of particular codes, but which remains dependent upon forces it can never fully integrate, Iser defines the literary text as a system capable of including its (own) exteriority, completely and without residue. And yet, his own "reading" of Luhmann exemplifies how treacherous such inclusion can be. For while *incorporating* Luhmann's text, *The Act of Reading* cannot be said to appropriate it. It ingests it, but does not digest its consequences: the nontotalizable particularity of all possible closure.

Institutionalization therefore remains a foreign body within Iser's text, pointing toward the inevitably inconclusive structure of all (its) conclusions and premises. For instance, that of an "intention underlying the selection" of extraliterary "norms" by the text; such an intention would have to be capable of surveying the whole from a superior, privileged vantage point in order to be in a position to make the correct selections. The notion of such a transcendent perspective is as incompatible with Luhmann's conception of institution as is that of "depragmatization," with which Iser seeks to characterize the relation of the literary text to its extraliterary referents. For Luhmann, such "depragmatization" would simply indicate *a different kind of pragmatics*, which in turn would have to be examined in the context of particular institutions. If Iser carefully avoids raising this question, he repeatedly demonstrates that such avoidance can itself be interpreted as a response to the desires (and fears) of a particular and identifiable group of readers, who have a special interest in legitimating their practice by according it *universal* validity. One such instance occurs at the end of his discussion of Compton-Burnett:

Thus the salient structure of the text controls the otherwise uncontrollable concepts prevalent in this ideational activity. In reacting to *the conditions governing his own ideas*, the reader *can regain the transcendental position he had temporarily lost but had always expected from a literary text*, and so he is able to acquire the detachment necessary for comprehension. (194, my emphasis)

It seems never to occur to Iser that "the conditions governing" the "ideas" of "the reader" might themselves be responsible for his "expectation" of acquiring a "transcendental position . . . from a literary text," which in turn is the condition of that "detachment necessary for comprehension." Iser never questions such an expectation but seeks only to respond to it. "Given the fact that we expect such comprehension when we read," *The Act of Reading* seems to say, "how can we best justify and legitimate that expectation?" Its response is to attribute to "the text" *in general* the power — as its intrinsic potentiality — of evoking and controlling such comprehension. But since *The Act of Reading* must at least illustrate this "power" by reading *particular* texts, it gets caught in the act it strives to control

For the texts it reinscribes and seeks to incorporate resist and disrupt the theory that seeks to integrate them. The result is that *The Act of Reading* offers us the spectacle of its own undoing by repeating the dilemma it endeavors, by means of its prescriptions, to banish. That dilemma involves not simply readers in general, as Iser would have it, but *particular groups of readers*: those, for instance, who have a vital stake in "regaining the transcendental position" they have "temporarily lost." Those readers, who are also the immediate addressees of *The Act of Reading*, can be identified as the professional students, scholars, and critics of literature, whose social and individual identities are largely determined by an institutionalized model of knowledge and learning based on the same universality and transcendence that Iser takes for granted. But this taking for granted occurs at a historical moment when precisely the efficacy of such norms is increasingly undermined by the practice of professional critics, a situation to which Iser refers only once, early in his book, and only in passing:

The moment the critic offers his interpretation he is himself open to criticism, because the structure of the work can be assembled in many different ways. A hostile reaction to his interpretation will indicate that he has not been sufficiently aware of the habitual norms that have oriented his consistency-building. The hostile reader, however, will be in the same position, for his reaction is liable to be dictated by standards that are equally habitual. (17)

The Compton-Burnett-Iser scenario comes into its own in this description, with a new twist, for the noncommunicating critics do not merely talk past one another, they engage in *hostilities*. The grounds for such conflict can hardly be explained by reference to a mere clash of "habits." *The Act of Reading*, however, is less interested in explaining such hostility than in arbitrating it, by "regaining" a "transcendental position." But such a position is only to be "regained" if it can be demonstrated to be already "there," *in* the text as its intrinsic *potential*. If the text can be said to control the reader, it is only because the text itself must be predetermined and controlled by something, or someone, else. If the reader can be said to actualize the text, this implies that the latter must already be actualization in potentia. And the form this potential assumes is that of a certain *intentionality*.

It is only when the literary text is considered to be an *intentional object* that it can be defined, axiomatically as it were, as the system that compensates for the deficiencies of all others, "balancing" out their deficits, integrating their exclusions. Such a notion of intentionality, however, carries with it the implied prerogative of a transcendent position, a vantage point from which selections and exclusions can be made and *surveyed* from the perspective of the *whole*. Paradoxically, it is this totalizing perspective that allows Iser to describe the "perspectives" of the text as "channeled views of an object," as filled-in places between which the "blanks" can take their (proper) place and exercise (legitimate) control over the reader. That place is *proper* and that control *legitimate* only insofar as they can be attributed to, and are expressive of, an original, constitutive, authenticating *intention*, which is authoritative precisely insofar as it is held to be above all partiality and particularity.

This intentional structure of the literary text is so self-evident to Iser that it is never submitted to discussion, but simply assumed:

> We may assume that every literary text in one way or another represents a perspective view of the world put together by . . . the author. It is also, in itself, composed of a variety of perspectives that outline the author's view and also provide access to what the reader is meant to visualize. (35)

The possibility of describing reading as a self-contained act, as a theoretical object capable of being treated in general, as the interaction of Text and Reader; the possibility of establishing reading as the actualization of a text that is, therefore, necessarily potentially present to itself and self-identical before and in order that such reading may take place; the possibility, finally, of "regaining" a transcendental position from which the dissensions and hostilities of critical controversy can be mediated, arbitrated, and comprehended—all this depends upon the assumption of an authorial, authoritative intention expressing itself authentically in and as "the text." If this assumption seems self-evident and is never submitted to discussion or question, it is because it is implicit in the most common gestures we make, for instance, in attributing a number of texts to "an author"; assigning a proper name to designate such texts ("The Compton-Burnett novel"). The act of thus identifying texts to be interpreted by thus inscribing them as *works of an author*, however common it may be, is anything but innocent: it has its presuppositions and, above all, its consequences. The *legal* fact of authorship is not necessarily determining for the hermeneutic status of a text as something that must be *read* and *interpreted*. And yet, the apparently incontrovertible self-evidence of authorship, and the equally apparent need to identify texts by naming their authors, function in actual critical practice to obscure the question of the text itself: to identify the text as the *work* of an *author* is to attribute to it, axiomatically, the status of a self-contained, homogeneous, and meaningful object, one that thereby *authorizes* the project of a critical discourse that seeks to *speak for the work itself*, i.e., in the name of the author.

It is remarkable, then, that *The Act of Reading*, which begins precisely by questioning the traditional conception of literature as a repository of univocal meaning, nevertheless gravitates toward the very position it sets out to criticize. And yet, such a shift is inevitable as long as the very notion of *criticism* itself is not radically questioned. For to criticize is to distinguish the truth of the work (or "text") from its others, and this can justify itself ultimately only by construing literature to be an intentional object, the product of a sovereign and transparent self-consciousness, the idealized projection of the consciousness to which literary criticism itself has always aspired.

Despite the ostensible emphasis on *the* reader, the definite article in its singularity prescribes the shift to come. For it is only possible to *describe* the Reader as a general and unified instance to the extent that one can *prescribe* that unity in terms of something else. That something else cannot be simply the "text," since the latter is open to the same equivocal plurality as is the "reader." No, the unifying principle must come from elsewhere, and it is here that the decisive appeal to the Author imposes itself.

But since the Author, like the Divine Principle of which it is the secular emanation, never speaks for itself, its unity is always entangled with the plurality and disunity of its interpreters, the critics. This entanglement surfaces when Iser seeks to demarcate his theory from that of the contemporary critic to whom he is perhaps the most closely related, Wayne Booth. Early in his book Iser cites the following passage from *The Rhetoric of Fiction*:

> "The author creates . . . an image of himself and another image of his reader; he makes his reader, as he makes his second self, and the most successful reading is one in which the created selves, author and reader, can find complete agreement." (37)

He then comments as follows:

> One wonders whether such an agreement can really work?
> . . . Would the role offered by the text function properly if it were totally accepted? . . . However, the suggestion that there are two selves is certainly tenable, for these are the role offered by the text and the real reader's own disposition. . . . Generally, the role prescribed by the text will be the stronger, but the reader's own disposition will never disappear totally. (37)

Small wonder that *The Act of Reading* has been welcomed in the land that has traditionally fancied itself the home of rugged individualism. But whereas Booth's model of literary creation and reception is overtly theological ("Let us make man in our own image, in the likeness of ourselves," Gen. 1:26), Iser reserves a space for "the real reader's own disposition, at the same time agreeing that "the role prescribed by the text will be the stronger." Thus, a semblance of secular pluralism is produced, within an atmosphere of liberalism, characterized by the systematic avoidance of the exclusions that structure its space. By ascribing such exclusions to "the text" ("the role prescribed by the text will be the stronger") the question of institutional power is neutralized and avoided. The discipline of literary studies can therefore breathe easier: its survival seems assured if only it accepts the "prescriptions" of the text, as they are *described* in *The Act of Reading.* The authoritative force of these descriptions presupposes a hierarchy of — in ascending order — reader, text, and author, to which correspond: students, teachers (and scholars), and finally, critical theorists. For only the latter are capable of laying down the law, of telling the rest "which courses should *not* be followed," and thereby marking out the space of (all possible, permissible, authentic) reading.

But the delimitation of this space never takes place as such, or in general; it is always doubled by the *particular place* it occupies, by the particular text it reads (albeit as illustration), by the particular set of figures with which it seeks to name that original, authorial intention. For despite all its pluralism and its liberalism, a theory that seeks to legislate the bounds of a discipline can, in principle as in practice, suffer no competition. It must establish its unique power *to speak for* the texts it describes if its authority is to impose itself. But to speak for the texts is to speak in the name of the Author, whose intention alone can guarantee that those texts have something to say. The problem, as already indicated, is that in order to be spoken for, texts must first be read. And such reading prevents *The Act of Reading* from ever getting its act fully together. As a final, particularly apt example, will show.

III

"In place of an introduction," *The Act of Reading* invokes Henry James's story *The Figure in the Carpet*, in which it sees prefigured the very situation to which it responds. For Iser, James's tale provides a "prognosis" both of the demise of traditional criticism and of its replacement by a radically new and more viable approach to literature. The two positions are identified by Iser with the narrator, "whom we shall call the critic" (4), and his friend Corvick. Both are concerned with elucidating the work of Vereker, a contemporary novelist, but in what for Iser are essentially different ways. The "critic" is guided by a conception that conceives the work of art as a repository of meaning, discursive in nature, "a 'thing' . . . that exists independently of the text . . . an esoteric message, a particular philosophy . . . or some 'extraordinary general intention' " (5). Corvick, by contrast, embodies a relationship to art in which its meaning emerges not "as an object to be defined, but [as] an effect to be experienced" (10).

From this initial resumé, it is clear that Iser's approach to *The Figure in the Carpet* does not merely identify the situation from which *The Act of Reading* will emerge; it also demonstrates its categories at work. For the working of the text depends upon a clash of "perspectives"· that of "the critic" and that of Corvick. That is, the text functions only by evoking a particular response in its readers, through which the latter can be said to "actualize" or fill in the "blanks" of James's story. Let us therefore retrace this process of actualization as Iser recounts it, The reader begins by embracing the perspective of the narrator ("the critic"). But two events force him to "detach" himself from this perspective: first, in a confrontation with the author, Vereker, the critic is told that his review is "the usual twaddle" and that he, like all his colleagues, has missed the point. Second, Corvick appears to have discovered what the critic has sought in vain, Vereker's secret. But this discovery is never expressed as such, discursively; only its effects upon Corvick are suggested, effects that seem to change his life. Corvick's death, before he can tell the critic just what it is he has discovered, creates the decisive "blank" that both "critic" and reader must seek to fill in. But here, Iser argues, their ways diverge: for whereas the "critic" rejects all the clues about the nature of that blank, by virtue of his historically limited conception of art, the reader "cannot avoid noting the signals that permeate the [critic's] vain search for meaning" (8).

In short, whereas the "critic" "sees nothing but blanks which withhold from him what he is seeking," the reader discovers something else. But this discovery is only possible because it has *already* been made by someone else: by Corvick, but above all, by "Vereker himself," who, Iser asserts, gives the "critic," and hence the reader, "the most important" of those "signals" that the reader "cannot avoid noting." The most important of these is contained in the following passage, which Iser cites:

> For himself, beyond doubt [i.e., for Vereker], the thing we were all so blank about was vividly there. It was something, I guessed, in the primal plan, something like a complex figure in a Persian carpet. He highly approved of this image when I used it, and he used another himself. "It's the very string," he said, "that my pearls are strung on." (8)

Iser does not hesitate to give us, his *readers*, the message that *his* reader, like Corvick, cannot help but understand: "Meaning is imagistic in character" (8). Expanding upon the meaning of this image of meaning as image, Iser observes:

> The formulated text, as Vereker and Corvick understand it, represents a pattern, a structured indicator to guide the imagination of the reader; and so the meaning can only be grasped as an image. The image provides the filling for what the textual pattern structures but leaves out. (9)

If Iser can then conclude that "such a 'filling' represents a basic condition of communication," it is only because he attributes to "Vereker" an authority identified with the work itself: it is "Vereker" who gives the "most important" signal, who "confirms" its significance and who "actually names this mode of communication" (9). And if one were to suggest that "Vereker" is a fictional name assigned to one of the text's "perspectives," Iser would simply point to the figure that stands behind this perspective, a figure that for Iser is obviously *not* in the least *fiction-*

al: "James," the *real author* of *The Figure in the Carpet.* This is evident in Iser's summary of the passage quoted, in which, he contends, "Vereker" emits, confirms, and names the "most important" signal in the text:

> The critic himself gives the key to this different quality of meaning, which James also underlines by calling his story *The Figure in the Carpet,* and which Vereker confirms in the presence of the critic: meaning is imagistic in character. This was the direction Corvick had taken right from the start. (8)

To this last assertion concerning Corvick I shall return in a moment. First, however, let it be remarked that in ascribing the text to an author, conceived as a self-consciousness constitutive of the text, Iser is able to identify "Vereker" not merely as a fictional author, but as the authoritative spokesman of a "real" author, whose authority presides over the text. Through this interpretive gesture—interpretive, and not simply descriptive (is there any such thing?)—Iser is able to present his reading as a mere rendering of the text itself. But such self-identity in turn depends utterly on the text being definable as the legitimate property of an author, that is, of a self-consciousness that "possesses" the object that its intentionality produces. As evidence of this expressive continuity of text and authorial intention, Iser points to the *title,* which is presented as a mark of *entitlement,* by which the author documents his possession of the text ("which James also underlines by calling *his* story"). The fact that this title *repeats,* or is repeated by, "the critic," does not seem to concern Iser, who asserts simply that the critic does not understand the import of his words. But while claiming that Vereker does understand, and that he permits the reader to uncover the true meaning of the story, Iser entirely ignores what is perhaps the distinctive feature of Vereker's response to the critic's conjecture: the fact that he "confirms" the critic's figure only by appropriating it with a new figure: "the very string . . . *my* pearls are strung on." Iser takes such appropriation for granted, as he must if he himself is to appropriate *The Figure in the Carpet* for *The Act of Reading.* For it is only by thus taking the meaning of the text *for granted;* only by constructing and hypostatizing an original, authoritative intention that *grants* meaning; only by identifying it first with the utterances of the fictional author, Vereker, who in turn is identified with the real author, James, that Iser can hope to avoid the dilemma he attributes to "the critic," who "sees nothing but blanks."

And yet, does not Iser thereby *act out* precisely what he criticizes "the critic" for trying to do: providing a discursive meaning in order to articulate the truth of the text? His assertion, "meaning is imagistic in character" remains a discursive statement even if what it seeks to articulate is said to exceed the bounds of discursivity. And it is this very discursivity that is charged with defining and prescribing the range of permissible response that will be admitted as "reading." If this is so, the only difference between "the critic" and the author (of *The Act of Reading*) would be that the latter claims to succeed where the former fails. But what, then, of the difference in "perspective" that the story, according to Iser, is intended to articulate? And above all, what, then, of the future of criticism?

IV

As already indicated, Iser's reading of *The Figure in the Carpet* depends entirely upon the radical opposition he attributes to the two characters, "the critic" and "Corvick": the former is obsessed with extracting the "secret" buried within the work, the latter is aware that "meaning is imagistic" and hence inseparable from the text ("this was the direction Corvick had taken right from the start" [8]). The critic, whose position Iser identifies with the "historical" norms of the nineteenth century, is both vain and vindictive: he seeks only to deprive the author of his secret, his rightful property, in order, parasitically, to benefit himself. "It is little wonder," Iser observes, "that he strikes us as a Philistine" (4).

But if Iser is uncompromising in his judgment of "the critic," what are we to say about his presentation of "the opposing perspective of Corvick". No doubt that the narrator is indeed introduced as a young man on the make:

> I pounced upon my opportunity — that is on the first volume of it. . . . This was his first novel, an advance copy, and whatever much or little it should do for his reputation I was clear on the spot as to what it should do for mine. (273)[8]

And yet in developing a critical approach, it is his older friend and colleague who advises the critic:

> For God's sake try to get *at* him. . . . Speak of him, you know, if you can, as *I* should have spoken of him. (274, author's italics)

If "getting *at*" Vereker characterizes the young critic as a "Philistine," it is *Corvick* who introduces the phrase, defining the former's task in terms of a certain imitation or emulation: "Speak of him, you know . . . as *I* should have spoken of him." The critic's dilemma, of course, is that he *does not* quite *know* how the other *should* have spoken — that is precisely the problem. To speak authoritatively, qua critic, is to become the spokesman of another, an alter ego, be it another, more established critic, or the author himself. But to speak with the voice of that other, one must first *know* how the other *would speak*:

> I wondered an instant. "You mean as far and away the biggest of the lot — that sort of thing?"
>
> Corvick almost groaned. "Oh, you know, I don't put them back to back that way; it's the infancy of art! But he gives me a pleasure so rare; the sense of" — he mused a little — "something or other."
>
> I wondered again. "The sense, pray, of what?"
>
> "My dear man, that's just what I want *you* to say!"
> (274–275)

"Speak like me — speak for youself!" This is the message that the critic receives, first from Corvick, and then from Vereker, "himself." It is precisely the game we have seen *The Act of Reading* playing: in order for (a certain) criticism to impose its authority, it must claim to speak with the voice of "the text," and ultimately for the author himself. But since that author never speaks for himself, since he must be *spoken for*, the spokesman can never establish his authority unequivocally. The authorized text either says too little or too much. *Too little*: "But he gives me a pleasure so rare; the sense of . . . something or other." The other, as author, is so self-identical, so *singular* and *unique*, that any predication would already be betrayal. This is what the budding critic, still in the infancy of art, has not yet understood. He thinks in comparatives, big and little, better and worse, more and less. He projects the hierarchical structure of the critical profession, in terms of which he introduces himself ("I had done a few things and earned a few pence . . . He had done *more* things than I, and earned *more* pence" [273]), upon his object. In so doing he has not yet recognized that the latter, if it is *to legitimize* the professional hierarchy, must not itself appear to be hierarchical or comparative; it must be *incommensurate*, identical-to-itself, and independent of all others. *Too much*: "the sense of . . . *something or other*." The predicate complement does not complete, it only points, tantalizing, toward a determination that is both indeterminate and overdetermined. Or, as Vereker will put it — and his discourse only echoes and continues that of Corvick — "my little point . . . the particular thing I've written my books most *for* . . . this little trick of mine" (281–282).

When Iser therefore asserts that Corvick pursues an "image," right from the start, he is quite right. What he does *not* say is that this image is by no means simply *opposed* to discursive language as such, but rather invoked in order to authorize a particular discourse.

All this is manifest in the final letter that Corvick, shortly before his death, writes to the "critic," in which he describes the project in which his great discovery is to be articulated:

> He had begun on the spot, for one of the quarterlies, a great last word on Vereker's writings, and this exhaustive study, the only one that would have counted, have existed, was to turn on the new light, to utter — oh, so quietly — the unimagined truth. It was in other words to trace the figure in the carpet through every convolution, to reproduce it in every tint. The result, said Corvick, was to be the greatest literary portrait ever painted. (302–303)

Corvick, who for Iser embodies that criticism of the future which *The Act of Reading* seeks to found theoretically, strangely resembles critics of the past. His criticism defines itself in a way no less conflictual and agonistic than that of the "critic" — indeed, its claims are even more absolute, since it seeks nothing less than to drive all competitors from the field. The "great last word on Vereker's writings" is to be both discursive and imagistic: it must be imagistic in order to impose its discursivity as a direct *description* of the figure, or rather face, of the Author. In advancing this claim, Corvick does in fact prefigure *The Act of Reading*, which also claims to describe what it has always seen and known. Its final response to all epistemological prodding could only echo the words of Gwendolyn Corvick, who, when pressed by the "critic" about her husband's discovery — "But how does he know?" — replies:

> "Know it's the real thing? Oh, I'm sure when you see it you do know. *Vera incessu patuit dea!*" (296)[9]

What all the perspectives represented in *The Figure in the Carpet* have in common — whether that of "the critic," "Corvick," "Gwendolyn Erme," or that of "Vereker" — is this conviction: the "real thing" can only be *known*, insofar as it has been *seen*, and it can only be seen insofar as it *shows itself*, in and through its *gait*. But, as the Latin word *incessu* suggests — signifying also *attack, invasion, or incursion* — to be witness to such a spectacle is not without its risks. And indeed, it is noteworthy that those directly associated with the great discovery in *The Figure in the Carpet* do not live to tell the tale. Whatever else may be said about that "extraordinary change" in which Iser sees the birth of a new criticism, its most palpable feature is to be fatal to those who experience it: Corvick dies suddenly, on his honeymoon (a marriage that has been made possible by the death of Gwendolyn's mother). Two years later, it is the turn of Vereker himself; and two pages following, of Mrs. Corvick. The only figures who live to *tell* and *hear* the story of *The Figure in the Carpet* are those who have never *seen* it: the "critic" and Drayton Deane (another critic and the second husband of Gwendolyn Erme). A curious fate is thus reserved for those who, as Iser sees it, carry the message of things to come.

But even more curious is the decisive scene in which the "critic" encounters the Author, Vereker. For Iser, the scene is decisive in that it demonstrates the futility and obsolescence of the "historical" norms that govern the critic's attempt to "get at" Vereker, at the same time providing the "key" to the new conception of aesthetic meaning as image and as experience. In Iser's version, the critic receives a decisive "rebuff" at the hands of Vereker, who rejects the former's notion that "the truth of the text is a 'thing' . . . that exists independently of the text . . . an esoteric message, a particular philosophy . . . or some 'extraordinary general intention' " (5).

And yet a quite different reading of that scene is not merely possible; it virtually imposes itself. If the critic is convinced that there is a secret to be discovered, Vereker not only does little to dissuade him, but does much to encourage just such a belief, as the following passage graphically demonstrates:

> "There's an idea in my work without which I wouldn't have given a straw for the whole job. It's the finest, fullest intention of the lot, and the application of it has been, I think, a triumph of patience, of ingenuity. I ought to leave that to somebody else to say; but that nobody does say it is precisely what we're talking about. It stretches, this little trick of mine, from book to book, and everything else, comparatively, plays over the surface of it. The order, the form, the texture of my books will perhaps some day constitute for the initiated a complete representation of it. So it's naturally the thing for the critic to look for. It strikes me," my visitor added, smiling, "even as the thing for the critic to find." (281–282)

If the critic is guided by a conception of the work as containing or comprising a "general intention," a "thing," a secret to be discovered, his meeting with Vereker only confirms him in this belief. What Vereker *denies* is not that such a "thing" exists, but rather that the critic — this particular critic, or any other — can ever find out what it is.[10] In so doing, he asserts his inalienable property rights, as author, over *his* work, "this little trick of mine." At the same time he encourages and even dares the critic to try. In this game of cat and mouse, as Vereker plays it, the critic cannot win. He protests:

> "But you talk about the initiated. There must therefore, you see, be initiation."

And Vereker replies: "What else in heaven's name is criticism supposed to be?"

The circle, as Vereker draws it, is closed — and, for the critic at least, it is vicious. Criticism, in order to justify itself, must be "initiation." But for there to be initiation, someone must already *be initiated*. The critic himself cannot initiate, he does not produce or create — that is the prerogative of the author alone. And yet if the author is the exclusive proprietor of his work, the critic can only be an intruder, and an interloper: "Besides, the critic just *isn't* a plain man: if he were, pray, what would he be doing in his neighbour's garden?" (282–283).

Vereker, the author, thus plays *cat and mouse* with the critic. And perhaps *this game* is the *key* to the "clue" he gives him:

> "My whole lucid effort gives him the clue — every page and line and letter. The thing's as concrete there as a bird in a cage, a bait on a hook, *a piece of cheese in a mouse-trap*. It's stuck into every volume *as your foot is stuck into your shoe*. It governs every line, it chooses every word, it dots every i, it places every comma." (283–284, my italics).

The critic is lured into the text — which he regards as the *author's work* — just as a mouse is lured into a mousetrap. But the "trap," of course, is that the critic can never be certain that he has *arrived* "there," where the "thing's as concrete . . . as a bird in a cage." Like the beast in the jungle, the trap is *sprung* precisely by *never springing*: in construing the work has a meaningful whole, the critic presupposes an authorial intention to which he can never, demonstrably, accede. And yet it is only the reference to such an intention that can *authorize* the critic's discoveries. The critic is caught, therefore, in an impossible place: in his own bedroom, as it were. For this is the site of the encounter, and both the time and place, as the critic later reflects, have been carefully chosen:

> "My dear young man," he exclaimed, "I'm so glad to lay hands on you! I'm afraid I most unwittingly wounded you by those words of mine at dinner . . . " I protested that no bones were broken; but he moved with me to my own door, his hand, on my shoulder, kindly feeling for a fracture; and on hearing that

I had come up to bed he asked leave to cross my threshold and just tell me in three words what his qualification of my remarks had represented. It was plain he really feared I was hurt, and the sense of his solicitude suddenly made all the difference to me. My cheap review fluttered off into space, and the best things I had said in it became flat enough beside the brilliancy of his being there. I can see him there still, on my rug, in the firelight and his spotted jacket, his fine, clear face all bright with the desire to be tender to my youth. I don't know what he had at first meant to say, but I think the sight of my relief touched him, excited him, brought up words to his lips from far within. It was so these words presently conveyed to me something that, as I afterwards knew, he had never uttered to any one. . . . The hour, the place, the unexpectedness deepened the impression: he couldn't have done anything more exquisitely successful. (279–280)

Having first demolished the critic in the presence of the "ladies," at the dinner table—at which, it seems, with the exception of author and critic, *only ladies* are present—the author, "kindly feeling for a fracture," accompanies the critic to his bedroom, asking "leave to cross my threshold." This sudden, unexpected *incursion* becomes the display of the true god—or, should we say, *goddess*? The distinction, precisely, is blurred by the "solicitude," of Vereker, of his "desire to be tender to my youth." But if this incursion is "exquisitely successful," that success consists above all in *the spectacle of a certain desire*, one which it is difficult to confine exclusively to the realm of aesthetics. For although the scene is bathed in "the brilliancy of his being there," Vereker's *Da-sein* is anything but purely ontological. This Figure is not simply "in" the carpet; it is *on* the carpet ("I can see him there still, *on my rug*, in the firelight"), and the difference is *de taille*. For this little *detail* marks the figure as more than just an image, an apparition, but rather as a *body*, the vulnerable object and subject of desire. Having incurred his wounds at the hands of the other (the Author), the critic now submits himself to the spectacle of his desire: abandoning the effort to speak for himself, he lets himself be spoken for, and above all, *spoken to*, as the exclusive addressee of the Author.[11] The Author thus becomes *his* Author, the image of his desire, "the desire to be tender to my youth." In view of the wounds he has inflicted, such tenderness is all the more in place, but also all the more passionate. The sight of the wounded critic, "flat . . . beside the brilliancy of his being there," becomes a *relief*: "I think the sight of my relief touched him, excited him, brought up words to his lips from far within." Flat, the bodily figure of the critic still presents a certain *relief*, and it is this that *touches, excites,* or *incites* something "far within" the other to rise — and shine. . . .

But the "words" that Vereker utters keep the critic effectively in his place, that no-place which is also his trap. Vereker dangles his secret in front of the critic, with sure-fire effect: "You fire me as I've never been fired . . . you make me determined to do or die" (283). The critic's fortune, however, is that in *not* doing, he lives to tell the tale. And yet, in this *not-doing*, he comes as close to discovering the Author's secret as one can come:

> I scratched my head. "Is it something in the style or something in the thought? An element of form or an element of feeling?" . . . He hesitated. "Well, you've got a heart in your body. Is that an element of form or an element of feeling? What I contend that nobody has ever mentioned in my work is the organ of life." (284)

And the critic replies:

> "I see — it's some idea about life, some sort of philosophy."

Were he to stop there, he might indeed be the critic that Iser takes him to be. But he immediately continues,

> with the eagerness of a thought perhaps still happier, "[unless it be] some kind of game you're up to with your style, something you're after in the language. Perhaps it's a preference for the letter P! . . . "Papa, potatoes, prunes — that sort of thing?" (284)

Vereker, "suitably indulgent," says only that the critic "hadn't got the right letter;" but the letter he chooses — or rather, that chooses him — is perhaps not simply *wrong* either. "Papa, potatoes, prunes" — but also the *organ of life* that figures the phantasmatic object of narcissistic desire: the penis or phallus.[12] Of the god, but also of the goddess. If the phallus can be considered to represent the transcendental signifier of narcissistic desire,[13] it may well be the privileged figure of the "game" being played out here, in the critic's bedroom. It is the game of the critic's desire to discover an object that is ultimately nothing other than *the desire of the critic*, in both senses of the genitive. What the signifier signifies is that *other* upon which the critic depends for his authorization: the transcendental Author, who dots all the i's, and in so doing (re-) places the critic's I.

But it is the outcome of this game that particularly merits our attention. Having dangled his secret in front of the critic; having played cat and mouse with him, and also hide-and-seek; having offered him the spectacle of "the loveliest thing in the world!" the author leaves the critic with the following advice: "Give it up—give it up!" And the critic comments: "This wasn't a challenge—it was fatherly advice" (285). It is advice that the critic, in a certain sense, accepts. Not easily, nor without ambivalence. But in however *perverse* a fashion and with whatever reserves, he now acknowledges that

> I *had* no knowledge—nobody had any. It was humiliating, but I could bear it . . . and I accounted for my confusion—perversely, I confess—by the idea that Vereker had made a fool of me. The buried treasure was a bad joke, the general intention a monstrous *pose*. (286)

It is this realization—for Iser the unequivocal mark of failure—that distinguishes the "critic's" path from that of Corvick and of Gwendolyn. For although he follows their efforts with considerable interest and excitement, he no longer pursues the secret himself. He accepts the fact that he has been *had* (and, we can add: by his "own" desire) and responds in the only way possible. It is a way that a contemporary of Henry James, Freud, described in his study of jokes. The victims of a bad joke, Freud writes, and in particular of those jokes that we call "shaggy-dog stories" (jokes on the joke, as it were, pure impostures), have only one choice: "They mute their irritation by resolving to become story-tellers themselves."[14] They pass the buck.

And this is precisely what "the critic" does, at the very end of the story, which is therefore also—its *beginning*. Having come to the realization that the other—in this case another critic, Drayton Deane—does not possess the secret either, that no one does and that nobody knows any more, or less, than he does, the "critic," in a certain sense, repeats, but also re-places the gesture of the author:

> My compunction was real; I laid my hand on his shoulder. "I beg you to forgive me—I've made a mistake. You *don't* know what I thought you knew . . . I had my reasons for assuming that you would be in a position to meet me." "Your reasons?" he asked. "What were your reasons?" I looked at him well; I hesitated; I considered . . . I drew him to a sofa . . . and, beginning with the anecdote of Vereker's one descent from the clouds . . . I told him in a word just what I've written out here. He listened with deepening attention, and I became aware, to my surprise, by his ejaculations . . . that he would

have been after all not unworthy to have been trusted by his wife. . . . So abrupt an experience of her want of trust had an agitating effect on him, but I saw that immediate shock throb away little by little and then gather into waves of wonder and curiosity — waves that promised . . . to break in the end with the fury of my own highest tides. I may say that today as victims of unappeased desire there isn't a pin to choose between us. (315)

There may not be a *pin*, but there is another "p" that distinguishes the two: the *pen*, which the "critic" has taken up in order to write "what I've written out here." Yet the pen that thus writes *out* is not necessarily the same instrument that expresses the interiority of an authorial intention. Earlier, the critic had asked Vereker about his pen:

Should you be able, pen in hand, to state it clearly yourself — to name it, phrase it, formulate it?

And Vereker had responded, characteristically, by turning the pen around:

Oh . . . if I were only, pen in hand, one of you chaps. (284)

The pen that the critic has finally — that is, all along — taken in hand, in order to write out the story we are reading, names no hidden secret, except perhaps the all too blatant one of an "unappeased desire."

That desire, as Iser has indicated, has something to do with the compulsive need to name which has traditionally informed criticism, and which is very much alive today. The question, however, that imposes itself through this reading of *The Act of Reading* and *The Figure in the Carpet* concerns the status of that naming. For, if there can be no question of simply assimilating the naming of criticism to that of the literary texts it seeks to identify, the question of their common fictionality, of their shared figurality, remains. "Critic," we may recall, is Iser's attempt to assign a proper name to the *anonymous narrator* of *The Figure in the Carpet*. Perhaps, however, the narrator of such a narrative can be named only *improperly*, by a reading that, as recounting and as reinscription, is forever caught in an act it can never quite get together.

NOTES

1. *Diacritics*, Summer 1980, devotes half of its pages to a presentation and discussion of Iser's work. And in the following issue, Stanley Fish notes that Iser's "two major

works, *The Implied Reader* [1978] and *The Act of Reading* [1978], outsell all other books on the prestigious list of the Johns Hopkins Press with the exception of *Grammatology*." *Diacritics* (Spring 1981):2.

2. Fish, *Diacritics*, Fall 1980, p. 12.

3. Ibid., p. 13.

4. Ibid.

5. The "givenness" of Iser's "perspectives" has been rightly criticized by Fish, in the article cited (pp. 7 ff.). However, the perspective from which Fish mounts his critique — that of a transcendent Community, origin, and arbiter of all interpretation — is, as I argue elsewhere, no less given. See "How Not to Stop Worrying," in S. Weber, *Institution and Interpretation* (Minneapolis: University of Minnesota Press, 1986).

6. "Isolation" is described by Freud (in *Inhibition, Symptom and Anxiety*) as a defense mechanism with a particularly intimate relation to the "normal thought-processes of conscious concentration: an objectionable thought, above all one involving self-contradiction or ambivalence, can be tolerated by consciousness on the condition that its disruptive consequences are split off from it. Freud suggests that such a process is at work in all logical thinking. For a discussion of this question see my *Legend of Freud* (Minneapolis: University of Minnesota Press, 1982).

7. For reasons that will presumably become intelligible in the course of this discussion, Iser reserves the title "critic" exclusively for the narrator, despite the fact that "Corvick" is also a critic. By contrast, those characters that represent "positive" figures for Iser are designated by their "proper" names: Corvick, Vereker.

8. The overdetermination of cultural artifacts — here Vereker's novel — as social booty and also prey (something to be pounced on) is only one instance of the more general process by which the established distinctions of a code meant to guarantee univocal meaning and intelligibility are systematically blurred and transgressed: spiritual and material, mind and body, subject and object, determination and indeterminacy, success and failure no longer conform to the logic of polar opposition; they are no longer mutually exclusive but rather tend to double or duplicate one another.

9. The Latin phrase is cited from the *Aeneid* (I.578), where Aeneas recognizes his mother, Venus, and then reproaches her: "Why do you mock your son so often and so cruelly, — with these lying apparitions? Why can't I ever join you, hand to hand, to hear, to answer you with honest words?" If this adequately expresses the desire of "the critic" and Corvick, is it not that of Iser's Reader as well? The new conception of aesthetic meaning as "image" that Iser discovers in *The Figure in the Carpet*, "links" the Reader "to the text," overcomes their separation and allows "text and reader thus (to) merge into a single situation" (9). If *The Figure in the Carpet*, however, figures anything at all, it is precisely the fatality of such a desire (as well, perhaps, as its inevitability). And it *figures* it not merely in the persons and scenes portrayed, but also, anagrammatically in the name of Gwendolyn *Erme* — "Mère" — whose mother must die in order that she and Corvick may be united in matrimony. Or in the name of *Ver*-eker, the author and object of the vision Gwendolyn describes, which echoes (or is echoed by) the *vera in-cessu*. . . . Such repetitions undermine yet another conventional distinction and opposition: that of father and mother, masculine and feminine. Is "the real thing" the one or the other? Or both and neither?

On this point I am indebted to Peter Lock's highly suggestive, but unpublished, paper, "*The Figure in the Carpet*: The Text as Riddle and Force."

10. "I almost live to see if it will ever be detected," Vereker tells his young interlocutor, "But I needn't worry — it won't!"

11. This exclusivity is one of the leitmotifs of the bedroom scene, in which the spec-

tacle of desire is inseparable from the—temporary—elimination of all rivals. Receiving the message of desire as the discourse of the other is, of course, one of the processes rediscovered by Lacan. If *The Figure* obviously invites a Lacanian reading, it would perhaps be even more suggestive to read Lacan through the perspective of this story, in which the relation of master/disciple is so effectively articulated.

12. As remarked by Lock, *"The Figure in the Carpet."*

13. James's work, and this tale in particular, give us what is perhaps the most concrete articulation of this Lacanian theme. Nor has this escaped the attention of readers, such as Edward Gathorne-Hardy (*An Adult's Garden of Bloomers, Uprooted from the Works of Several Eminent Authors* [London 1966]), of whose collection I shall cite only the following passage, from Roderick Hudson: " 'Oh, I can't explain!' cried Roderick impatiently, returning to his work. 'I've only one way of expressing my deepest feelings —it's this.' And he swung his tool." James's tool, evidently, was his pen.

14. Sigmund Freud, *Jokes and Their Relation to the Unconscious* (New York: Norton Library, 1963), p. 66. See also my *Legend of Freud*.

9

UNIVERSITY ENGLISH TEACHING
Observations on Symbolism and Reflexivity

David Punter

M y no doubt contentious claim for this article is that it represents research into the teaching of English in universities. A stress on this claim is necessary because such research, in the sense of work that asserts a basis in empirical evidence, is very rare; or at least, it rarely results in written production.[1] The relevant fields appear to be fragmented beyond repair. There is, of course, plenty of research into education, and even into tertiary education; but it rarely permeates academic disciplines. There is a certain amount of research into the nature of universities as organizational systems, but it is widely disparaged by the members of those institutions.[2] And there is a concept of "research" within English, although it is now being increasingly disclosed as a fiction, built around an obsolete system of higher degrees, tending to reinforce the individualist and amateur ideology that is the site of most pedagogic activity in English, and now being in any case rendered irrelevant by economic constraints.[3] These comments on the political resistance of the discipline of English will form part of my subject matter, as well as acting as a framework of assumptions.

A HISTORICAL STARTING POINT
The most useful approach to the location of English as a university discipline remains that of Perry Anderson in "Components of the National Culture," first published in 1968;[4] and the historical supersession of the 1960s, which has been a major ideological imperative of university life in the succeeding decade, makes it hardly surprising that Anderson's pioneering but sketchy article has not been followed up.[5] His central claim about the societal and pedagogic/reproductive role of English is summarized in the following passage, which succeeds an

analysis of the discipline of anthropology as the first home of that quest for epistemological totality which in turn resulted historically from the failure of the British intelligentsia to develop either a classical or a Marxist sociology of any heuristic power:

> Suppressed and denied in every other sector of thought, the second, displaced home of the totality became literary criticism. Here, no expatriate influence ever became dominant. Leavis commanded his subject, within his own generation. With him, English literary criticism conceived the ambition to become the vaulting centre of "humane studies and of the university." English was "the chief of the humanities." This claim was unique to England: no other country has ever produced a critical discipline with these pretensions. They should be seen, not as a reflection of megalomania on the part of Leavis, but as a symptom of the objective vacuum at the centre of the culture. Driven out of any obvious habitats, the notion of the totality found refuge in the least expected of studies. The peculiar status of literary criticism, as conceived by Leavis and his pupils, is itself evidence of the global anomaly of the system. A preliminary definition would be to say that when philosophy became "technical," a displacement occurred and literary criticism became "ethical."[6]

Anderson's argument, however, needs to be regarded as structuralist in what has come to seem an old-fashioned sense: it deals in diagrams and maps, and there is an absence of concern for educational process, for the actual ways in which a structure perceived, perhaps, by the educators is passed down and remolded by the workings of institutions. Leavis's major tenets actually had very little impact, and now have still less, on the run of author-oriented books on the library shelves which students are instructed to vest with authority. Also, although Anderson mentions the crucial term "displacement," he does not follow up the psychopolitical implications: that this act of displacement has produced an educational process that hinges on a set of classifiable imaginary gratifications, embedded in modes of teaching and learning; and that displacement characterizes the self-constructions of the academics and students who are the participants in these modes. We may hypothesize that the discipline of English is in any case structurally displaced in the following sense: that there is only a very distant correlation between the nature of the psychological investment effected in fictions by people between the ages of fourteen and eighteen, which has much to do with the vicarious experiencing of alternative selves and ways of being, and

with the evasion of aspects of familial authority, and that kind of investment which is presumed by university English departments, which has
more to do with induction into various largely unstated authority structures through the dual medium of text and faculty member.[7] The fact
that neither "teacher" nor "lecturer" would be fully appropriate terms
in this context, but would have to be replaced by a categorization that
has little to do with the experience of the student, is itself evidence of
the displacement of concepts of instruction and learning that is integral
to the university teaching of English; such concepts are uneasily replaced by untheorized notions of "learning by contagion," "scholarly
contact," and other formulations characteristic, most of all, of a kind
of modern alchemy.[8]

TEACHING AND LEARNING

But we can trace displacement, and simultaneously the ideological
purposes that the discipline of English serves, more accurately through
a survey of specific modes of teaching and learning. None of these
modes needs to be considered as peculiar to English; but such is the
social and educational prestige of English that modal variations in the
wider academic structure are often spinoffs from English departments,
and even when they are not they are often referred back to a mythicized
version of English as an archetypal process of intellectual exchange. I
shall try briefly to describe the psychopolitical implications of these
modes.

The Tutorial

The serial one-to-one encounter between academic and student is
now actually very rare, but continues to function in the imaginary life
of English departments, thinned though that often is, as an ideal. It
fulfills various functions. Effectively, it disposes of controversy, first by
privatization and second by reducing flexibility in the authority
structure to an absolute minimum. Since in a one-to-one situation
authority becomes essentially unquestionable (except through absence),
it is safe to invest such encounters with a certain cosiness which fulfills
regressive wishes of the student. For once, he or she has one parent, and
a parent, furthermore, of a kind believed to be admirable, all to
him/herself. The student is grateful; the academic is freed, away from
the exacting standards of colleagues, to be mischievous, even to see
himself once more as young and eager.[9] The institution and its demands
can be distanced, even waved away with a magic wand; we enter a
world of make-believe, wherein there is the absolute security of
knowing that whatever takes place can have no relation at all to the

world outside. In a wider sense, the tutorial provides a model against which the rest of "mass society" can be found wanting, and reinforces privilege, on both sides; tribal dreams of the old sitting around campfires imparting the wisdom of the centuries to the burgeoning generation can be held up as compensation for the exigencies of competitivity, the job market, and so forth. Some participants never fully recover.

The Lecture

The disturbing peer-group demands exiled from the tutorial are removed to the lecture room, where the academic, needing compensation for the implicit suggestion (for no imaginary gratifications are perfect) that his time is worth the equivalent of a single student's, may experience the emotional benefits of textual exposition to a large audience without, again, significant controversy or feedback. Lecturing is a passive-aggressive mode of relating; all fantasy power is invested in the lecturer, while the member of the audience is allowed to experience total irresponsibility.[10] Having savored a spurious adult equality in the academic's study, he or she is now reminded of a childlike state, in which almost no action, including leaving the room, produces any effect on the lecturer. Omniscience confronts nescience, and the text is effectively recuperated by the proper custodian of culture.[11] Together, lecture and tutorial perform a symbolic act necessary for social functioning:[12] they habituate the junior participant to powerlessness, and render him or her grateful for the condescension that may occasionally palliate the operations of absolute power.

The Seminar

There is, however, a sense in which this symbolic activity is incomplete since it rests on an archaic, feudal mode of production. Authority cannot be devolved; it can only be held or graciously dispensed, and thus comes into conflict with what may have been perceived as a more liberal structure of school studies, in which a premium may have been set on discussion and peer-group articulacy. The seminar allows for gratifications more in tune with the team spirit necessary in the later operation of a more sophisticated economy. The justifications for seminar teaching in English are many, and some of them are contradictory. It permits collaboration; or, it exposes the student to the experience of hard competition. It allows for exposure of the leader's weaknesses; or, it demonstrates his skill in manipulating a conscious group. It foregrounds the literary text as a present, tabled object over which all may pore; or, it subjugates the text to the development of argumentative articulacy. All these claims have in common an assumption about the similarity of effects on individuals in a group of twelve, fifteen, or thirty students. The reality is somewhat different, since the seminar acts as a winnowing machine, and, used as an instrument for pure discussion with methodological instruction reduced to a minimum, it tends to winnow in accordance with a pre-existing structure of skills and abilities.[13] Students do get better or worse at "participation," but generally along already laid down trajectories. What is offered instead of genuine development is confirmation of prejudice, which can be very useful in the process of self-formation. Individual roles are readily available—the earnest student, the joker, the brilliant interpolator, the silent majority —and comment becomes shaped to the production and sustenance of these roles. It is significant that a seminar-based system often appears to lessen the amount and quality of literary discussion outside the seminar room; it has been argued that this is the mark of the satisfied consumer, but it seems to have more to do with a willingness to engage in debate in a forum where these fixed roles may be threatened or unavailable. Seminars also permit a satisfying indulgence in resentment between articulate and comparatively inarticulate, and thus confirm hierarchy. On the other hand, individuals must fight to hang on to their possession of the text, or part of the text; they often experience other individuals' contributions as theft or violation, and erect systems of defense within which they may hug "their" texts, or their perceptions, to their bosom. The nature of the symbolic act here is perhaps obvious: that the student is being reconciled to a muscular, free-market view of society, in which you need to fight for what you have and what you can get, or resign yourself to a sullen withdrawal. The department may turn out students in whom these self-constructions are already far advanced, and in whom the experience of so-called choice has already been revealed as a variant of surreptitious Darwinism.

Reading

Students are encouraged to "read privately," or "in their own time," as though certain parts of their time physically belonged to someone else. There is an implication that an essential part, perhaps *the* essential part, of the study of English is incommunicable; and, further, that if an element of richness appears from time to time to be lacking from the practice of the syllabus, this may be referred back to a private failure to water the garden in which the seeds of knowledge have been helpfully sown. At the same time, it is made clear that this activity of private reading is, in unstated ways, different from the kind of reading that may have been practiced previously; it is more informed, more judicious. No information is given about how to discover this pleasure of the text, yet lack of enthusiasm may be regarded with gravity. Reading becomes extremely difficult for many students of English, for it is predicated on an unformulated functionalism, even where this is strenuously denied by the educators. But, of course, the gratification is obvious: the student is being trusted on his or her own, given power over an essential part of the course, even perhaps being allowed to continue to revel in fantasy on his or her own, although this might be frowned upon in public. A definition of leisure is being offered: it has to do with the contradictory requirement that good use be made of unstructured time, even when this time is at all points contiguous with structured time, and even when the content of leisure is heavily recommended by those in power. The carrot is escape; and thus the most sophisticated arguments about the societal importance of fantasy, arguments which have a bearing on the whole of literary study, fall foul of the implications of the very process of learning itself.

Writing

> We may realise that the forms we teach in continue to mirror an earlier world: the lecture, being an image of the renaissance schoolroom, or the Victorian factory, prolongs that model into our students' future behaviour as managers, teachers, broadcasters. We continue to write, and require students to write, in modes which have been superseded by changes in communication: the article, the essay, barely exist outside academe.[14]

The modes already mentioned do almost nothing to help students to understand what literary *work* might be; they all, after all, offer a large degree of optionality, and an ambiguous and hesitant relation between student and text. This displacement of work results in an enormous weight being placed on written production, and at the same time this production is required to fit into pre-established molds. Many students believe that they are being offered an implicit choice: between writing as they would want, and writing as their teachers desire. This opposition is to an extent imaginary, since the first choice is never formulated and the second is rarely given precise limits; this produces a situation of alienation within the production, where the only thing that may be clear to the student about his or her work as writing is that it belongs to someone else, it is not what they would really *like* to write. This is a useful protection for the privatized self; it also protects academics in their dealings with written work, for they are allowed to know that nothing is invested in it. The code thus becomes free-floating: what is signified is never stated, while the signifiers are wound continuously upward on a spiral that often ends in an unspecifiable parody, unspecifiable because its models, the critical books, are often caught in the same spiral themselves. In the student essay, an alienated self, formed according to the imagined desires of the institution, attempts to speak to another alienated self, caught between subjectivity and convention; somewhere a little way away, two people look at each other in bewilderment around the sides of this looming example of unintelligible communication, which appears to have been written by, and addressed to, entirely fictional characters.

THE PSYCHOPOLITICAL STRUCTURE OF "ENGLISH"

My claim is thus that the structure of English as a practiced and experienced discipline may be read reflexively as a text. Anderson should not really have been surprised to find this "critical" discipline lodged at the heart of a decentered intellectual life, for several reasons: first, because a purely critical stance is the remnant of what, more dialectically considered, could be a fully *reflexive* discipline; second, because the particular discipline concerned is that which should, above all, be capable of dealing in a many-leveled way with narrative, and the emptied center that *is* English thus stands as an overall symbol for the refusal of sequential historical truth which, as Anderson persuasively argues, has been the great achievement of the English bourgeoisie;[15] and third, because the displacement of the study of the written and lived culture from an aspect of education to a central pillar of induction is obviously of major importance from the point of view of a subservient intelligentsia. The truly extraordinary feature disclosed is that, as well as converting the study into an anti-creative parody, this intelligentsia has also managed to retain it as the most desirable course of study in the universities; a facade of "development" has been generated, behind which disruptive fantasies can be accommodated and transformed into socially useful intellectual skills — reconciliation, the practice of humility, specific channelings of resentment. The historical role of English in the transmission of a socially stable liberalism has now been transcended, and a far more complex set of tasks handed to literary academics, which involves simultaneous self-vaunting and self trivialization.[16] We have only to think generally about the public image of Oxford and Cambridge, or specifically about a cultural event like the Cambridge structuralism row earlier this year, or about an academic novel and television series like *The History Man*,[17] to see how very successful the university teacher of English has become at colluding in the promulgation of this contradictory nexus of private pride and public humility which is the very model of the nondisruptive modern citizen.

The *text* as such is essential in this process, because the authority which it is said to possess, the announced policy of noninterference between the individual student and the book, is the essential cover story that conceals the real authority relations at work in the university teaching of English, which are in fact of a highly sophisticated kind, and relate to a series of specific self-constructions (which can themselves, of course, also be discussed and "criticized" in a literary way).

What I am suggesting is that the discipline of English has taken on the contours of a model for certain kinds of social mystification; the academic's relation to the text, or to the body of literature, is seen as priestly, in that he may hold the keys to interpretation, or even to a quasi-carnal knowledge, but the student cannot obtain these keys simply by asking. The duty of the academic is to guard a mystery; notionally, an elite of those who display some "natural" aptitude may aspire to priestly status, but apart from that the progress of a student through a university English course is often experienced as a progressive alienation from the text, from the mysterious communion, and thus stands as a model for the degree of control that society may come to exercise over the fantasy life. Intimacy becomes distantiation; and under these circumstances, increasing optionality within a particular course often only reinforces the separation between those who already possess a chart and those who are constantly informed that no chart is available, or, indeed, appropriate. The important categories of amateur and professional, leisure and work, are elided, which circles back to the evasion of a definition of work or task which is a central feature of the impotence of English.

The structure of the type of authority that the academic guards and exercises is intimately bound up with the nature of literary-critical practice. Naming is crucial: criticism, appreciation, interpretation, deconstruction, may well figure as important distinctions within the trade, but present themselves to students as a chain of definitional evasion, as a "bad infinite." The question of what the student is to *do* with a text is classified as a tasteless instrumentalism, thus preparing for a later situation in which the meaning of labor can be presented as an unnecessary question. Types of criticism that seek to address the inner workings of a text are clearly more "dangerous" (intellectually and sexually) than those that merely seek to reproduce value judgments; but it is no coincidence that they are bound to a version of the "technical" that is linguistically inaccessible to the student. Students of English are often tacitly or otherwise encouraged to lodge the essential features of their self-construction in areas peripheral to their actual study, in theatrical participation, for instance, or in amateur journalism; thus the central mystery is preserved, and focus is replaced by diffusion, while the student defines him/herself increasingly as "nonacademic," thus perpetuating the notion of an absolute incommensurability between the activities of the academic and those of the student. Bourdieu and Passeron's remarks about the unreality of "difference" in educational process seem particularly applicable to education in English, and are appropriately situated centrally in the boundary area of the life of the graduate student:

> the same habitus which engenders a particular practice can equally well engender the opposite when its principle is the logic of dissimilation (e.g. in apprentice intellectuals, who are inclined to play the intellectual game of self-demarcation in a particularly direct fashion, the same privileged-class habitus can generate radically opposed political or aesthetic opinions, whose deep unity is betrayed only in the modality of their declarations of their position or their practices).[18]

It is hardly surprising that, in a situation where students (as children) are denied access to the principles on which they might achieve self-differentiation, whereas academics (as parents) claim a precision of differentiation that can almost never be glimpsed in practice, graduate students (adolescents in this system) are forced into a manic search for identity which is nonetheless predicated on a fearful sharing of language and assumptions. Differentiation and identity, the essential processes of metaphor, are confounded, as they are in the everyday experience of the student who is constantly criticized for practicing a kind of criticism that is *always either* too "immanent" (because a totality of knowledge is not anyway available) or too "extrinsic" (because "English," as presently constructed, does not actually make sense without structural support from other disciplines, other areas and modes of knowledge).

WORK AND GROUPS

The approach to the Real is at best fitful, the retreat from it into this or that form of intellectual comfort perpetual.[19]

There are many resistances to politicization (I take the word to be a synonym for an "approach to the Real") in university English teaching; here I want to focus on only two, the evasion of work and the evasion of the sense of the group, and on some of the connections between them. My hypothesis, and my experience, is that both operate in terms of collusion between academics and students; the essential emphases of this collusion are amateurism, which ensures that work cannot be properly conceived as a focus of activity, and individualism, which ensures that groups of people cannot be conceived as operating according to certain demonstrable laws (except a meaningless law of identicality). Yet there is, of course, a body of knowledge about these areas of work process and group behavior;[20] and in the remainder of this essay I wish to suggest some ways in which this body of knowledge might be brought to bear, and to report on an experience of trying to do so. To become skilled in these areas requires concrete financial resources, and these resources are not habitually made available by university English departments; I would therefore argue that the sketchiness of my approach, although reprehensible, is nevertheless unavoidable under the circumstances in which I work, and this is itself a feature of the situation of English studies.

I take it that all groups of people brought together to work on a specific task react by in various ways resisting attention to that task, and that a major reason they do so is that work requires organization and that organization requires the deployment and acceptance of authority. Authority is resisted because it can only be conceived according to psychical models, and thus to accept it would require a personal and group interrogation of the familial past, and the attempt to resist beginning this interrogation is the motivational basis of much human activity. The simplest things to do with the unwanted demands of authority are either to collude with it, often in the hope that there will be a future painless usurpation, or to denigrate it in the hope that it will wither away. The dictatorship of the proletariat and the withering away of the state can be considered as the twin faces of desire; if we wait long enough, parents will die and we will come into our golden empire. Regrettably, we do not have that long; and in any case, in a university expectations are reversed, for aging academics will continue to be there long after the departure of a particular group of students.

The group life of a university may be considered a series of mirrors, whose job is to ensure the reflection of static fantasies. Thus the students' exaggerated rejection of the authority of their teachers is reflected at a "higher" level, at which the inidivudal department ascribes all blame for constraint to the wider school of studies, which in turn refers difficulty to the misdeeds of the university Senate. It also, of course, operates downward: academics in positions of considerable institutional authority (and untrained for such roles) tend to refer to entire departments as "dissident" in much the same terms as those used by individual academics about a fantasized student body. This fear of incipient replacement by a lower level of hierarchy (a lower form of life?) is accompanied by a desire for the feared situation: students will be characterized as difficult and reviled for insufficient independence of mind in the same breath.

Although much work exists on the formation of group myths and their organizational consequences, I have space here only to consider one particular example of an insight into the operations of groups, and to suggest how it might be applicable in particular to the process of university English teaching. This passage describes one among several sources of group conservatism, and concerns the handling of the experience of loss and its relation to anxiety:

> At the same time that [a] familiar and relied upon figure is lost both externally and in the private world of subjective experience, there is also an experience of *anxiety*. From an external point of view this anxiety may be described as a fear of the unknown; subjectively, however, it is a fear of all sorts of hobgoblins and foul fiends that may spring out of the unknown. Where once the individual felt optimistic about the world he was in, as if he contained within him a benign and reliable "good mother" who would look after him, he now feels fearful of what the world may hold for him and very ill-prepared to deal with it. This change from a self-confident person to a pessimistic misery can be triggered off by the loss of a present-day attachment figure, as if the external loss caused not only an equivalent and additional internal loss of a "good" figure but also her displacement by a host of "bad" and threatening ones. No wonder, therefore, that groups try to preserve their membership and sanctify "things as they are" for the sake of familiarity. Changes threaten to remove people or social structures and so to revive experiences of undermining grief; changes also threaten a degree of the unknown which at once becomes peopled with horrors.[21]

At the level of the seminar group, this structure will be most obviously marked in terms of dependency relations. The impulse is frequently contradictory, in a way that has obvious familial parallels: the group will wish to fix the leader into a specific role, but will simultaneously want to drag him from that role, to make him show a "human" side. His authority is forced to rely on either dehumanization or becoming "one of the boys." This relates to attitudes toward the text, which is either talked about as though it were written yesterday by a friend, or as a monstrous corpse. In critical terms, this often manifests itself as an ambivalence about biography: the relation of facts about an author's life becomes invested with taboo in parallel with the "real life" of the seminar leader. Between object and subject, there is no link and very little territory, for it would be in that territory that personal choices, quasi-sexual relations, would have to be made; and it is also that territory which is infested with "hobgoblins and foul fiends," unprogrammed forces that can be avoided by assuming that the leader knows all the answers. The "change from a self-confident person to a pessimistic misery" is, I would suggest, a familiar structure for public student progress through the university, and can also be seen as a characterization of an individual student's entry into a seminar group; he or she often leaves optimism at the door, setting up and colluding with a lowest-common-denominator set of expectations. The consequent conservatism evidences itself in resistance to reflexivity on the part of educational participants: changes that may actually occur in student or academic as part of the process of engagement with literature are outlawed from the approved discourse and are replaced by the forces of static positioning.

DUET: AN INTERTEXT

It follows from what I have said above that there are profound difficulties in developing the university teaching of English by working within the established modes, because they tend to prohibit a dangerous and difficult reflexivity, even though current developments in literary criticism and theory itself appear to permit real advances in self-awareness of process. The Development of University English Teaching project, which was set up in the light of these difficulties, therefore functions through workshops, and its existence is justifiable principally in terms of the actual process of these workshops.[22] Reporting on it thus runs the risk of intrinsic paradox. I have therefore chosen to avoid a discursive or judgmental mode; what follows is an intertext, composed of excerpts from the program for the most recent workshop, interspersed with commentary. Academics in universities and related institutions, involved in teaching English and related subjects, are drawn together for a week; the primary task is:

> to provide opportunities within the Workshop setting for participants to examine and develop their experience and their practice as men and women who teach English or related subjects in institutions of higher education. (1)

The staff, which contains workers in university English and in group relations, undertakes to address itself throughout to this task to the best of its ability; and in particular to provide opportunities to explore connections between the literary and, in a wide sense, the social context, as we perceive it.

> The challenge for us . . . is to confront the context in the terms that literary people use. . . . The sense of loss, and passivity in the face of it, seem to be partly historical. It is as if we were grieving not merely for present ills but for our lost empire and loss of creativity — lost parents or gods, perhaps. Numerous recent books are about the empire, or exist as quotations of books that were written within it: J. G. Farrell's *Siege of Krishnapur*, Susan Hill's *Strange Meeting* (Wilfred Owen) and Paul Fussell's *The Great War and Modern Memory*, John Fowles's *The French Lieutenant's Woman* (*Persuasion*, Hardy, etc.), Frederick Bush's *The Mutual Friend*, *Apocalypse Now*. . . . This is not surprising: Peter Marris in *Loss and Change* draws continuous parallels between individual bereavement, and the effort societies must make to rediscover meaningfulness as they change, now, at a rate faster than the change of generations. (5)

Trying to interpret the context necessarily involves taking account of the present situation of universities, and of the unconscious processes that we (especially as people concerned with the literary) may discern operating within that situation:

> Suppose we ask what unconscious purpose for society — what purpose as a great writer would apprehend it — is being served by the contraction of education now? The contractions, instead of giving birth to new life, are punishing it; and this punishment recurs at other levels, in centres for retaliatory detention, in the unemployment of school-leavers. It is as though there were a general attack on young people, underneath the permissiveness, the declared concern, the commercial blandishments.
>
> The implied myth is of sacrifice: the young (and their mentors) are to be sacrificed to redeem the excesses of the 60s? or perhaps as a way of rejecting the future, ensuring it does not arrive? Yet sacrifice does not involve killing merely: it is sanctification. Perhaps we are seeing the sacralisation of certain groups in society — the unemployed, the young, the black — so as to permit other groups to be unholy. . . .
>
> An alternative reading (or writing) of the situation, a student suggests, would be in terms of propitiation: making sure,

by virtuous thrift and stern measures, that the future does arrive, albeit in a slimmed-down form. Propitiation of the gods would go along with "deterrence" at many levels: instead of an achieved sacrifice, a static threat — to withhold education, or employment, or love, unless the generations behave themselves; ultimately, a threat to blow the world up, unless. (6)

The specifically literary task of perceiving and interpreting social symbolism and metaphor, it is assumed, cannot be achieved by respecting the apparently equally specific separations enforced by the classification of disciplines; nor by respecting the barriers between work and play, production and leisure, which are themselves contingent on a historically particular division of labor.

Our subject is "creative," playful; but how can we insert that into academic curricula? or into graduate work and hence the next generation of teachers? . . . (7)

Our subject is close to "life": it leads directly into socially vital skills — song, drama, the articulation of the unseen, sharpening the ear to the complex symbolisms of marriage, or of management. Yet it is difficult to declare this, even in a university, without embarrassment. Lower down in the system some schools are beginning to fear that English may be designated a luxury subject which the state cannot afford. . . . (8)

We assume then that the resources of people engaged in the advanced study of English and related subjects, and the materials and institutions they work with, are rich in potential; but the potential is not being fully realised. Scholars and students have capacities for creativity, for the generation of ideas, and for skilful work in a wide range of occupations; they have access to dynamic theory; and they are based in departments which are powerful organisations both in themselves and as models of institutional behaviour. Above all, they are learned in symbolic meaning. But constraints limit the realization of these resources. Some constraints come from the larger context of recession; others from the defensive ethos of universities, from the climate of the subject itself or from the inhibitions that an individual may meet in putting his or her potential to work on a text, in a department, with a colleague or student. (11)

Constraints, of course, are always with us; the assumption is that as individuals and as groups we will find the nature of these constraints filtered through a complex web of projection and introjection, and that it will only be by *practice*, within the workshop and within the home environment of members, that these constraints can be further understood, and that development within and beyond them may be fostered.

So the Workshop itself is offered as a model — not in the sense of ideal, but a working model, a text. Members are invited to treat it as the main material for study; to take part in the events and use their contents for professional purposes, but also to "read" their process as a text, rather in the sense that Barthes advocates in Section XII of S/Z on "The weaving of voices":

> The five codes create a kind of network, a "topos" through which the entire text passes (or rather, in passing, becomes text). . . . We are, in fact, concerned not to manifest a structure but to produce a structuration.

That statement is echoed in a book on schoolteaching:

> The primary objective of teaching should be to re create the *primary* virtues of "disciplined" thinking, namely ability to structure complex subject matter and to sustain extensive networks of reference points and concepts. . . . The capacity of the mind to pick out the shape of an event or a fact from the environment, to distinguish figure from ground, is prior to the existence of subjects. . . . Works of art and fiction are good examples of networks of symbols around which a boundary has been placed in order to facilitate intense internal cross-referencing. . . . Subjects are yet more elaborate symbol systems. . . . The problem for the teacher is to devise situations in which students are led to create for themselves sustained structures of thinking rather than merely trying to master extracts of pre-structured subject matter. (11–12)[23]

The different concepts of "discipline" raised by this passage may be vital: that within the term, the criteria of specialization and general applicability have been conflated in an attempt to reinforce the fragmentation of knowledge, and to place barriers between the person and his or her process of learning.

Within the workshop, members participate in three interwoven events: the Development Event, the Group Event, and the Review Event, which serves to provide opportunities to reflect on the activities of the workshop as a whole. The Development Event consists of sessions in which particular modes of teaching are demonstrated and subsequently practiced by the members in small groups: there are sessions on the teaching of fiction, on ideology and myth, on structure and subjectivity, on stylistics, on student-centered learning methods, on "literary practice." This last, which is in fact chronologically an early component of the workshop, aims to develop the creativity of members in interrelation with experience of the formation of groups for teaching and learning; to offer creativity, in fact, as a major mode through which viable and productive learning groups may be formed:

> These sessions will be conducted independently in each seminar group: but there is a common objective. That is, to provide opportunities for participants to engage together in the practice of writing and the formation of a working seminar.
>
> The emphasis, then, will be on practical ways of forming a working group; of eliciting imaginative or descriptive writing; and occasionally on communal reading as performance and exploration.
>
> The assumption is that these practices are related: that attention to people as members of a working group, and to their imaginative and expressive resources, may activate a more developed and committed kind of criticism, and a kind of writing which is related to people: a society rather than individual genius. (20)

There is no space here to move through each of the sessions or foci, but all hinge to an extent on providing opportunities for clarifying the relations between structure and subjectivity.

> The responses expected by the New Criticism, and even its *Scrutiny*-based British parallel, have become mechanical, turned into what Deirdre Burton has called "competitive sincerity." One remedy is deeper subjectivity; another is sharper instrumentation. By attending to structure in specific ways, we give ourselves a set of tools. They serve when intuition fails; they are explicit, and sharable. (22)[24]

In connection with the teaching of fiction, our assumption is that we now have to hand methodological skills that have developed vastly over the last twenty years:

> Over the same period, a major change in the body of fiction itself has been towards a more conscious manifesting of narrative

methods and authorial presence, associated with the "nouveau roman" in France, and in the USA with such labels as "fabulation," "metafiction," "the fictive." John Hawkes is an example of a writer who looks outside narrative conventions for principles on which to establish a type of fiction: when he talks about his work, the connexions with literary *theory* are foregrounded:

> My novels are not highly plotted, but certainly they're elaborately structured. I began to write fiction on the assumption that the true enemies of the novel were plot, character, setting, and theme, and having once abandoned these familiar ways of thinking about fiction, totality of vision or structure was really all that remained. And structure—verbal and psychological coherence—is still my largest concern as a writer. Related or corresponding event, recurring image and recurring action, these constitute the essential substance or meaningful density of my writing. However . . . this kind of structure can't be planned in advance but can only be discovered in the writing process itself. The success of the effort depends on the degree and quality of consciousness that can be brought to bear on fully liberated materials of the unconscious. I'm trying to hold in balance poetic and novelistic methods in order to make the novel a more valid and pleasurable experience. (26–27)[25]

I hope it should be clear by now that there are many points of contact between Hawkes's conception of text and the project of the workshops.

> This [Hawkes's] discourse about creativity is contiguous with other, more "theoretical" discourses: "totality of structure" is central to both Marxist/Althusserian and non-Marxist variants of structuralism; correspondence and recurrence remind us of older magical systems, but are also terms which underlie the "metahistorical" writing of Foucault and others; the materials of the unconscious clearly belong in a Freudian discourse, along with the neosurrealism of the method Hawkes advocates.
>
> Our suggestion, therefore, is that the explosion of theorizing in the last few decades need not place us at a greater distance from texts, but rather that theory, text and teaching can be mutually informing. We think that ready access to the text, and an essential

intimacy with it, are best achieved not by amateur discussion, or by imitating others' criticism, but by practicing the use of some of the powerful implements now to hand. (27)

Whereas the Development Event focuses on actual and possible developments in the practice of university English teaching, the Group Event provides opportunities for a different kind of experience and perception:

Teaching English is not just a matter of understanding and enjoying literature and language, nor of applying particular educational techniques — though both are necessary. It is also something that takes place in a human encounter between men and women in a particular social context — a meeting, or series of meetings, within an educational institution open to the influences of a wider society. What the student perceives and learns depends on many personal, social, organizational and political factors.

The Group Event is intended to open up this dimension of teaching and learning for examination within the Workshop. It provides opportunities to gain further insight nto the processes shaping the life of educational institutions, including the Workshop itself; to explore, for example, problems of freedom and control, structure and spontaneity, dependence and autonomy, involvement and withdrawal, order and chaos, power and authority, masculinity and femininity, and of making and ending relationships.

The "syllabus" for the Event cannot be determined in advance, since it is created by the participants in the Workshop. In some form, however, we can expect to have opportunities to examine:

— the influence of myth, fantasy, and unconscious processes upon the relations between the members of a group or institution
— the ambiguities and anxieties of offering and accepting direction and insight
— the way individuals are assigned roles, or mould them for themselves, within the social system of a group
— the tacit beliefs about learning, teaching and knowledge which shape the life of educational institutions. (37)

It is, perhaps, a point in this last passage which should bear a final emphasis: that the workshops are posited as open systems, in which the learning of an individual cannot be predicted. Setting up such a situation produces frustrations, disappointments, anger; but it also allows a territory within which genuine development might take place.[26]

SOME DANGERS AND DOUBTS

It seems appropriate to conclude by rehearsing some questions about university English teaching. First, how are we to disclose the authority relations that structure such education as takes place? Reflexivity about the essentially social process within which teacher, text, and learner are meshed is clearly a goal to be striven for; but the clear danger here is that the text becomes a poor third partner. Reception theory, it seems to me, can be used as a pedagogic instrument, in this sense: that if the text can itself be construed as a web of actual and potential relations (between author, narrative voice, characters, implied reader, and so forth), the study of the actual situation within which the text is read, transmitted, discussed, may be perceptible as congruent. Literary texts, after all, are from one point of view frozen models of social process, even at the point where that freezing appears at first glance to have been accompanied by a draining of recognizable social intercourse.

Second, how are we to frame modes of literary work? The danger of the Frankfurt-influenced rejection of "instrumental knowledge" has always been that it would be accompanied by a political retreat into a stance of contemplation; and for students of literature, this process, which regards analytical work as destructive, can find resonant and still powerful reinforcement in the ever-present aftermath of romanticism. The equation of dissection and murder can be invoked readily, and is accompanied by a specific division of knowledge whereby that which can be labeled "technical" is exported and downgraded.[27] One path through would be by attempts at sophisticating the category of the subjective; obviously those responses that students regard, and are encouraged to regard, as "their own" are themselves the products of specific educational process, whereas the alternative category of "structure" is actually no less influenced by interpersonal factors within the field of perception.

Third, how are we to come to authoritative judgments on the issue of resistance? Within a specific piece of group educational work, the identification of resistance will always depend on skills unavailable to practitioners of English teaching, since they involve training in the recognition of projections and introjections. There is also an issue here of permanence: to establish a reflexive process within a temporary educational institution may be possible, but this will be largely conditioned precisely by its temporariness. There are deeply embedded resistances having to do with the necessity of institutional continuity which operate against any kind of reflexivity that may appear to threaten the internal and external boundaries of a relatively long-lasting institution, which has come to regard its own authority structure, wrongly, as the essential prerequisite of its existence and effective functioning. The embeddedness of this conservative tendency seems likely to get worse in times of economic and social constraint.

But it is, I suggest, to questions of this kind that we need to turn our attention if we are to effect any development of English as a "discipline" in the socially important sense of that word.

NOTES

1. There are, of course, exceptions: see, e.g., J. Axelrod, *The University Teacher as Artist: Towards an Aesthetics of Teaching with Emphasis on the Humanities* (San Francisco: Jossey-Bass, 1973).

2. See, in particular, N. MacKenzie, M. Eraut, H. C. Jones, *Teaching and Learning: An Introduction to New Methods and Resources in Higher Education* (Paris: UNESCO, 1976); R. M. Beard and D. A. Bligh, *Research into Teaching Methods in Higher Education* (London: SRHE, 1971); G. C. Moodie and R. Eustace, *Power and Authority in British Universities* (London: Allen and Unwin, 1974); A. K. Rice, *The Modern University: A Model Organisation* (London: Tavistock, 1970); *The University as an Organization*, ed. J. A. Perkins (New York: McGraw-Hill, 1973).

3. In referring to economic constraints, I have the United Kingdom in mind, as I shall have throughout; but many of the arguments are, I suspect, transferable in one degree or another to other "advanced" economies and their collective situation.

4. *New Left Review* 50 (1968):3–57; reprinted in *Student Power: Problems, Diagnosis, Action*, ed. A. Cockburn and R. Blackburn (Harmondsworth, Middx.: Penguin, 1969), pp. 214–284.

5. The only real attempt at this task is T. Nairn, "The English Literary Intelligentsia," *Bananas* 3 (1976):17–22; but this does not seriously take on the universities as such, and is in any case marred by a conclusion that is either absurdly optimistic or a badly misplaced irony.

6. Anderson, *NLR*, pp. 50–51; the concept of "expatriate influence" is important, and suspect, throughout the article.

7. I am aware that not all school and student careers are based on the conventional age structure; but, with honorable exceptions, most university teaching of English is, and the shape of British educational policy now makes it unlikely that our small gains in differentiating the pattern will be sustained.

8. A particular example of this confidence in magic would be from a recent external examiner's report to my own School of Studies:

> One candidate whose course work as well as exam paper I had the pleasure of reading showed himself as able as any man [sic] reading English at any English university in the course of a number of years: and he had clearly profited less from seminars than from the generous conversation of the individual lecturer

> or lecturers capable of drawing him out. . . . It looks as though nothing really educates the intelligent mind but conversation between one human being and another.

This has, of course, to remain unattributed.

9. I have chosen to characterize "the student" with both genders, since this reflects both fact and myth; "the academic" with male gender, since this reflects the myth and, to an extent that may fairly and richly be termed tragic, the fact.

10. To an extent, these remarks follow ones made by the UEA English Studies Group (David Punter, David Aers, Robert Clark, Jon Cook, Thomas Elsasser) in a recent presentation. See UEA English Studies Group, "Strategies for Representing Revolution," *1789: Reading Writing Revolution*, ed. F. Barker et al. (Colchester: University of Essex, 1982).

11. The ambiguities of "recuperation" as a literary-critical and role-descriptive concept perhaps need to be pointed out.

12. For the meaning of "symbolic act" that I have relied on throughout, see F. Jameson, *The Political Unconscious: Narrative as a Socially Symbolic Act* (Ithaca, N.Y.: Cornell University Press, 1981), esp. pp. 74–102.

13. This is, of course, a comment not on the ideal seminars described in much of the literature (see, e.g., the relevant sections in *University Teaching in Transition*, ed. D. Layton [Edinburgh: Oliver and Boyd, 1968]), but on actual seminars. See the rather frightening implications of L. S. Powell, *Communication and Learning* (London: Pitman, 1969), pp. 35–45, despite his bland conclusions; and, throughout, E. Richardson, *Group Study for Teachers* (London: Routledge and Kegan Paul, 1967).

14. This is the first of many quotations from *DUET 2: Workshop Programme* (1981), and is from p. 7; see note 22 below.

15. See Anderson, *NLR*, pp. 8, 13ff.; cf. Nairn, "The English Literary Intelligentsia," p. 18.

16. See Nairn, "The English Literary Intelligentsia," pp. 18–19.

17. These examples may be rather specific to Britain. I refer to a "cause célèbre" in which the nonreappointment of a particular Cambridge academic became the symbolic occasion for a reactionary public explosion against structuralism and Marxism; and to the academic novel by Malcolm Bradbury that became a popular television series in Britain. I would couple them symbolically as elements in a process of self-punishment/scapegoating.

18. P. Bourdieu and J.-C. Passeron, *Reproduction in Education, Society and Culture*, trans. R. Nice (London and Beverly Hills: Sage, 1977), p. 35.

19. Jameson, *The Political Unconscious*, p. 284.

20. See Richardson, *Group Study for Teachers*; W. R. Bion, *Experiences in Groups* (London: Tavistock, 1961); R. H. Gosling, D. H. Miller, P. M. Turquet, D. Woodhouse, *The Use of Small Groups in Training* (London: Codicote, 1967); and essays in *Exploring Individual and Organisational Boundaries*, ed. W. G. Lawrence (London: Tavistock, 1979) and *Training in Small Groups*, ed. B. Babington Smith and B. A. Farrell (Oxford: Pergamon, 1979).

21. Gosling, "Another Source of Conservatism in Groups," in *Exploring Individual and Organisational Boundaries*, ed. Lawrence, p. 78.

22. DUET was initiated in 1979 by John Broadbent, with financial assistance from the University of East Anglia and the Nuffield Foundation. I would like here to record my debt to him, and to the other DUET staff with whom I have worked: Joan Coleman, Colin Evans, Vimala Herman, Geraldine McLoughlin, Barry Palmer, Gordon Read, Nicola Townsend, Karen Vermeulen. *DUET 2: Workshop Programme*, from which the

ensuing extracts come, was multiply authored, and is the responsibility of the staff of DUET 2. The present essay is, of course, *not* multiply authored; and it should not be taken as an authoritative statement on behalf of DUET. Cf. J. Broadbent, "Untwisting all the Chains: An Account of the 'DUET' Workshop by its Director," *Quinquereme: New Studies in Modern Languages* (1981):225–230.

23. The quotes within the quote are from R. Barthes, *S/Z*, trans. R. Miller (London: Cape, 1975), p. 20; and G. Chanan and L. Gilchrist, *What School Is For* (London: Methuen, 1974), pp. 92, 96, 97, 99.

24. Cf. D. Burton, *Dialogue and Discourse: A Sociolinguistic Approach to Modern Drama Dialogue and Naturally Occurring Conversation* (London: Routledge and Kegan Paul, 1980).

25. The quote within the quote is from an interview with Hawkes; see R. Scholes, *The Fabulators* (New York: Oxford University Press, 1967), pp. 68–69.

26. For my meaning of "open systems," see in particular (although it is not directly related to the "educational") E. J. Miller, "Open Systems Revisited: A Proposition about Development and Change," in *Exploring Individual and Organisational Boundaries*, ed. Lawrence, pp. 217–233.

27. The specific reference, of course, is to Wordsworth; but no account of the formation of modern British intellectual life could be complete without a more wide-ranging description of the penetration of romanticism and its continuing but changing ideological functions.

10

BETWEEN POWER AND DESIRE
The Margins of the City

Donald Preziosi

In her study of the building habits of the !Kung people of West Africa, the anthropologist Leila Marshall notes that

> it takes the women only ¾ of an hour to build their shelter. But half the time at least, the women's whim is not to build shelters at all. In this case, they sometimes put up two sticks to symbolize the entrance to the shelters so that the family may orient itself as to which is the man's and which the women's side of the fire. Sometimes, they don't bother with the sticks at all.[1]

Cities and their parts endlessly ostensify, replicate, and palimpsest the differences by which solidarities and individualities are cued and construed. In creating and filling rhetorical space with a telling order of objects, the built world is a theater of presentations and representations, exfoliating models of causality in every dimension and at every size and scale. Consisting of the sum of what is appropriatable from the planetary biosphere, including our own and other bodies, it entails positions of and for subjects, scaffolds for the erection of our selves, and at the same time serves as a member of the cast. The city is always the staging of sexual difference.

The truth of the city is that it is forever false. A city is not a city unless it occludes the laws of its composition and the rules of its games.

Steeped in tension, we are persuaded both that it created itself and that it is the creation of a hidden or long-absent god. We play and are played out through the constant metamorphosis of sceneries, players, and texts which both mediate and create scenarios and desires. At the same time tool box, stage set, Wunderkammer, and Wunderblock, the made world works to constitute its subjects by spatiotemporal difference, deferral, and the perpetual occlusion of completion and resolution. With a logic for every contingency, every ability and need, the city is the only game in town.

The built environment establishes topoi so that thought may have topics with which to weave the tropisms of daily life. Unfolding metonymically, anaphorically, metaphorically, and with symbolism, iconism, and irony, it carves from and gives to airy nothing a local habitation. It houses all the temples of entelechy we could desire, packaging them as institutions, disciplines, narratives, and theaters or theories to see from. In drawing a cord across the void so that we may know what is above — below, before — after, inside and outside, the city is a topology of irony, situating us in only one place at a time while endlessly drawing us on to other places, other desires.

Its unfoldings teem at every moment with the burden of the whole, oscillating everywhere between swift changes of desire and direction, and fetishistic consolidations. It is both the trace left by these alternations and the trace that engenders them, the perpetual circuit between opacity and transparency. Child of ideology masquerading as a father without progenitors, the city builds act upon act in the manner of terraces, opening avenues for narration that are forever cul-de-sacked, invariably returned to points of departure and emergence. We cannot think ourselves to a space beyond the city or to a time back before it, any more than we can camp outside language.

In Calvino's city of Eudoxia was a miraculous carpet, preserved in the temple, whose eveyr arabesque, the augurs claimed, replicated in ideal miniature every nook, cranny, anguish, and desire of the whole urban fabric as well as the patterns of the stars in the sky according to their true constellations. Others suggested that the true image of the universe was the city itself, in all its deformity and deponency.

It has become imperative to study together the history of the road and the history of writing. But not as it were with the hope for establishing some unified field theory of voice and thing, nor still less in order to realign all the old concepts in -er and in -ed by interposing some Mirror or Middle Voice between active and passive, or between the city as text-to-be-read and city as that which establishes the architectonic conditions for the emergence of textuality. Nor, it should be added, in order to resuscitate those faded esperantos of encapsulated desire, the humanistic disciplines; the city is not reducible to speech, nor voice to the built environment.

Should there be a "discipline" of the made world in all its variety and complexity? We are heir to a mosaic of instituted discourses comfortably settled into a gentlemanly division of labor across the surface of the visual: art and architectual history and criticism, the languages on cinema, theater, dance, costume, the anthropologies of things and technologies — all those petites semiologies jostled together over institutional space-time like so many prophets conjuring up *in parvo* the oblique glimpses of a messianic portrait hoping to be embodied. Yet it is clear that writing and the city must be thought together; their meditations must be seen to be inseparable, at the same time avoiding the double binds of the game of origins.

Here I find myself at the intersection of other texts, of avenues of stories told oneself or which one has had oneself told in the game worlds arranged by caregivers and others, within which were conjured all those *imagines agentes* peopling our itineraries. Three stories or games are most immediately palpable.

First, the game of the Father, the Leonardo game of claiming that in every whirl of the grain on the parquet floors of childhood one will see all past and future things and worlds in miniature. Set in motion by the "one will see," one never ceases being the *flaneur*, the Benjamin tracing out of his life on the cafe table with pencil and paper, drawing endless labyrinths.

Next, the game of the Mother who with pencil adds ears and eyes to the shadows on the page, conjuring rabbits, wolves, flowers, and, by turning the page upside down, a portrait of oneself. Different laughters becoming ironic in juxtaposition.

Or the third story, in a thirty-year-old anthology of science fiction, of a crystal, translucent city on a far planet, with chiming, crystalline creatures floating in air around the uppermost spires high in the clouds. There are many entrances into the city, but each is shaped like the profile of every conceivable being. One enters the only one possible into a room of expected proportions. After becoming accustomed to the light and air, a further door is perceived which, with some slight contortion, may be taken to a second room minutely stranger than the first. And so on, each space increasingly odd and impossible, yet in due order familiar, traversible, penetrable, and on and on until one's own body is metapmorphized in form and substance, emerging from the highest tower to join the aerial flight of the crystalline creatures, at one in form and substance with the city itself, skywriting what appeared far below to have been clouds. The game of the City.

Vitruvius describes how in the Greek theater there were positioned some three rows of thirteen vases tuned to particular notes, in order to amplify and transmit evenly throughout the great semicircle of seats the slightest nuance of voice and music emanating from the orchestra. Those vases placed on the lowest row were tuned to the enharmonic scale, the middle row to the chromatic, and the highest to the diatonic scale.

This was an attempt to relate the varying distance between stage and individual vase, and embodies the Greek fascination with the relationship between the length of a string and musical or vocal pitch — which is to say between space and voice. The interest is reflected in Aristotle's *De Anima*, where he notes that an object affects the air around it in the same way that a seal affects wax: the object seen progressively affects all the air moving away from it until it reaches the sensitive pupil of our eye, which is also affected, being full of liquid. Although it might seem that Aristotle comes close to the modern notion that vision is based on the transmission of waves through a medium, the impetus for the theory was primarily to synchronize and coordinate vision and hearing, the voice and the visual.

This concern for the coordination of vision and voice underlies our own designs for the theater of the disciplines, itself a synecdoche for the utopias of our urban stagings. Resonance, synchronization, the alignments of texts and objects — the various sciences of the visual (our little semiologies) work in the final instance as potteries for the manufacture of resonating vases. Metonymies perpetually at work on the same metaphor. The ghostly voice in the vase; the vase embodying, disseminating voice along the entire warp and weft of the urban fabric and its several sciences. (The Minotaur always bellows out of sight, always just around the next corner.) In the sciences of the visual, in the game worlds in which we have been weaned, the high priest has always been the art historian with his cargo-cults, his holding up of every *objet* as a landing strip for the Logos.

Do we need to rehearse the dreary decades of our wandering in a logocentric labyrinth? Need we reiterate that the inmates of that maze have long been hypnotized by a graffito on the wall of a cul-de-sac that reads, "since all languages are made up of words and all words are signs, all things made up of signs must be languages"? Daedalos knew what he was doing in fashioning a prison for the Minotaur, no doubt foreseeing the day, four thousand years down the road, when more would have wanted to break in than escape.

Shall we situate ourselves in and among the battlefields of the semiologies of the visual and place odds on the outcome of the contemporary theoretical and methodological struggles? Given the inevitable inertia (which is to say resistance to theory) of the institutions that have framed and partitioned the visual, it has been an easy temptation on the part of these combatants to consider their disciplines as boats that are in the process of reconstruction while being kept afloat — a plank-by-plank procedure retaining at any one time the greater bulk of the vessel. This comfortable and collegial perspective (which it should not be forgotten has always been one of the very enabling mechanisms and strategies of the academy) resonates with a tale told about the ancient Argonauts in the story of Jason and the Golden Fleece. Under divine constraints to complete their long and arduous journey in the good ship *Argo*, the Argonauts were faced with the problem of a continuously deteriorating vessel. However, as archetypically clever Greeks (or as prototypical semioticians), our heroes found that they could trick the gods by replacing their entire ship one plank at a time, so that by the end of their journey they would have a completely new vessel, albeit one of identical name and form.

It might be instructive at this point to listen closely to the argot of the visual disciplines. In all its various costumes, visual signification has been taken to be a nonverbal correlate of an idealist speaker/message/listener schema, wherein the position of the speaker or addresser is taken to correspond to that of the designer, maker, or fashioner of works; the made object or artifact or appropriated topos is taken to be a message or communicative token; and the viewer or beholder or user has been taken to be an addressee or receiver/consumer of message-objects.

There are a great many variants on this formula in the field of visual studies, but almost without exception the maker of a work is seen as addressing users or viewers through some type of artifactual mediation. Of course the "addresser" and "addressee" may be individuals or groups, and what constitutes the message may be as small and as temporary as an eyebrow flash or as large and as permanent as a pyramid.

But what tends to remain constant in this schema is not a set of conventionally agreed-upon units or, if you will, some constant form of content, but rather the topology of relationships among the three categories making up the formula. What tends to remain constant in the visual disciplines as a whole is also a pervasive movement toward the naturalization of this schema, which survives in ever new and amazing forms across shifts in theoretical and methodological posturings.

We need not dispute the evident fact that formations are made and used, and that in certain societies at particular times, maker and user may be different individuals or collectives. And unquestionably, makers and users construe made formations as communicative, as semiologically bounded or syntactically complete, or as components in larger transmissions which can include the coordination of signals in other media. Nor need we dismiss as without pertinence the notions of fields of functional dominance in semiotic events such as the Jakobsonian sextuple of phatic, emotive, metalinguistic, conative, referential, and poetic or aesthetic orientations, or even the multifunctional "horizons" of Mukařovský's schema for architecture, upon which the Jakobsonian system was metaphorically modeled thirty years later.

What is of importance is the fact that behind these jugglings of functionality in semiosis, we are confronted with what is an essentially linear or transitive chain of semiosis wherein the object or message is taken primarily as a trace of the intentions of an active fashioner, whose intentions and conditions of production are to be reconstituted by users or beholders. The game of the Father.

In this (often very long and extended) chain of assumptions, artifacts are construed as reflections or re-presentations of originary mentifaction; the signifi-ed existing somewhere in the mind of the producer/speaker. The semiologies of the visual are in this regard entirely complicit with the paradigms of traditional art theory over the past several centuries. There have been a variety of different metaphors (or, if you will, ideological encodings) for the paradigm, among which have been noted the following.

1. The maker is seen as inspired articulator of collective values; privileged servant of a social order symbolized by powerful patrons; prophetic or bohemian rebel dissidently marginal to conventional society; independent manufacturer offering her private products to amenable audiences; or worker-engineer or bricoleur on a fraternal footing with a usership.

2. The object is encoded variously as product, practice, process, medium, symbol, epiphany, gesture, index, icon, or as the message in a code of expectancies.

3. The process of making is viewed alternately as manufacture, revelation, inspiration, labor, play, reflection, fantasy, or reproduction.

4. Usage is encoded as consumption, magical influence, arcane ritual, participatory dialogue, passive reception, spiritual encounter, translation, or mechanical decipherment.

5. The user of an object is characteristically seen as a reader, consumer, or receiver of a transmission that may or may not have been directly aimed at him or her.

We are dealing essentially here with figural variants of the same underlying metaphor. Close attention to the history of writing on the visual will reveal far fewer images for the user than for the maker, the object, or the mechanisms of production and reception. In most cases the user is seen as an essentially passive reader or consumer of objects and images: the end of the paradigmatic line, so to speak, the destiny, fate, or terminus of the work.

But there is a sixth component of the schema, namely the critical incubus, the manipulator of signs and symptoms; the legitimate communicator of readings, effects, and prescribed interpretations. The critic/historian plays a vital role in the formula, and this component is in effect the enabling mechanism that gives life and direction to the formula itself. What is not at question is the fact that makers may construe their own activity as more or less expressive or communicative, or that users (when different) may do the same.

What is of pertinence in the history of the sciences of the visual is the characteristic slant given this and similar metaphors not only in traditional discourse but also by the latter-day semiotician. By and large, the triadic paradigm of maker/object/viewer is given a trajectory so as to privilege the maker, author, or fashioner of works, the *auteur*, as essentially an active originary force in complementary contrast to a largely passive or receptive consumer of works. The vase in the Vitruvian auditorium.

It involves no great leap of the imagination to see that the paradigm simultaneously serves as a validating device so as to privilege the role of the art historian, critic, or semiotician as a diviner of intentionality on behalf of lay beholders.

It must also be observed that the transitive triadic paradigm is frequently masked by certain rhetorical maneuvers whereby the source or origin of the work is situated "behind" a producer as conscious designer or fabricator. In the history of visual discourse, this movement has characteristically gone in two directions. First, so to speak, "externally," into Zeitgeist, ethnicity, or economic or social forces of which the producer is the instrument. Secondly, it has gone into an "internal" domain, which as often as not has consisted of wellsprings of creative or libidinal impulses and energies of which the maker is as often as not unconscious, and (again) for which he or she serves as instrument.

In visual studies, and most especially in art and architectural history, this latter "internalizing" movement has gone in the direction of the legitimization of a homogeneous selfhood, all of whose products are construed as complementary evidence for biographic unity, self-identity, the unity of the spirit or Voice. Indeed, one of the primary items on the hidden agenda of art criticism and art history has been precisely the erection of evidence for the validation of a unary, homogeneous selfhood on the part of producers. It takes next to no imagination to understand that such a notion serves as a keystone in the operations of the art-commodity market: how could one sell a Caravaggio if there were times when he painted like Michaelangelo? Since Morelli began his studies of fingernails over a century ago, the bulk of art historical writing has consisted of a jockeying for territorial and sacerdotal position and the playing out of an impulse to catapult oneself into a position proper to speaking *dans le vrai*. This tendency has continued unabated, and indeed in recent times has if anything accelerated in pitch, with higher and higher financial stakes.

But these impulses have not come from some libidinal void; they are an already-prefabricated stance manufactured by the metaphorical mechanisms double-binding the disciplines of the visual (but most especially art criticism and history).

The transitivity of the triadic production schema informing critical practice has more recently evinced an opposite but equal tendency toward a privileging of the viewer or user. In such a framework, the user comes to be established as a prime (or in some cases the only really pertinent) orchestrator of signification, with the product or object seen as primarily an occasion for work on the part of the viewer who treats them as material for a transfinite freeplay. In this formula, what is past is fore-play.

Historically, the contemporary attention to the site of construal of objects and to theories of visual reception has come about in a number of complex ways and has resulted from a number of conditions specific to visual studies. While encouraging because an increased focus upon the complex realities of what viewers and users actually do with artworks has promised a release from the tedious Michaelangelism of a previous generation, by and large much of the work in this area has been idealist and reductive.

It might have been expected that visual reception theory could address questions of perception and cognition on both an individual and a collective basis; instead it appears that interest is focused primarily upon the reception of works by prior generations of art and architectural critics, and the movement has become a supplement to studies of historical and social "contexts" of works. There are two fronts on which writing is proliferating — the semiological, concerned in a more focused manner on individual aesthetic perception; and the Marxist, which, almost without exception, while attending to the reconstitution of historical and social or ideological conditions of production and reception, remains entrapped within an instrumentalist metaphorical frame wherein both works and producers resonate and transcribe broader external forces in a unidimensional manner. Back to the echoing vases in the Vitruvian auditorium; nearly all the writing within a Marxist critical framework has been complicit with the logocentrist, triadic, communicational paradigm.

This is not to say that work within a more explicit semiological frame has offered a more sophisticated alternative. With the user or viewer attended to as a decoder or cryptanalyst of messages in a code, as a dual consequence of promoting an extreme autotelism of the object and a privileging of the artist/author as originary transmitter, there has come about a tendency to occlude both the processes of production and reception and their social and historical circumstances.

In effect, the latter movement has served to perpetuate a closure against history; by reducing the circumstances of production and reception to (what to date has been) an extremely narrow construal of semiosis as mechanical personal process, much writing has been blind to the fact that all messages and codes are always already articulated by means of ideological fixities and prefabrications.

As far as psychoanalytic theory is concerned, apart from the exemplary work being done in cinema over the past decade and a half, work in traditional areas of the visual arts has strenuously sought to preserve against all decenterings a notion of the subject as transfixed upon the sunny stained glass window of homogeneous selfhood.

For some time now, the sciences of the visual have labored intensively to teach dumb buildings and mute stones to speak in phonemes and morphemes. And the current interest in the semiology of the visual arts has offered what can be seen largely as a response to an already-prefabricated agenda and practice — an iconography in cybernetic costume, but an iconography nonetheless, still steeped in a Gestalt psychologism long discredited elsewhere in the academy.

In its long and complex history since the Renaiisance, what is now referred to by hindsight as the discipline of art history and criticism has been in thrall to several major themes. Among these may be noted the themes of genesis, continuity, resemblance, evolution, and periodization. We may see played out various impulses toward dualities and binarisms, tendencies to speak in terms of primitive and sophisticated, simple and complex, monumentality and ordinariness, uniqueness and replication. The history of the discipline speaks to us of inventions, changes, problem solving, transformations, the gradual (or abrupt) emergence of one visual logic out of or against another, and euclidean theorems concerning orthodox mappings between objects and surrounds or systems of social, cultural, or individual values.

In point of fact, art history has always been a system of value pertaining to the nature of history, sociality, production, consumption, exchange-value, perception, cognition, and, above all, origins. Historically, its protocols have been primed so as to make inevitable and natural the idea of Art as an Object in its own right, as distinct from other objects—the body, the state, the made world, the "natural" world. It is imperative to attend to the mechanisms of those stratagems that have made certain kinds of artifactual behavior accessible to knowledge (and therefore institutional control). The central logocentric paradigm has worked to establish and position artwork and art historian relative to each other, and its metaphorical conundrums have served precisely to validate paradigms that are at base metaphysical and theologic. Not least of these notions is that of the world itself as the artifact of an Ideal Artificer.

Historically, the discipline has served as a mechanism to produce certain kinds of viewing subjects—ideally passive consumers or receivers, or, more recently, educated and discerning cryptographic connoisseurs. It has worked as a system for the investiture of certain groups of individuals with interpretative, semiotic, and exegetical power. It has also, and by no means accidentally, worked as a factory for the manufacture of regnant ideology, serving as a site for the legitimization and validation of various kinds of political and economic regimes. We need not be reminded that in its present formats, art history and criticism achieved their hegemony during the heyday of Euroamerican mercantilism and imperialism; it is no lamentable historical accident, no mere quirk of fate, that the discipline today has become one of the principal shunting yards in the circulation of elitist commodities. It is in no way marginal to a politics of repression.

None of this of course is news. But what has become clearer, in so small measure because of the growth of contemporary theory, is the set of mechanisms whereby institutionalized visual sciences have achieved their power and poignancy. Their sources of power are not centralized but diffuse, operating by means of epistemological knots, ideological double bindings, and co-optive metaphors and tropes. By and large, their developments and evolutions over the past several generations have come to be seen much more clearly as a series of dreary oscillations between antithetical "theoretical" or "methodological" perspectives which are already-prefabricated options set in motion by a pervasism logocentrism. (We would seriously delude ourselves were we to claim that all of this emanates from some central office, academy, or network of old boys and girls charged with enforcing a party line on the arts; the latter, after all, are but ghosts in a machine of metaphors, a gameworld of language always already present.)

But let us also be clear that there is no way to blithely step out of the forest of symbols and metaphors into some value-neutral, dispassionate, nonpolitical clearing where we might erect unhindered some Adamic metalanguage. Were we to pretend to do so, we would invariably fall into the very trap laid down by the structure of prefabricated metaphorical options, which have historically constituted our disciplinary protocols and stratagems, not to mention those strategies of containment through illusory option of consumerist political ecnomies — playing the preppie to some hippie only to be punked in turn. We need in fact to avoid the trap of erecting some counterobject, some negative theology. And in this eschewal, it is imperative to be clear that there is no methodology, no theory that does not entail some implicit definition and delimitation of prescribed relationships among "analyst," "analysand," and the circumstances and conditions of the social production and reception of the built environment. To speak of methodology is to speak of ideology, and our talk about how we talk about methodology is an infralanguage whose very instruments are the metaphors we seek to deconstruct.

The game of the City: the juxtaposition of the games of the Father and of the Mother, their embrace and interaction, their inescapable rivalry, their circling around each other in perpetual orbit. This is not a simple addition or summation, but rather that which engenders the condition for the emergence of the twin games, the complementary siblings whose embrace is never a fusion.

How should we begin this imperative meditation on the game of the city, on the history of the road and that of writing?

We have always been taught to be enamored of those devices like old vacuum-tube radios that could be taken apart so that all their components could be *seen* in a telling order: function, operation, taken as the diagrammatic geometry of form; a field of forces whose condensation engenders a formation. Weaned as graphologists whose every fixed object is a temple of entelechy, whose every gaze will orchestrate stars into constellations, *imagines agentes*, our agendas have been wound up to play out scenarios with keys manufactured by Aristotle and Quintillian.

Aristotle (*de Anima*, 432a): the object affects the air around it in the same way that a seal affects wax.

Quintillian (*Institutio Oratoria*, XI, ii, 20): we use places as wax and images as letters.

But the habit of visualizing writing on places (*loci*) has been more than merely an *ars memorativa*, which involved the active cultivation of cognitive maps on the part of rhetoricians for the memorization of long and complex orations. This "method of *loci*" encouraged orators to affix portions of a speech onto regular and syncopated portions of a building or city such that by means of an imaginary walk through that temple or neighborhood the various *topics* of one's argument could be evoked. And the arts of memory formed the fundamental basis for the medieval arts of religious representation—the church as a Summa within which were painted and sculpted all the virtues and vices, all the itineraries of the paths to heaven or hell. From the arrangement of rhetorical topics along the measured porticos of a building conjured up in memory to the orchestration of artifacts to conjure up the memory of didactic lessons. In the latter case, figural art employed *imagines agentes* or striking, moving images to cue the memory of a lesson or story: grammar was a severe old woman carrying a knife and file with which to remove children's grammatical errors: All of this reached its grandest application in the Renaissance Memory Theater of Giulio Camillo, whose seven tiers of seats, divided into seven arcs, were intended to encapsulate all of the world's wisdom to a spectator placed at the center of the orchestra.

The latter is more than merely an architectonic encyclopedia peopled with classical mythological figures in a bewildering array of poses embodying all that there is to know about the world and its history. It is in fact one more in a chain of choreo-graphics intrinsic to the history of the Occident which unites its metaphysics and its technics; yet another of those embodiments of metaphorical topology that serve to encatalyze, crystallize, and broadcast the Logos.

The Theater of Memory; its obverse yet equivalent, the panoptical Academy; the game of the City. Where better to situate ourselves in a meditation on its history than on that site, that *topos* which was the first Summa and embodiment of western metaphysics, the Athenian Acropolis.

The ostensible aims of the building program for the Acropolis (occupying most of the second half of the fifth century B.C.) were the erection of a new city sanctuary over the ruins of previous buildings destroyed in the Greco-Persian war, a struggle decisively won for Greece by the Athenians off the island of Salamis earlier in the century. Abandoning the preferences of a previous political generation who felt that the best monument to the survival and victory of Athens over the Persian empire was a destroyed sanctuary, the generation of Pericles embarked on a project to make of the Acropolis a monument and sacred temenos for all of Greece. Employing funds from the levies imposed by the city on its allies in order to strengthen the defensive forces of Greece, the city government completely redesigned the old city sanctuary.

Buildings were erected, such as the Parthenon, Erechtheon, Propylaea, temple of Athena Nike, and various minor sanctuaries and votives, which to varying degrees embodied a fusion of mainland Greek doric and eastern Greek ionic styles.

What was effected was a large-scale orchestration of elements that in their individual morphology and in their compositional relationships epitomized at the same time classical philosophy, ethics, theology, and political ideology. Each of the three major buildings — Parthenon, Erechtheon, and Propylaea — embodied a synchronization of theories of perception (optics) and protocols of ritual performance.

The Acropolis was composed so that the Parthenon would appear both as the embodiment of the citadel itself — its proportions, unique for a temple of the period, are in fact those of the Acropolis rock itself — and as the climax of all ascents, all processional movements up to and on the citadel. The latter is reinforced by the sculptural program on the building: the well-known frieze depicting the very Panathenaic procession that periodically flowed around the building from its western end to its eastern front door. This section of the Panathenaia represented the final stage in a procession that began in the city of Eleusis to the west of Athens and wound its way through the lower city along an avenue passing through the Agora before ascending the Acropolis rock. The southwest corner of the building was the pont where the sculpted frieze began — a pont which also marks the limit of vision for the spectator/participant approaching from the Propylaea.

The building known as the Erechtheon is also unique as a temple building. Its quadripartite asymmetry and irregular internal plan served to house four distinct cults and included enclosed as well as open-air spaces. It stands on the north side of the central empty space of the Acropolis, a counterpoint to the Parthenon on the south side of the citadel platform. The Propylaea, or entrance gateway, stands at the western end of the Acropolis, marking the ascent and transition from lower secular space to the higher sacred platform.

On the face of it, the Acropolis presents itself as a perfectly canonical temenos, despite the curiously shaped Erechtheon and the unusual size and proportions of the Parthenon. And the Propylaea is rather grander than other temple precinct gateways up to this time, but in most other respects presents a familiar face.

And yet, if we look more closely at the Acropolis, its general orthodoxy dissolves into a picture wholly at odds with its canonical appearance. The visual environment orchestrated on the citadel is at base a fiction, which becomes evident at the very point of transition from outside to inside, namely the Propylaea. At the entrance to the building is a sudden rupture in the linear and modulated procession into the sanctuary, a radical rent in the otherwise deftly woven urban fabric.

This occurs precisely at the point where the entrant passes the outermost angles of the embracing dual arms of the building, which is also the point where the zigzag ramp ascends to where it will turn up and into the central longitudinal axis of the Propylaea. On either side, the porticos of the structure present a perfect symmetry; the colonnade on each glank is a mirror image of the other. That on the south curtains a space beyond which is a blank wall, a space serving in part as a kind of vestibular transition to the tiny temenos of the temple of Athena Nike on the southwestern bastion. That on the north marks a transition to a room known as the Pinacotheca, serving as a gallery of paintings.

The latter is in no way unusual except for the fact that its door and side windows are curiously off-center. I cannot think of any other example of a Greek building in which the alignments of doors, windows, and intercolumnar spaces are not axial.

If we return to that point of entrance to the Acropolis noted before, we will find that the door and windows of the painting gallery are in fact positioned to appear between the columns of the portico precisely and solely from that point.

And that point suddenly becomes the orchestra of a theater, defined solely by the passage of a spectator walking up the ramp. But — the gateway to a temple sanctuary as a theater? What is to be seen? What may be seen is the hidden agenda of the designers of the new sanctuary, namely a sculptural composition that epitomized, which embodied the political reality of Athenian hegemony over Greece itself. A choreographic rhetoric whereby the position and alignments of objects served as a memory-trace, cueing the vision of what should not be forgotten and which at the same time should not be spoken — that the Athenian democracy had become an imperium.

At the point referred to, fixed and focused upon by the entrance to (what else?) the picture gallery, the entrant gets the first full glimpse of the great gold and ivory monumental statue of Athena Promachos; the warrior goddess/patron embodying the Athenian victory over Persia. The statue would have faced directly out through the longitudinal axis of the Propylaea. But not to meet the eyes of the entrant; rather, to look through the Propylaea out to the west and the island of Salamis (the site of the Athenian victory-battle), which itself becomes visible for the first time at the very point we are stopped.

This sudden rupture of the geometries of classical architecture, this abrupt gaze of a building upon its spectators, reveals the whole structural composition as a *theatron*, a theater for seeing. But not in such a way as to position the spectator on a tier of seats; rather, to place the individual at the orchestral center, at the site for the orchestration of meaning, where the individual gaze measures all things. The Propylaea is the obverse of the theater of Dionysos on the Acropolis's south slope.

Earlier propylon buildings on this spot had quite different orientations, and served solely as simple transition points between the profane and sacred realms. But the new Propylaea works as a viewing platform, a vantage point from which all that is the city is brought into a telling order, a grand sculptural composition. The Propylaea oscillates between its role as a hinge between the secular and the sacred and its role as a pivot, the new center of an *urbs* and its *orbs*: a temple of entelechy, a *theoria* of the city.

And yet by this sudden focus upon the individual entrant, the participant in the religious drama is equally a fiction, a democratic myth — for it is in fact the state and its visible but unspeakable imperialistic ideology that is the true orchestrator of this rhetorical choreography, this heightened political drama within which the individual citizen has become transformed into a bit player reciting lines written elsewhere. Beneath the text of man as the measure of all things is a countertext wherein the individual is the measured captive of the state.

Scripted by whom? By Pericles himself, and his master-planner Pheidias. Yet it was soon to be the case that the opacity of the schema was to become all too transparent: Pheidias was to be banished for the impiety of carving portraits on the shield of Athena on the statue in the Parthenon that bore an uncanny resemblance to Pericles and himself — an irruption of the historical and political into the domain of the divine.

Lest this rhetorical-spatial dramaturgy lapse in our eyes into melodrama, it is well to recall our own very recent history. I do not allude to the scandal and impiety of the new Vietnam War Memorial in Washington and the rush toward its cosmeticization, but rather a telling event central to (but now completely forgotten since) the most recent administrative inauguration: namely the dramatic moment of illumination of several national monuments in the city of Washington. You might recall the climactic moment when the new inauguree, standing at the war memorial in the Arlington National Cemetery, pressed a button that triggered a set of laser beams radiating out to the tops of the White House, Washington and Jefferson Monuments, and the dome of the Capitol. Illuminated from the central perspective of a war monument, we are spectators to a chilling realignment of national priorities.

The history of writing and of the arts of memory — the method of loci (which is to say the game of the City) are inseparable, and nowhere is this more evident than in the fifth-century orchestration and embodiment of the polis, the Athenian Acropolis. The *ars memorativa* is the hinge around which swing the laminated leaves of Occidental metaphysics and technics. Our attention to the history of these laminations and scripted choreogrpahies is an urgent task of deconstruction.

Indeed, to continue to pursue the history of writing and the history of the city along separate avenues comes to be as futile as trying to trace with a pencil the shadow of the tracing pencil.

NOTE

1. Leila Marshall, "!Kung Bushman Bands," *Africa* 30, no. 4 (1960):342–343.

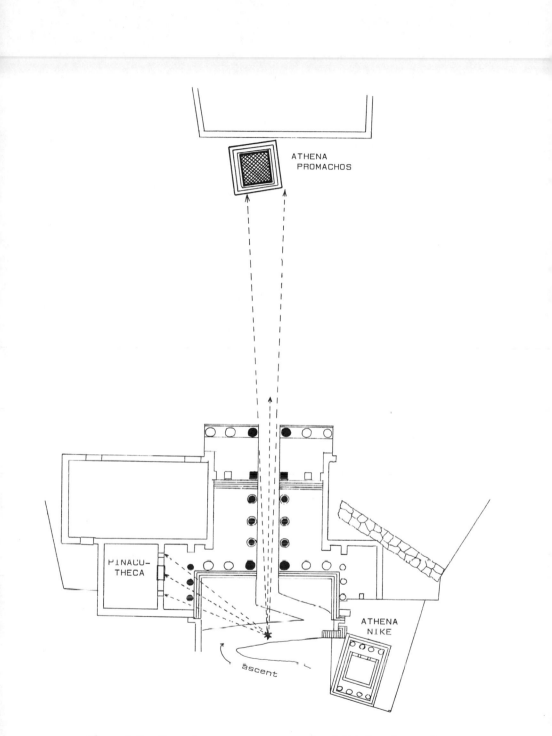

ATHENA
PROMACHOS

PINACU-
THECA

ATHENA
NIKE

ascent

Plan of the Propylaea entrance onto the Athenian Acropolis

CONTRIBUTORS

Tom Conley is Professor and Chair of the Department of French and Italian at the University of Minnesota. He has published essays on Montaigne in *Oeuvres et critiques*, *MLN*, and *Diacritics*.

Jacques Derrida teaches philosophy at the Ecole des Hautes Etudes en Sciences Sociales (Paris) and is a member of the faculty of Yale University. The essay published in this volume is part of a series of studies dealing with institutional aspects of philosophy and literature.

Malcolm Evans is Senior Lecturer in the Department of Language and Literature, Polytechnic of North London. He has contributed articles on Shakespeare and English Renaissance drama to *Shakespeare Quarterly* and *Shakespeare Jahrbuch West*, and his "Deconstructing Shakespeare's Comedies" is forthcoming in *Alternative Shakespeares*, edited by J. Drakakis. He is currently working on two books to be published by Harvester Press, the first on Shakespeare (entitled *Signifying Nothing*) and the second on the relationship between speech and writing.

Peter Middleton, a free-lance lecturer and writer, has published essays on William Blake and various contemporary poets. He is currently a lecturer in English at Southampton University and is working on a study of the poetics of free verse.

Donald Preziosi is Professor of Art History at the University of California, Los Angeles. He is the author of *The Semiotics of the Built Environment*, *Architecture, Language & Meaning*, and *Minoan Architectural Design*, and is currently writing a book about the origins of art and a book on recent theoretical developments in art history.

David Punter is Senior Lecturer in English Studies at the University of East Anglia in Norwich. His published books include *The Literature of Terror: A History of Gothic Fictions from 1765 to the Present Day*; his new book, to be published by Routledge, is *The Hidden Script: Studies in Writing and the Unconscious.*

Ruth Salvaggio, an Assistant Professor of English at Virginia Polytechnic Institute, is the author of *Dryden's Dualities* as well as several essays on Restoration/eighteenth-century literature and critical theory.

Henry Sussman is Professor of Comparative Literature at the State University of New York at Buffalo. He has written *The Hegelian Aftermath: Readings in Hegel, Kierkegaard, Freud, Proust, and James* and *Franz Kafka: Geometrician of Metaphor.*

Samuel Weber teaches critical theory at the University of Minnesota. His most recent book, *Institution and Interpretation*, is to be published shortly by the University of Minnesota Press.

Robert Young teaches English at Southampton University. He is the editor of *Untying the Text: A Post-Structuralist Reader* and the founding editor of *The Oxford Literary Review*. The present essay forms part of a larger study of history and representation in English Romantic literature.